Edexcel GCE History

A World Divided: Superpower Relations 1944–90

Steve Phillips

Series editors: Martin Collier   Rosemary Rees

Unit 3 Student Book

A PEARSON COMPANY

Published by Pearson Education Limited, a company incorporated in England and Wales, having its registered office at Edinburgh Gate, Harlow, Essex, CM20 2JE. Registered company number: 872828

www.heinemann.co.uk

Edexcel is a registered trade mark of Edexcel Limited

Text © Pearson Education Limited 2009

First published 2009

12 11 10
10 9 8 7 6 5 4 3

British Library Cataloguing in Publication Data
A catalogue record for this book is available from the British Library

ISBN 978 0 435308 12 4

Copyright notice

Edited by Florence Production Ltd, Stoodleigh, Devon
Designed by Florence Production Ltd, Stoodleigh, Devon
Typeset by Florence Production Ltd, Stoodleigh, Devon
Produced by Florence Production Ltd, Stoodleigh, Devon
Original illustrations © Pearson Education Limited 2009
Illustrated by Florence Production Ltd, Stoodleigh, Devon
Picture research by Maria Joannou
Cover photo/illustration © Alamy/Interfoto
Printed in Malaysia (CTP-VVP)

Acknowledgements

The author and publisher would like to thank the following individuals and organisations for permission to reproduce photographs:

Alamy/RIA Novosti, p. 77; British Cartoon Archive/University of Kent, pp. 16, 48; Corbis/ Bettmann, pp. 44, 87, 91, 108, 131; Corbis/Hulton-Deutsch Collection, p. 170; Corbis/National Archives/Bettmann, p. 6; Corbis/Swim Ink, p. 126; Crown Copyright, p. 98; David King Collection, p. 2; Fotolibra/Time Magazine, p. 147; Getty Images/AFP, p. 181; Getty Images/Central Press, p. 141; Getty Images/Keystone, p. 9; Getty Images/Library of Congress, p. 50; Getty Images/Popperfoto, p. 73; Jeff Koterba, p. 180; Library of Congress, p. 160; NASA/Marshall Space Flight Center, p. 137; PA Photos/AP, p. 166; Rex Features/ Alexander Grachtchenov, p. 155; Rex Features/Roger-Viollet, pp. 32, 103; Rex Features/ AS/TS/Keystone USA, p. 175; The School of Slavonic and East European Studies, University of London, p. 48; Topfoto/Ullsteinbild, pp. 28, 53; Unknown, p. v; USAF, p. 106.

Written sources

p. 52, p. 62, p. 67, p. 67, p. 113: Extracts from John Lewis Gaddis, *We Now Know*, OUP, 1997. By permission of Oxford University Press; p. 147, p. 150, p. 162, p. 174, p. 189, p. 189: Extracts from John Lewis Gaddis, *The Cold War*, 2005, p. 191, pp. 198–9, p. 227, pp. 244–5, p. 236, p. 238. Copyright © John Lewis Gaddis, 2005. Reproduced by permission of Penguin Books; p. 155, p. 161, p. 184, p. 188: Extracts from J. Hanhimaki and O.A. Westad, *The Cold War*, OUP, 2003. By permission of Oxford University Press; p. 87, p. 126, p. 126: Extracts from N. Khrushchev and E. Crankshaw, *Khrushchev Remembers*, Andre Deutsch, 1971.

Every effort has been made to contact copyright holders of material reproduced in this book. Any omissions will be rectified in subsequent printings if notice is given to the publishers.

Disclaimer

Contents

Introduction

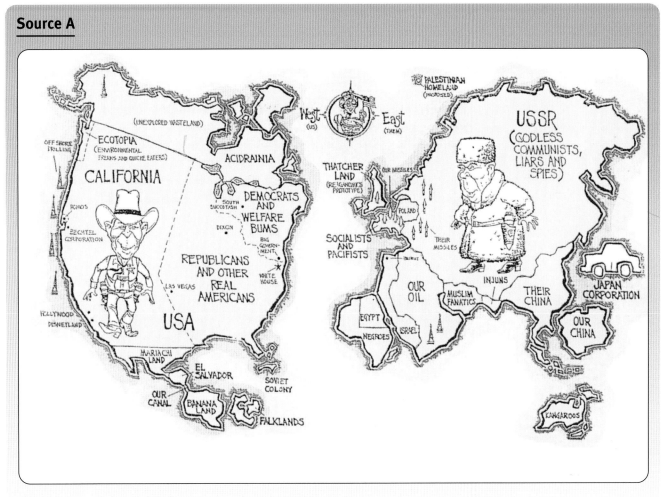

'The US view of the world', from an American newspaper, 1982

Discussion points

- What does Source A tell us about American attitudes towards the USSR?
- What does this source tell us about American attitudes towards the rest of the world?
- What message is the author of this source trying to convey about superpower relations?

International relations from 1944 until the collapse of the Soviet Union in 1991 were dominated by the superpower rivalry that existed between the USA and its allies on one side and the Soviet Union and its satellite states on the other. This rivalry was to divide a large part of the world's surface and its population. It was a division that was not confined to the more economically developed world but spread out to involve and entangle the so-called Third World as many of its countries struggled to find solutions to the development of their own economies and found the superpowers offering alternative models of development.

During this period of superpower rivalry the Cold War developed, a war where the two sides did not come into direct armed conflict but attacked each other through propaganda, non-cooperation and economic measures. These methods of attack are those that Source A highlights in a comic form. This would seem to imply that the Cold War lacked the dangers of previous conflicts, but this was far from the truth. The capability of both superpowers was at a level that had never been reached before – economically, with the ability to mobilise vast amounts of resources, but also militarily. From the first use of atomic weapons on Hiroshima and Nagasaki in August 1945, international relations were dominated by the potential use of nuclear weapons to support conflict. The vast destructive power of these weapons made the stakes much greater and the Cold War a division that threatened the very survival of the planet and its people.

The focus of this book is on international relations in the second half of the twentieth century, a period that was dominated by the emergence of two superpowers, the USA and the USSR, and the tensions created by their co-existence and rivalry. The book aims to stimulate debate on the key issues of this topic and to examine two of the key historical controversies surrounding superpower relations in this period:

1 the debate over the causes of the Cold War from 1944 to 1953, which will be explored at the beginning of this book

2 the debate over the sudden ending of the Cold War in the 1980s (examined in Unit 9).

These controversies provide opportunities to weigh up differing interpretations of issues that stir strong opinions in historians.

Although it has been the origins and endings of the Cold War that have provoked fierce debate, superpower relations in the long period between these developments were equally important and also raise serious issues for discussion.

The Cold War emerged out of the ashes of the Second World War. The defeat of Nazi Germany at the end the Second World War had left a power vacuum in Europe in 1945. The tension that developed between the USA and the USSR was in large part due to attempts by both countries to fill this vacuum. The USSR saw control over Eastern Europe as necessary in order to safeguard their country from further attack from a hostile capitalist

Source B

Map of the world showing the USA and the USSR and their allies

West. The USA saw a strong need to prevent Europe falling into the hands of communism, a political system that was seen as a threat to the freedoms of capitalism in the West. Europe thus became a battleground between two different political ideologies.

The misunderstanding and lack of trust that marked relations between the two superpowers was to add to the growing hostility between them. The result was not only a deterioration in relations but a hardening of the division between Eastern and Western Europe that produced the so-called 'Iron Curtain'.

Although the hostility between East and West stopped short of direct military conflict between the superpowers, the Cold War was, nevertheless, to see tension fluctuate considerably. In the 1950s and 1960s the Cold War affected other parts of the world, notably South East Asia where serious wars occurred in Korea and Vietnam. The Cuban Missile Crisis of 1962 illustrated the dangers of nuclear conflict posed by superpower rivalry.

By the 1950s there were also developments that promoted an easing in relations and led to the so-called '**Thaw**', which was to develop into Détente by the late 1960s. Superpower relations were to become complicated by the emergence of China as a third superpower, a communist state but one unwilling to support the USSR in international affairs.

The superficial nature of Détente was revealed when superpower relations deteriorated rapidly after the Soviet Union invaded Afghanistan in 1979. The so-called Second Cold War of the early 1980s showed how little trust existed between the USA and the USSR. Yet the constant war of words was to be replaced by much more productive talks when Mikhail Gorbachev became Soviet leader in 1985. His foreign policy, while promoting a more friendly relationship with the West, allowed the governments of Eastern Europe greater flexibility to pursue their own policies. Greater freedom in the USSR as well as most parts of Eastern Europe was to lead to popular demonstrations calling for democracy and an end to communism. Gorbachev made it clear that Soviet forces would no longer be used to prop up unpopular governments. Stripped of support both at home and abroad, the communist regimes across Eastern Europe, including the Soviet Union itself, collapsed. The fall of the Soviet Union in 1991 marked an end to the Cold War and the ideological differences that had given the conflict its distinctiveness.

Definition

The Thaw
The term given to the easing of superpower relations that occurred after the death of Stalin in 1953 and came to an end with the Cuban Missile Crisis of 1962.

Timeline of the key moments in the Cold War

The Cold War develops

1945

February	Yalta Conference
8 May	VE Day (end of Second World War against Germany)
17 July–2 August	Potsdam Conference
6 August	Atomic bomb dropped on Hiroshima

2 September	VJ Day (end of war against Japan)
1946	
5 March	Churchill gives 'Iron Curtain' speech at Fulton, Missouri
10 September	Greek Communists launch civil war against royalists
1947	
March	Launch of the Truman Doctrine
June	Marshall Plan established
1948	
February	Communist coup in Czechoslovakia
June	Berlin Blockade begins
1949	
April	NATO established
May	Berlin Blockade lifted

The Cold War spreads to the Far East

September	Communists take over China
1950	
February	Sino–Soviet Alliance signed
25 June	Start of the Korean War
1953	
5 March	Death of Stalin
27 July	Ceasefire agreed in Korea

The 'Thaw'

1954	
July	Geneva Agreement on Indochina
September	Taiwan Straits crisis develops
1955	
May	Warsaw Pact established
July	Geneva Summit (Khrushchev and Eisenhower)
1956	
November	Soviet troops invade Hungary
1958	
August	Crisis develops in Taiwan Straits
1960	
May	U-2 spy plane shot down over USSR
1961	
12 April	Yuri Gagarin becomes first man in space
17–20 April	Bay of Pigs Invasion

June	Vienna Summit (Kennedy and Khrushchev)
August	Berlin Wall erected
1962	
October	Cuban Missile Crisis

Détente

1964	
August	Gulf of Tonkin Resolution leads to increased US involvement in Vietnam
1968	
August	Soviet invasion of Czechoslovakia
1969	
March	Sino–Soviet border clash at Damansky Island on the Ussuri River
August	Sino–Soviet clashes at Xinjiang
1972	
May	SALT I signed
1975	
August	Helsinki Accords signed

The Second Cold War

1979	
December	Soviet invasion of Afghanistan
1980	
December	Martial law introduced in Poland in response to Solidarity
1983	
1 September	South Korean airliner KAL 007 shot down by Soviet air force

The collapse of communism and the end of the Cold War

1985	
11 March	Gorbachev becomes Soviet leader
1987	
December	Washington Summit (Reagan and Gorbachev)
1989	
January–December	Collapse of communist regimes in Eastern Europe
9 November	Berlin Wall opened
1991	
25 December	End of the USSR

1 The seeds of conflict 1917–44

What is this unit about?

This unit focuses on the early development of relations between the USA and the USSR before the Cold War emerged in the period after 1945. This will help to give you a sense of the long-term factors that influenced relations between the superpowers and provide the context for the breakdown in relations that was to occur after the Second World War. In this unit you will:

- explore the differences in ideology between capitalism and communism
- discover what tensions existed between the USA and the USSR in the period 1917–44
- find out how these tensions were affected by the Second World War
- discover which individuals played a key role in relations between the superpowers at the end of the Second World War.

Key questions

- What differences in ideology were there between capitalism and communism?
- To what extent had relations between the superpowers broken down by the end of 1944?

Timeline

1917	Bolshevik Revolution – Lenin comes to power in Russia
1918	Woodrow Wilson issues the Fourteen Points, US war aims
1919	Comintern established by Bolshevik Russia
1939	Second World War starts
1941	Nazi Germany invades the USSR
	Grand Alliance (GB, USA, USSR) formed against Germany, Italy and Japan
1943	'Big Three' meet at Teheran

Definitions

Bolshevik

The name of the political party that seized power in Russia in October 1917. It had been led by Lenin since 1903. The Bolsheviks were believers in communism. In 1925 they changed their official name to the All-Union Communist Party.

The Cold War

The term given to the conflict that existed between the USA and the USSR after the Second World War. It was a conflict that involved economic measures, non-cooperation and propaganda but no direct armed fighting between the two sides. Thus, despite a breakdown in relations between the superpowers, 'hot' war was avoided. With the advent of nuclear weapons, both sides used a range of less destructive methods of conflict.

USSR

The Union of Soviet Socialist Republics, also known as the **Soviet Union**. The USSR was introduced in 1923 as the official title of the areas of the old Russian Empire that were now under communist control. It was made up of 15 different republics but was dominated by Russia, the largest in size and population. The USSR collapsed in 1991.

Source A

Тов. Ленин ОЧИЩАЕТ землю от нечисти.

1.1 A Soviet cartoon from the 1920s: the caption reads 'Comrade Lenin sweeps the earth clean of scum'

SKILLS BUILDER

1 What is the message of the cartoon (Source A)?
2 Source A was produced by the **Bolshevik** government in the early 1920s. How might governments in the West have viewed this source?

The Cold War, a period of international tension between the USA and the **USSR**, developed out of the end of the Second World War in 1945. Yet, as Source A demonstrates, the seeds of this conflict were sown before the Second World War. The ideology of communism was, in 1917, to provide the new **Bolshevik** government of Russia with a view of the outside world that made increased hostility between them highly likely.

What differences in ideology were there between capitalism and communism?

Historians often link the emergence of the Cold War to the unique circumstances produced by the Second World War, but in fact the seeds of its conflict are more evident in the developments that were promoted by the First World War. The ideologies that the USSR and the USA were to symbolise during the Cold War were to emerge on the world stage during the First World War.

It was the chaos unleashed upon Russia by the First World War that was in large part responsible for the Bolshevik Revolution of 1917. The Bolshevik seizure of power in Russia was to lead to the establishment of the world's first socialist state, a state whose government saw the ideas of communism as its guiding principle. These principles were aimed at improving the lot of the industrial working class by ending their exploitation by the middle classes and the governments that acted in their interests. Communism was viewed by many governments in the rest of Europe as a highly destabilising force that threatened social and political order, a perception that was reinforced by many communist groups advocating revolution. Lenin, the leader of the Bolshevik Revolution, was to represent all that was feared by the governments of **the West**: a threat to the existing social and political order. Those governments that wished to halt the spread of communism, and had made political reforms to extend the franchise, were beginning to present a case to their own electorate and on the international arena in terms of upholding the freedoms of democracy and capitalism. In Britain Prime Minister Lloyd George had talked of political and social reform as 'an antidote to Socialism'. Thus, underlying the hatred that was to develop between the West and the Soviet Union, as Bolshevik Russia was to become, was a conflict between opposing **ideologies**.

Based on the ideas of Karl Marx, communism provided a framework of economic and political principles that directly opposed those traditionally held in the West. Communism had developed out of Marx's critique of capitalism, the economic system that had developed in Europe during the Industrial Revolution of the eighteenth and nineteenth centuries. Capitalism, according to Marx, involved the exploitation of the working class proletariat for the benefit of the middle class bourgeoisie. Communism, which sought to end this exploitative system, was, in essence, an attack on the power structure of Western society. What gave Marxists encouragement was the belief of Marx that the capitalist system was inherently unstable, producing boom periods but also inevitable recessions that would sow the seeds of its own destruction. The fall of capitalism was therefore, according to Marx, only a matter of time.

Economic differences

Communists, such as the Bolsheviks, saw capitalism as responsible for the division of society in the West into different classes. The emphasis on private ownership of businesses was seen as producing the division between the rich factory owners and the poorer working classes. To do away with this inequality, communists believed that all factories, businesses and land should be taken over by the government on behalf of the people. This process of nationalisation would enable the goods generated by the economy to be more fairly distributed according to need. The principle of a state-owned economy was the opposite of private enterprise, encouraged by capitalism, whereby individuals had the freedom to own their own businesses and to keep the majority of the

Definitions

The West
The term given to the capitalist countries of western Europe and North America during the Cold War. The United States was the principal power of the West.

Ideology
A set of ideas and beliefs that forms the basis of an economic or political system. The Cold War involved conflict between two competing ideologies: communism and capitalism.

profits. In capitalist economies the incentive of individual gain was a direct contrast to the community responsibility encouraged by communism. To the owners of businesses, factories and land, the process of nationalisation represented a threat to their wealth, status and power, and it was these people that often dominated the governments and political elites of countries in the West.

Political differences

As well as differences in economic ideology, there was an important contrast in terms of political system. The West saw itself as upholding liberal democracy. This political system was valued because it upheld important freedoms, such as the freedom to vote, freedom of speech, freedom of worship and a free press. In this sense liberal democracy gave people a choice of government and the chance to vote an unpopular government out of office. To the communists, political parties were the result of different and conflicting classes. In a communist state, where a classless society was being created, there was no need for different political parties. Thus a communist system was a one-party state, with the Communist Party ruling on behalf of the people. Communism also promoted the principle of class unity rather than nationalism. Thus, workers were encouraged to unite without regard for national boundaries. This made the threat of communism particularly destabilising for existing governments in the West, who saw their freedoms as under attack.

Communism's emphasis on government control over the economy and a one-party state to further the interests of the industrial workers provided a sharp contrast with the economic and political freedoms taken for granted in the West.

International relations

Marxist ideology said little directly about the conduct of international relations, but after 1917 the Bolshevik government was in a position where it had to define some guiding principles for dealing with a hostile outside world. Communists believed that conflict between capitalism and communism was inevitable because they represented completely opposed systems. If communism was to succeed, it had to bring about a worldwide revolution and this meant helping to bring about what Marxists saw as the inevitable collapse of capitalism. In March 1919 Lenin stated: 'We are living not merely in a state, but in a system of states: and it is inconceivable that the Soviet republic should continue to exist for a long period side by side with imperialist states.' In order to further the cause of communism and aid the collapse of capitalism, the **Comintern** was set up. Its role was to coordinate communist groups throughout the world and to support their attempts to undermine capitalism by all available means, including revolution. Thus, the ideology of communism was inherently hostile to the West and the values it stood for.

Definition

Comintern

An organisation set up in 1919 to facilitate contacts between communist groups throughout the world. The Soviet government was able to control its activities, and the West feared it was being used to undermine capitalism and spread communist revolution. It was also known as the Third International, as it replaced the Second International that had existed before 1919.

Wilsonian liberalism

At the same time as communist ideology was being put into practice the First World War saw the emergence of a much clearer vision of US attitudes towards foreign policy than had hitherto been seen. In January 1918 the US President Woodrow Wilson issued his Fourteen Points. This was a statement of America's war aims, those values in international affairs that America was prepared to join the First World War and fight for. Although the Fourteen Points was a list of specific aims, it also presented an ideological framework for international relations in 1918. Wilson's liberalism promoted the principles of:

a) *self-determination* – the right of all national groups to decide their own form of government according to the democratic wishes of its people

b) *open markets* – markets that require the dismantling of trade barriers and spheres of influence that limited the freedom of capitalism throughout the world

c) *collective security* – a grand vision of a world peace-keeping organisation that would guarantee the safety of any country under attack.

Source B

Woodrow Wilson's address to Congress, 2 April 1917

We shall fight for the things which we have always carried nearest our hearts – for democracy, for the right of those who submit to authority to have a voice in their own governments, for the rights and liberties of small nations, for a universal dominion of right by such a concert of free peoples as shall bring peace and safety to all nations and make the world itself at last free. To such a task we can dedicate our lives and our fortunes, everything that we are and everything that we have, with the pride of those who know that the day has come when America is privileged to spend her blood and her might for the principles that gave her birth and happiness and the peace which she has treasured. God helping her, she can do no other.

SKILLS BUILDER

1 Which of Wilson's principles are addressed in this speech and how?

2 Explain how Wilson's principles would lead to a greater world role for the USA.

3 What does this source indicate about the seriousness of Wilson's desire to uphold these ideas?

4 Explain how Wilson's principles could be seen as a criticism of European countries at this time.

Wilson's ideas were not original and, with the exception of the principle of collective security, were based on traditional American values of personal and economic freedom (i.e. democracy and capitalism). What was different, however, was the vision of these ideas on a world scale. Wilson believed that the USA had a moral duty to spread its values to the rest of the world. This marked a clear shift away from the traditional US foreign policy of keeping out of foreign affairs with the exception of Latin America, which it regarded as its own sphere of influence.

Yet Wilson's ideas were, in the short term, to have a limited impact. In 1919 the US Senate rejected the Versailles Treaty, which had tried to apply Wilson's ideas. The USA then turned its back on Europe, returning to a policy of isolation. For the longer term, Wilson had laid down a vision that others could, and would, pick up.

Thus, Lenin's concept of world revolution and Wilsonian liberalism represented two widely differing models for the conduct of international relations. The seeds of future conflict lay in the hostility generated between these two competing views. When the circumstances were created to let these competing views flourish, the Cold War was likely to follow.

Source C

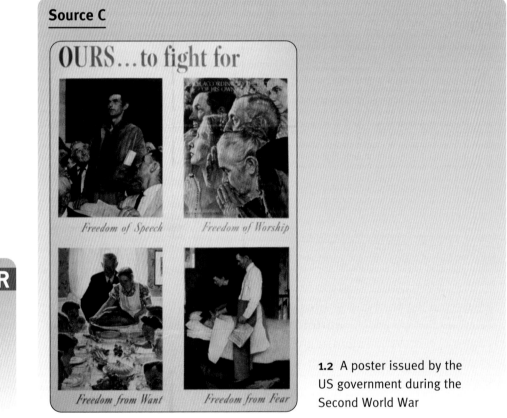

1.2 A poster issued by the US government during the Second World War

SKILLS BUILDER

Explain how communism could be seen as a threat to the American freedoms presented in Source C.

What tensions existed between the USSR and the capitalist world in the 1920s and 1930s?

Although not the dominant theme in international relations, the ideological differences between communism and capitalism were to cause tensions between the USSR and the capitalist world in the 1920s and 1930s.

Relations between the Soviet Union and the West were to remain poor throughout the inter-war years, with important consequences for international relations in Europe when Hitler's foreign policy threatened to engulf the continent in a major conflict at the end of the 1930s.

Causes of tension

1 The ideological differences, already outlined, between capitalism and communism were a source of tension. Not only were the two sets of ideas different but they were seen as diametrically opposed. Communism was seen as a direct threat to the privileges, status and power of the elites that formed the governments in the West.

2 The decision of the Bolshevik government to pull Russia out of the First World War and the resulting **Treaty of Brest-Litovsk**, March 1918, was another cause of tension. It led to a feeling of betrayal amongst the Allies. Britain and France were desperate to keep Russia in the war to avoid having to face the might of Germany alone.

3 The refusal of the Soviet regime to honour the debts owed to the West by previous Russian governments was a source of tension in international relations. The Soviet government's policy of nationalising key sectors of the economy resulted in many foreign companies losing their investments. This particularly affected France, where investors in the Russian economy put pressure on the French government to recover these losses.

4 The Bolshevik government had taken the decision to execute the Tsar of Russia and his family. Tsar Nicholas II was a cousin of King George V, and the British King was reluctant to undertake any communication with his cousin's murderers.

5 The Allied countries of Britain, France, the USA and Japan had all sent help to the enemies of the Bolsheviks in the Russian Civil War of 1917–21. The Bolsheviks did not forget that these countries had been active in plotting the downfall of their government.

6 The activities of Comintern, or Third International, raised tension. The organisation issued a stream of anti-capitalist propaganda that often incited people to overthrow their government in the name of communism. As communist groups in countries such as Spain and France grew in strength often as a response to the hardships of the Great Economic Depression of the 1930s, the USA became increasingly alarmed.

7 Mutual mistrust and hostility constantly undermined attempts by Britain and France to work with the Soviet Union. In the 1930s the rise of an aggressive Germany under the leadership of Hitler made this a serious issue. The USSR was highly suspicious of Britain's policy of **appeasement** towards Germany, seeing it as an attempt to placate Hitler and turn his attention away from the West and towards the USSR. When Hitler had demanded parts of Czechoslovakia in 1938 and 1939, Britain and France had proved ineffective in standing up to him.

Definitions

Treaty of Brest-Litovsk, March 1918
The Bolsheviks had gained a lot of support because they promised to take Russia out of the First World War. An armistice was agreed in December 1917, leading to negotiations between Russia and Germany. In March 1918 the Bolsheviks reluctantly agreed to the terms of the Treaty of Brest-Litovsk. The Germans imposed a harsh treaty on Russia.

Appeasement
The policy adopted by Britain towards Germany in the 1930s. It involved negotiating with Hitler and trying to reach accommodation with his demands for territory where they seemed reasonable. Stalin saw it as a sign of Britain's lack of enthusiasm for halting Hitler's foreign policy advances, especially when they might be made at the expense of the USSR in eastern Europe. This method of dealing with Hitler failed to prevent the outbreak of the Second World War. After 1945 political leaders such as Truman and Churchill thought a more hard-line approach towards aggressors would be more effective. This attitude was to influence policy towards the USSR during the Cold War.

Discussion point

Did the fact that the USSR was communist make a difference to relations between it and the West? What other factors made relations between them hostile?

8 The result of this mistrust and suspicion was to push Stalin, who had emerged as leader of the Soviet Union after Lenin's death in 1924, into the Nazi–Soviet Pact of August 1939. This was an accommodation with Hitler that limited the threat of a German invasion of the Soviet Union and gave Stalin time to prepare for a war he believed was inevitable. Britain and France condemned Stalin's actions in signing the Pact but they had pushed him towards Hitler by their own half-hearted attitudes and ineffectual policies. For Stalin it was a 'marriage of convenience' that gave the USSR the opportunity to gain parts of Poland as well as sign a non-aggression pact.

The tension and hostility that existed between the USSR and Britain and France in the inter-war years remained largely on the level of propaganda or spats over trade, but the consequences of this hostility were to be crucial to the future of Europe. The main victor in the war of words between the USSR and Britain and France was Nazi Germany, which was able to exploit these divisions in order to help secure success for Hitler's invasion of large parts of Europe.

What were the strains in the Grand Alliance?

Given their differences in ideology, the Soviet Union and the capitalist West could hardly be considered natural allies. Nonetheless, circumstances were to draw the two sides into an alliance.

When Hitler launched his invasion of the Soviet Union on 22 June 1941, the Second World War was transformed. The USSR found itself on the same side as Britain in resisting the might of Nazi Germany. When Japan bombed the American naval base at Pearl Harbor in December of the same year, the USA joined the war against the Fascist powers. Thus, by the end of 1941, the Soviet Union, the USA and Britain were allies against Germany, Italy and Japan. Previous hostility between East and West was to be temporarily forgotten, or at least swept under the carpet, until the defeat of the Fascist powers was secured by the formation of what was to become known as the Grand Alliance.

The leaders of the three countries that made up the Grand Alliance – Winston Churchill (the British Prime Minister), Stalin (the Soviet leader) and Franklin D. Roosevelt (the American President) – were to overcome differences between themselves to establish a working relationship in order to secure victory against Fascism. Realism dominated the attitudes of the leaders. Churchill recognised that the war could not be won without an agreement with the Soviet Union. Stalin needed a second front to be opened against Germany to relieve the pressure on the USSR. Roosevelt wished to concentrate on winning the war rather than argue about what would happen afterwards, an issue where disagreements would be much more obvious.

The 'Big Three' met in Teheran in November 1943 to agree on several issues concerning Poland. Yet despite this level of cooperation, divisions remained between the three leaders and were to remain a source of tension in the relationship.

Further strains were:

1 The opening of a Second Front. One key strain in the Alliance was over the timing of opening up a Second Front against Germany. Stalin was concerned first and foremost with the security of the Soviet Union. Since June 1941 the Soviet Union had borne the brunt of the fighting against Germany and had suffered severe losses both in human and material resources. To Stalin, the need to open up a Second Front in Western Europe against Germany to relieve the pressure on the USSR in the East was an urgent necessity. Yet the refusal of Britain and the USA to do so until the time was right led Stalin to be suspicious of their motives.

2 The issue of Poland. Strains also developed when discussion of post-war arrangements got down to specific details. As the tide was turned against Germany, these issues came to the fore. Due to its geographical position, Poland was of immense importance for the security of the Soviet Union. Poland had been the route of three invasions of Russia in the twentieth century. The Soviet Union was not prepared to see an unfriendly government in Poland. A provisional Polish government had been set up in exile in London by those who had fled the country in 1939, but there was also the Union of Polish Patriots, a prospective 'communist-friendly' government based in the Soviet Union.

1.3 The 'Big Three' (Churchill, Roosevelt, Stalin) at the Yalta Conference

One of the key points of debate between the leaders of the Grand Alliance was therefore over where the borders of Poland should be drawn and the nature of the government that should be established in the country.

The strains in the Grand Alliance were never very serious until the end of the war but they did enable critics to voice discontent with the Grand Alliance. In the United States there were those, such as the Vice-President, Harry S. Truman, who hated communism and were uncomfortable with the whole idea of working closely with the Soviet Union. In 1941 Truman had stated: 'If we see that Germany is winning the war we ought to help Russia, and if Russia is winning we ought to help Germany, and in that way let them kill as many as possible'. This was not a view shared by President Roosevelt, but it did represent the viewpoint of a sizeable part of the American public.

Thus, despite the appearance of the Grand Alliance as a union of states fighting together against common foes, the mistrust and tension that had been evident before the Second World War remained. With the defeat of Nazi Germany the reason for the Alliance had come to an end. It was at this point that the previous hostility between the two sides was to reassert itself.

To what extent had relations between the superpowers broken down by the end of 1944?

By the end of 1944 the seeds of the Cold War were in place. Long-term causes of conflict had existed since 1917: two superpowers had emerged that represented directly opposed ideologies, and the imminent defeat of Nazi Germany had started to create a power vacuum in Europe into which both countries were drawn to protect their own interests. Nonetheless, despite the existence of these factors, the Cold War had not yet developed and its development was by no means inevitable.

Tensions and hostility between the USSR and the USA were kept to a minimum because neither country took on a world role in the period before 1941. The reasons for this were different for each country.

The USA had the capability to play a world role after 1918, but neither the US establishment nor the American public had the will to do so. Instead, the USA ignored the wishes of Woodrow Wilson and returned to a policy of isolationism.

SKILLS BUILDER

Study the table of information on the 'Big Three'. Use this information to highlight aspects of each individual that might (a) cause tension and (b) reduce tension in international relations.

Joseph Stalin (1879–1953)

Born 1879 in Georgia in the south of the old Russian Empire. His family were from peasant stock.

Leadership and personal qualities Shrewd, manipulative, coarse, practically minded, an effective administrator and ruthless.

Career Joined the Bolshevik Party in 1903, appointed General Secretary of the Party in 1922. Emerged as leader of the USSR after the death of Lenin in 1924. Undisputed leader of the Soviet Union from 1928.

Domestic policies Harsh but effective industrialisation, collectivisation of agriculture, systematic use of terror, heavy censorship and propaganda. By the end of the Second World War his policies had turned the USSR into a world power.

Foreign policy Highly suspicious of the West and viewed the capitalist powers as anti-Bolshevik. Determined to safeguard the country against foreign attack.

Franklin D. Roosevelt (1882–1945)

Born 1882 in New York.

Leadership and personal qualities Energetic, enthusiastic, optimistic. Roosevelt was struck down by polio in 1921 and was thereafter confined to a wheelchair. This gave him an understanding of the position of the disadvantaged in society.

Career Attended law school and then joined the Democratic Party. Roosevelt was liberal in attitude. Governor of New York 1928–33. President of the United States from 1933 until his death in April 1945. Re-elected an unprecedented three times.

Domestic policies Introduced a set of measures known as the New Deal, which attempted to address the problems caused by the Great Economic Depression after the Wall Street Crash. Targeted help at the disadvantaged in society. Increased state involvement in the economy in order to create jobs.

Foreign policy Brought the USA into the Second World War after the Japanese attack on Pearl Harbor. He was prepared to negotiate directly with Stalin during the Second World War, and he was optimistic that this arrangement could continue after the war.

Winston Churchill (1874–1965)

Born 1874 in Oxfordshire.

Leadership and personal qualities Phenomenal energy, inspiring, willing to get directly involved, humane.

Career Served as a cavalry officer in the army during the Boer War. Originally a Conservative, he served in the Liberal governments of 1906–14. Rejoined the Conservative Party in 1922 and became Chancellor of the Exchequer 1924–29. Excluded from office in the 1930s but took up the cause against Fascism. Prime Minister of Britain during the Second World War from 1940 to 1945. Returned as Prime Minister 1951–55.

Domestic policies President of the Board of Trade and Home Secretary under the great reforming Liberal governments of the years 1906–14. During the Second World War he left home affairs to Labour members of the wartime coalition government whilst he focused on the conduct of the war.

Foreign policy Strongly anti-communist, but nonetheless was prepared to work with the Soviet Union against Nazi Germany. Met Stalin several times and established a sound working relationship with Stalin. In the post-war world Churchill was deeply suspicious of Stalin's motives and in 1946 his 'Iron Curtain' speech called for an alliance between Britain and the USA to prevent Soviet expansion.

The USSR, on the other hand, lacked the capacity to play a world role in this period. Devastated by the impact of the First World War, Bolshevik Russia then had to fight a civil war. The USSR spent the inter-war years trying to ensure its own survival rather than spreading world revolution.

The Second World War forced both countries onto the world stage, whether they wished it or not. Yet the circumstances of the war gave them common ground. The War provided a threat, in the form of the Axis powers of Germany, Italy and Japan, to the security of both countries.

It was the defeat of Germany, Italy and Japan in 1945 that led to the re-emergence of tensions and open hostility between East and West. The USA and the USSR were now in a position where they possessed both the will and the ability to impose their ideology on a European, if not yet global, scale.

It was the attitudes and policies that both the USA and the USSR were to develop towards each other during and after 1945 that led to the final breakdown in relations.

Unit summary

What have you learned in this unit?

Ideological differences existed between capitalism and communism. These differences gained in importance after the Bolshevik Revolution of 1917 and Woodrow Wilson's Fourteen Points in 1918. Although these differences caused tension in the inter-war years, the level of hostility was limited. The Second World War brought the USA and USSR together against the threat of Nazi Germany and its allies. It was at the end of the war that tensions between the 'Big Three' became prominent. Dealing with the post-war world was likely to highlight the differences between the wartime allies as they struggled to adjust to a Europe that had been ravaged by war and was in desperate need of reconstruction.

What skills have you used in this unit?

You have been introduced to some of the key skills you will be developing through this topic. You have used a range of sources to explore attitudes between the West and the USSR. Material will have been used to identify and discuss the factors that caused tension between the two sides and those factors that drew them together. You have also had an opportunity to think about the value of one of the sources by reference to its origins and purpose.

Exam style questions

Although this unit has been concerned with setting the context for the main issues and controversies of this topic, rather than answering the central questions that you will face in the exam, it is still useful to plan for part of an answer that may be set on the controversy about the origins of the Cold War.

The questions centred on this controversy will appear in Section B of the exam. They will ask you to use two or three sources and your own knowledge to make a judgement on an interpretation. For example:

- How far do you agree with the view that the origins of the Cold War in 1945 and 1946 owed much to ideological differences and little to personalities and conflicting national interests?

To answer this question you will need to examine the events of 1945 and 1946 that you will go on to read about in the next unit. In preparation for this, use the material you have covered in this unit to identify the key points you need to look for. You may find it useful to list these points under the headings:

- ideological differences
- personalities
- conflicting national interests.

Exam tips

Before you start to write an answer you should draw up a plan. This can save you a lot of time later on and can help ensure that your efforts are not wasted. There is nothing worse than spending a lot of time on an answer that gets a low mark. Sound planning can help guarantee good results.

A useful tool for planning is that of *deconstructing questions*.

How to deconstruct a question

Break the question down into its constituent parts. Look for the following:

1 the *instruction* (I) e.g. 'how far', 'assess'.
2 the *topic* (T) e.g. the Cold War 1945–46, the Korean War.
3 *Keywords* (KW) that need to be focused on in your answer.

Example:

Question: How far do you agree with the view that the origins of the Cold War in 1945 and 1946 owed much to ideological differences and little to personalities and conflicting national interests?

- I – 'How far'
- T – the origins of the Cold War in 1945 and 1946
- KW – 'ideological differences', 'personalities', 'conflicting national interests'.

RESEARCH TOPIC

The Teheran Conference of November 1943

This marked the first meeting of the 'Big Three' leaders. Although relations between the leaders were generally productive, the conference highlighted some of the issues that were to rise to the surface later. Your task is to research this conference in order to identify these issues. Try to find out:

- Why had Stalin not wanted to meet Roosevelt and Churchill until 1943?

- Why was Teheran chosen as the place to hold the conference?

- What was agreed?

- Why were agreements reached relatively easily?

2 How did the Cold War develop between 1944 and 1953?

What is this unit about?

This unit focuses on the development of the Cold War between the superpowers in the years 1944 to 1953. This will give you an understanding of how relations between the superpowers deteriorated in these years and the key events in this process. In this unit you will:

- explore the legacy of the Second World War and its impact on the superpowers
- find out how relations between the superpowers deteriorated in this period
- discover how the tensions of the Cold War extended to the Far East after 1949
- examine the key confrontations between the superpowers during this period: the 'Iron Curtain' speech; Truman Doctrine; Berlin Blockade; the Korean War.

Key questions

- How did the Cold War develop between 1944 and 1953?
- What role did the key confrontations of this period play in the development of the Cold War?

Timeline

1945	
February	Yalta Conference
8 May	VE Day (end of Second World War against Germany)
17 July–2 August	Potsdam Conference
6 August	Atomic bomb dropped on Hiroshima
2 September	VJ Day (end of war against Japan)
1946	
5 March	Churchill gives 'Iron Curtain' speech at Fulton, Missouri
10 September	Greek Communists launch civil war against royalists
1947	
March	Launch of the Truman Doctrine
June	Marshall Plan established
1948	
February	Communist coup in Czechoslovakia
June	Berlin Blockade begins

1949	
April	NATO established
May	Berlin Blockade lifted
September	Communists take over China
1950	
February	Sino–Soviet Alliance signed
25 June	Start of the Korean War
1953	
5 March	Death of Stalin
27 July	Ceasefire agreed in Korea

Introduction

Source A

2.1 A British cartoon from 1946

Discussion points

- What does Source A suggest about relations between Britain and the Soviet Union after the Second World War?
- How does the cartoonist portray communism?

In October 1944 Churchill met Stalin in Moscow to talk about war strategy. Their minds were already looking forward to what would happen when Germany was defeated. Churchill proposed what he termed a 'naughty document' to list their interests in the countries of Eastern Europe. It was an effort to limit the influence of the USSR and uphold that of Britain without any reference to the peoples of the countries involved. In Greece, Britain would have a 90 per cent interest and Russia 10 per cent; in

Romania, the percentages were reversed. In Hungary and Bulgaria, Churchill agreed to an 80 per cent Russian interest. Stalin ticked the percentages in agreement with Churchill, but he must have been amused because the position of the Red Army in Eastern Europe would make Soviet influence a reality in Eastern Europe whether Churchill or the Americans liked it or not.

Agreement between the West and the Soviet Union was still possible in 1945. At the wartime conferences of Yalta and Potsdam substantial progress was made in attempting to lay down a basis for post-war Europe. Yet events were to quickly bring about a deterioration in relations. By the end of 1947 American and Soviet policies had hardened the stance of their respective governments, and there seemed little chance of avoiding further tension. Soviet actions over Berlin in 1948–49, the communist takeover of China in 1949 and the Korean War of 1950–53 seemed to confirm to the Americans that world communism under the leadership of Stalin was intent on expansion. In return, the 'Iron Fist' approach of US President Truman and the development of the policy of containment was seen in Moscow as evidence that the USA was adopting an aggressive stance towards the USSR.

> I think it is a mistake to believe that you can, at any time, sit down with the Russians and solve questions. I do not think that is the way that our problems are going to be worked out with the Russians.
>
> Dean Acheson, the US Secretary of State,
> speaking in the US Congress, April 1947

Acheson's statement illustrates the change in superpower relations that had occurred since 1945. The Cold War had developed, and division replaced cooperation. Winston Churchill's concept of an 'Iron Curtain' dividing the continent had quickly become a reality.

How did the legacy of the Second World War make a Cold War more likely?

Events in history are often, perhaps usually, seen as driven by the actions of individual leaders. Leaders are, however, a product of their circumstances, and their actions are very much dictated by the circumstances that they find themselves in. In terms of the development of the Cold War between 1945 and 1950, the key personalities were Stalin, Truman, Roosevelt and Churchill. The circumstances in which they were to play out their roles were conditioned by the Second World War.

The Second World War created a power vacuum in Europe into which the USA and the USSR were both drawn. The War had resulted in the defeat of Nazi Germany. At its height Nazi Germany had conquered most of the continent of Europe. Its defeat, therefore, left large areas of Europe without any meaningful government or administration. The traditional forms of government in Europe had been discredited, especially in Eastern Europe where resistance to Nazi conquest had been particularly ineffective.

Definitions

Second Front

The name given to the idea of a campaign against Nazi Europe in the west in addition to the Russian Front. Since the Nazi invasion of the Soviet Union in June 1941, the Germans had been able to concentrate most of their military resources on the Eastern Front. This had put an enormous pressure on the Soviet Union. Stalin therefore pushed Britain and the USA to open up a Second Front against Germany in France that would distract Germany from the Russian Front and thus help to relieve the pressure on the USSR. This proposed new front in France was known as the Second Front.

The purges

The wave of terror that Stalin and his supporters used to remove enemies. The targets were so-called enemies of the state and included leading Communist Party politicians such as Bukharin, Kamenev and Zinoviev. Many members of the Soviet armed forces were also purged, as were the secret police themselves. The purges reached a peak of activity in the years 1936–39.

The Second World War had left much of Europe economically devastated. The industrial heart of Europe had been laid waste and over 16 million people were left homeless. Europe was in desperate need of reconstruction. The USA and the USSR were to provide the inspiration for alternative methods of bringing about the economic recovery of Europe.

The War had left Europe devastated but it had also highlighted the emergence of the USA and the USSR as powers with the capacity to dominate Europe. Both powers were determined not to let the other fill the power vacuum completely. The USA had emerged from the war as a world superpower: it produced over 50 per cent of the world's manufacturing output, owned a navy as big as the rest of the world's navies put together and was in sole possession of the atomic bomb. The USSR was in a state of severe economic hardship in 1945, but its Red Army of over 11 million troops occupied most of Eastern Europe: it was in a position to enforce its will on large parts of the continent. The result was a division of Europe into spheres of influence, and tensions were to develop over the relative limits and extent of these different spheres. Thus, the power vacuum caused by the defeat of Nazi Germany was a short-term cause of the Cold War.

It was ideological differences that gave attempts to fill the power vacuum in Europe an additional edge. Roosevelt was willing to use US influence to ensure peace based on the principles of Wilsonian liberalism (See Unit 1 page 5). He desired to promote international cooperation and spread democracy as the basis of world peace. The United Nations (UN), it was hoped, would be a world organisation of free, independent democratic nations. The opening of economic markets was seen as essential to protect US trading interests after the dislocation of the war. The USSR was now in a better position to pursue its foreign policy aims of securing its borders and spreading communism by a process of territorial acquisition.

Another legacy of the war was the deep distrust and suspicion that had developed between the wartime allies. Cooperation between the USA and the USSR had focused on the practical issue of ensuring the defeat of Nazi Germany, but alongside this was a growing mutual suspicion. Stalin had been deeply suspicious of Britain and America's delay in opening up a **Second Front** against Hitler. He had concerns that the West wanted to use Hitler to weaken communism. On the American side, the government was uneasy with Stalin's ruthless policies, especially **the purges** of the late 1930s. This did not fit well with the USA's view of the Second World War as a fight to preserve freedom in the world.

Distrust and suspicion were to be heightened by another legacy of the war, the development of the atomic bomb. The power of destruction shown by the impact of the nuclear bombs dropped on Hiroshima and Nagasaki in 1945 sent a clear message to Stalin about the military superiority of the USA. Although the decision to drop the bombs was made in relation to the war with Japan, the failure of Truman to inform Stalin of his decision added to Soviet suspicions of US motives. Stalin was determined to develop

Soviet nuclear capability as soon as possible. The end of the Second World War had ushered in the nuclear age.

The circumstances produced by the Second World War in 1945 were in many ways unique. The superpowers were drawn into a Europe where a power vacuum now existed, and its devastated economies meant that it was desperate for reconstruction. Yet the legacy of the Second World War was an increase in mistrust and suspicion between the superpowers in a situation where cooperation and agreement were called for. Thus the situation provided plenty of opportunities for a Cold War to develop.

Discussion point

In what ways did the situation in 1945 draw the USA and the USSR into greater involvement in European affairs?

What were the attitudes of the main powers to the situation in Europe in 1945?

The actions taken by both East and West after 1945 were conditioned in large part by their attitudes and perceptions of each other and the situation posed by the end of the war. These attitudes were to provide the most important short-term causes of the Cold War.

1 Soviet attitudes in 1945

Although Stalin was a communist who professed world revolution, his foreign policy after 1945 was to be conditioned above all by the severe losses endured in the Second World War. Over 20 million Soviet citizens had died as a direct result of the war. Whole cities had been reduced to rubble, countless villages obliterated, and machinery and livestock decimated. Thus Stalin's main aim was to safeguard and rebuild the Soviet Union.

Stalin's foreign policy was based on the aim of taking advantage of the military situation in Europe to strengthen Soviet influence and prevent another invasion from the west. This policy resulted in occupying as much of Eastern Europe as possible. To nations of the West this was seen as evidence of the expansionist nature of communism, but Soviet aims were based on attitudes that were more complicated than this.

Russia had been invaded from the west three times in the twentieth century: by Germany in the First World War; by those helping the Whites during the Russian Civil War; and by Germany again in the Second World War. Each time Russian losses had been substantial, but the sacrifice required during the Second World War was unprecedented. The need to ensure such a devastating war was not again inflicted upon the Soviet Union was undoubtedly a weighty and pressing concern. The situation in Europe in 1945 provided Stalin with an opportunity to establish a buffer zone of Soviet-influenced states in Eastern Europe, which would act as a barrier against further invasion of the USSR from the west.

This Soviet obsession with security was difficult for the American government to understand. To the American government, the USSR was more interested in spreading communism. While it would be understandable for a communist state to want to spread its own ideology when the opportunity presented itself, this does not seem to have been Stalin's prime concern. The Soviet Union's foreign policy had long since been concerned with ensuring survival rather than spreading world revolution. The prospects of the latter were seen as minimal after 1921.

Stalin's aims were therefore more traditional. He believed that what the USSR got after the war should be determined by the degree of losses it had endured. The USSR should regain the territories it had lost to Germany during the war and hold onto those areas gained under the Nazi–Soviet Pact of 1939 (i.e. the Baltic States, eastern Poland, parts of Romania and Finland). In addition Stalin expected economic assistance from the USA.

The problem with Stalin's aims was that they would result in Soviet domination over a large part of Europe, which would be unacceptable to the USA as it developed its own foreign policy aims to account for the situation in 1945 and to play a more active role in it.

2 US attitudes in 1945

The attitudes of the US government were to change in 1945 as Truman replaced Roosevelt as President. This change in attitude was from one of accommodation to one of confrontation.

Roosevelt had brought the USA into the Second World War under the propaganda slogan of fighting for freedom. Roosevelt was well aware that the Soviet Union hardly matched his ideal of freedom.

Although later criticised for being too soft on communism, Roosevelt's approach to the Soviet Union was realistic given the circumstances. Roosevelt recognised that America had to seek some sort of working relationship with the USSR. With the Soviet Red Army stationed in most of Eastern Europe and in the atmosphere of war-weariness that enveloped the USA in 1945, Roosevelt saw negotiation and compromise as the most effective methods of safeguarding Western interests while avoiding having to commit substantial resources to Europe.

Roosevelt's personal relationship with Stalin could well have seen this approach succeed, but Roosevelt was not a well man. When he died in April 1945, Roosevelt was replaced as President by **Harry S. Truman** (see page 22). As Vice-President, Truman had been kept out of foreign affairs, and as a result he found himself suddenly catapulted into a position he was not prepared for. This gave Truman a sense of weakness, which was increased by the growing pressure exerted within America by anti-communist groups. The result of Truman trying to assert his authority was the adoption of a more openly hostile attitude towards the Soviet Union, which was to find its justification in George Kennan's 'Long Telegram' of February 1946. **George Kennan** was the United States Deputy Chief of Mission at the US Embassy in Moscow. His 'Long Telegram' (see Unit 3, Source C, page 50) provided an analysis of Soviet foreign policy which

Biography

George Kennan (1904–2005)

Deputy Chief of Mission in the US Embassy in Moscow in 1946. Kennan's analysis of Soviet foreign policy was given in the Long Telegram of 1946. He saw the USSR as aggressive and suspicious and recommended firm action by the USA against what he viewed as Soviet expansion in Eastern Europe. The 'Long Telegram' was to be highly influential on Truman's foreign policy and led to the policy of containment. Kennan later returned to the Soviet Union as US Ambassador in 1952–53.

emphasised the role of communist ideology. He saw the Soviet leadership as suspicious and aggressive; insecurities that stemmed from their view of the outside world. Given this outlook, there could be no compromise with the USSR. From this point the American government dropped the prospect of compromise in favour of a policy of **containment**.

There were other factors that pushed Truman into dealing firmly with the Soviet Union. His hard-line approach, which was to become known as the 'Iron Fist', was a reaction against the policy of appeasement that had been pursued by the British against Nazi Germany. The lesson learnt by Truman was that the best way to stop dictators was to stand up to them.

Economic considerations pushed the USA towards greater involvement in Europe. The consumer-based US economy was concerned to see a revival in Europe to ensure a free market for American goods. The spread of communism and a subsequent closure of these markets to free trade needed to be avoided. Fears of an economic recession made US industrialists keen to protect this potential market from Soviet expansion.

The arms industries had done well out of the Second World War but now feared a downturn in orders with the end of the conflict. Thus for some businesses there was a definite advantage in talking up the international tension that was developing with the Cold War.

The growing mistrust of the USSR by the American government was increased by the failure of the USA to understand the Soviet Union's obsession with security. Due to geographical considerations US security had not been threatened directly during the Second World War. There was no comparison with the extreme suffering and hardship endured by the Soviet Union. The failure of the American government to comprehend the Soviet demand for security from further attack led them to interpret every action as part of the USSR's desire to dominate Europe and spread world communism. This misinterpretation was to add to the hostility that developed during the Cold War.

Despite these pressures pushing the US government towards making a greater commitment to Europe, there remained many among the American public who favoured returning to the traditional US policy of isolationism after 1945. These attitudes were driven by a desire to avoid war and a distaste for European **imperialism**. The future of US foreign policy was in the balance in 1945.

3 British attitudes in 1945

The Second World War had left Britain a great power in name only. The severe exertions of the war had produced a tripling of the national debt and a bankrupt economy. Yet Britain still had the commitments and responsibilities of a great power. This practical consideration was to greatly influence Britain's attitude to Europe. The British government knew that it would find it impossible to limit Soviet influence unless the USA could be persuaded to play a key role in the reconstruction of Europe.

> ### Definitions
>
> **Containment**
>
> The US policy of actively seeking to prevent the spread of Communism. It was heavily promoted by George Kennan's 'Long Telegram' and became the basis of US foreign policy under Truman.
>
> **Imperialism**
>
> Building an empire of dependent states.

Winston Churchill feared that the Americans, tired of fighting, would return to a policy of isolationism, as they had after the First World War. He realised that even with US support there was little the West could do to prevent Stalin doing as he wished in Eastern Europe. This explains why Churchill hoped that a personal agreement with Stalin might limit his actions.

In July 1945 Churchill was ousted as Prime Minister of Britain after a general election that saw a landslide victory for the Labour Party. To the general public, domestic policy, especially the establishment of the welfare state, was the priority. Yet there was little difference in how the Soviet Union was viewed by the new government, headed by **Clement Attlee**. Neither Attlee nor his foreign secretary Ernest Bevin ever showed the slightest sympathy with communism at home or abroad. Bevin made several attempts to get the USA to make a greater commitment to Europe by pointing to the danger of the Soviet threat to Iran as well as Eastern Europe. By 1946 the foreign policies of Britain and the USA were more in step with each other over the need to stand firm against the threat from the Soviet Union.

In 1945 the attitudes of the three main powers were hardening as they started to focus on post-war issues. When the two sides tried to reach agreement on the details of the post-war settlement hostility, coupled with misunderstanding and distrust, was to lead quickly to a breakdown in relations.

Questions

1 For each of the following countries write a short report stating the hopes and aims of their government for Europe in 1945:
   a) the USSR
   b) the USA
   c) Britain
   What similarities are there between the hopes and aims of these countries?

Biography

Clement Attlee (1883–1967)

Prime Minister of Britain between 1945 and 1951. He had been Deputy Prime Minister to Churchill in the wartime coalition government, when he was concerned with domestic policies. As leader of the Labour Party Attlee was a socialist but he did not share any sympathies with communism or the Soviet Union. Attlee believed in reform not revolution, and democracy rather than dictatorship, as the way to bring about change. He replaced Churchill as Prime Minister during the Potsdam Conference, after the 1945 election. Like Churchill he distrusted Stalin's motives and worked to secure a firmer commitment from the USA to help Western Europe stop the spread of communism.

Biography

Harry S. Truman (1884–1972)

US president from 1945, after the sudden death of Roosevelt, until 1952. A member of the Democratic Party, he served as Roosevelt's vice-president after 1944. His political career had been concerned with domestic issues and he knew little about foreign affairs when he suddenly became president. Under pressure from critics of Roosevelt's approach to Stalin, Truman adopted a more hard-line attitude to the Soviet Union. He took firm action during the Soviet blockade of Berlin in 1948–49 and entered the Korean War in 1950 to prevent the spread of communism in the Far East. At the end of his presidency he was under pressure from Red hysteria, a wave of strong anti-communist feeling promoted by Senator Joseph McCarthy.

How did the Cold War develop in Europe between 1945 and 1950?

The alliance of the 'Big Three' lost its reason for being as soon as Nazi Germany was defeated in 1945. The tensions and differences that had been kept below the surface during the Second World War came quickly to the fore. By 1950 there was a deep rift between East and West. As the Soviet Union acted to secure its hold over Eastern Europe, US involvement in Europe increased. The US government had, through the Truman Doctrine of March 1947, offered to intervene wherever communism threatened to impose itself in Europe, and by the Marshall Plan in the same year, he made a firm commitment to help restore the economies of Europe. The atmosphere of limited agreement and negotiation that had existed in 1945 was replaced by one where fear and mutual suspicion had gained the upper hand and had resulted in a deep division that proved impossible to repair.

What were the stages in this process of diplomatic breakdown?

Stage 1: the Yalta and Potsdam Conferences, 1945

In August 1941 Britain and the USA had agreed to the Atlantic Charter, a general statement of liberal principles on which the post-war international settlement was to be based. These principles included economic collaboration, a general security system and the drawing of national boundaries with regard to the wishes of the local population. These were broad principles that the Soviet Union had little trouble in supporting. But Stalin's attitude to fine principles was one of ambivalence: 'A declaration I regard as algebra, but an agreement as practical arithmetic. I do not wish to decry algebra, but I prefer arithmetic.' Differences in the interpretation of the general principles were to become obvious when at the Yalta Conference of February 1945 the leaders got down to the business of refining details.

Stalin was on home soil when he met with Churchill and Roosevelt at Yalta in the Soviet Union. The personal relationship between the three leaders was still sound enough to result in some significant agreements.

The main source of disagreement was over Poland. When the Soviet Red Army liberated Poland from Germany, a communist government was set up, based at Lublin. This was despite the fact that there was a government in exile in London that was ready to return to Poland as soon as it was safe to do so. At Yalta Stalin agreed to allow members of the London-based government into the new Lublin administration. The West hoped that Stalin's promise to uphold free elections would reduce the influence of the communists in the government.

Despite the agreements reached at the Yalta Conference, relations between East and West were to deteriorate quickly thereafter. When Roosevelt died in April 1945 his enemies accused him of having been soft on communism. Soviet actions in Eastern Europe after the conference seemed to indicate

> **Agreements reached at the Yalta Conference, February 1945**
>
> - the establishment of the United Nations
> - the division of Germany, Berlin and Austria into zones of occupation
> - the principle of free elections in Eastern Europe
> - agreement by the Soviet Union to join the war against Japan in return for the southern half of Sakhalin island and economic rights in Manchuria
> - the setting of the borders of post-war Poland so that substantial areas were given to the USSR.

that Stalin's word could not be trusted. Truman, the new American president, was determined not to make the same mistake. Less than a fortnight after taking over the presidency Truman told **Molotov**, the Soviet Foreign Minister who was visiting the United States, that the Soviet Union must keep to the agreements reached at Yalta. Truman is said to have used 'the language of a Missouri mule driver', and Molotov complained that he had never been spoken to in such a manner before. Truman's reply was that if the Soviet Union carried out its commitments he would 'not get talked to like that' again.

When the former wartime allies met later at Potsdam in July 1945 attitudes had hardened still further. The conference was to mark a severe cooling of relations. Stalin now faced Truman, who was still struggling to come to grips with the demands of the presidency, and Churchill, who was ousted as British Prime Minister by a general election and replaced by Clement Attlee while the conference was taking place. Faced with two relative newcomers to foreign affairs, Stalin had a clear advantage.

Truman and the British government were annoyed with the actions the Soviet Union was taking in Eastern Europe. Stalin had been allowed to incorporate some Polish territory into the Soviet Union. He then proceeded to transport Poles – who now found themselves in the USSR – west behind the new Polish–Soviet border. The USA and Britain finally agreed to move the western frontier of Poland to the Oder–Western Neisse line; 5 million Germans were subsequently expelled from Poland by the USSR and forcibly moved west into Germany. Throughout Eastern Europe communist groups were being positioned in important government roles. These actions worried Truman, in particular, and he determined not to inform Stalin of the decision to drop the first atomic bomb on Japan, an event that happened only four days after the end of the conference. The bombing of **Hiroshima** was the result of calculations made by the Americans in terms of how to bring the war against Japan to an end with the minimum loss of American lives. Yet Truman was fully aware that the atomic bomb could be a powerful weapon by which pressure could be exerted on the Soviet Union. The enormous destructive damage caused by the bomb on Hiroshima shocked the world. Truman called it 'the greatest thing in history'. It was hoped that Stalin would take notice and become more amenable in Europe. Stalin saw the failure of Truman to at least inform him of the bomb as a deep insult, and far from making Stalin more amenable, it increased his suspicions and distrust of America's motives. Stalin was, after all, a wartime ally of the United States and, it could be argued, had a right to be informed. When a second atomic bomb was dropped on the Japanese city of Nagasaki on 9 August, the United States was able to bring about the surrender of Japan without the need for Soviet assistance. Stalin was therefore denied a part in the occupation of Japan.

Events were to prove that the atomic bomb had little impact on Stalin's policies. While encouraging the Soviet Union to develop its own atomic bomb as soon as possible, Stalin regarded the atomic bomb as a weapon of bluff that was unlikely to be used in Europe because of its huge destructive power. Thus, the threat of America using its atomic bombs was to harden Stalin's attitude of mistrust towards the USA without softening his policies.

Stage 2: Russian influence in Eastern Europe 1945–47

At the end of the Second World War the Soviet Red Army was stationed in large parts of Eastern Europe. Given the political and military vacuum that existed after the defeat of Nazi Germany, the Red Army was well placed to exert influence in Eastern Europe. Its presence was a source of much anxiety on the part of the West, who realised that it provided Stalin with a powerful weapon by which he could stamp his policies on the region. In actual fact, the Soviet Union was to be demobilised rapidly from an army of over 11 million in May 1945 to about 2 million in early 1948. Sixty Red Army divisions remained in Eastern Europe to fulfil a policing role. Although not aimed against the West, these divisions played an important role in imposing communist regimes on the region. Pro-communist governments were set up in Poland, Hungary, Romania, Bulgaria and Albania. The events that led to this situation differed slightly in each country, but the usual pattern was one of pressure applied by the Soviet Union to allow communist politicians to hold key positions in **coalition governments** before elections were held. With posts such as that of interior minister (responsible for the police force and law and order) in communist hands, elections could then be manipulated to ensure communists controlled the levers of power. To strengthen Communist parties, they were often encouraged by Stalin to merge with other, often bigger, socialist groups, who found 'merge' to mean, in reality, takeover. By the end of 1947 every state in Eastern Europe was controlled by a communist government with the exception of Czechoslovakia.

Stalin had gained control over what he considered to be a legitimate sphere of influence for the Soviet Union. To have governments unfriendly to the USSR on its borders was seen as unacceptable because this was unlikely to guarantee security against future attack. To the United States this development was viewed differently. Stalin had failed to keep his promise to hold free elections in Eastern Europe. The US government was suspicious of Stalin's intentions and was worried that there was a serious threat of Soviet expansion across Europe. These fears were also raised by Churchill.

Stage 3: Churchill's 'Iron Curtain' speech, March 1946

The call for firmer action by the West against the threat of communism was made by Churchill, the ex-Prime Minister of Britain. In a speech delivered at Fulton, Missouri, in the USA, Churchill declared: 'From Stettin in the Baltic to Trieste in the Adriatic an **Iron Curtain** has descended across the continent' (see Source F, page 33). In order to meet this Soviet expansion, Churchill called for an alliance between Britain and America.

Definitions

Coalition government

A government made up of the representatives of more than one political party. They were often set up in the countries of Eastern Europe immediately after the Second World War in the interests of national unity but provided a useful foothold for Communists to gain control.

Iron Curtain

The name given to a figurative line that divided the communist East from the capitalist West in Europe. The term was made popular by Winston Churchill in 1946 when it was used in a speech at Fulton, Missouri (see map on page 26).

Iron Fist

A term used by Truman to describe a tougher approach to the USSR. It was a reaction to the approach adopted by Roosevelt, his predecessor, which was seen by Truman as too soft on communism.

Warmonger

Someone who wishes to provoke war. Stalin accused Churchill of warmongering after his Iron Curtain speech.

Churchill gave the speech as a private individual: Attlee was not informed of its content beforehand but did not disagree with its message and later thanked Churchill. Truman had read the speech before it was delivered and was present when it was given. Public opinion in America was not favourable to the call for an alliance with Britain, but Churchill had stated what Truman and his advisers privately thought, and it fell into line with Truman's **Iron Fist** approach: 'Unless Russia is faced with an iron fist and strong language, another war is in the making.'

In Moscow the speech received a hysterical response. Stalin saw it as deliberately provocative and accused Churchill of being a **warmonger**. Relations between East and West reached a new low.

Source B

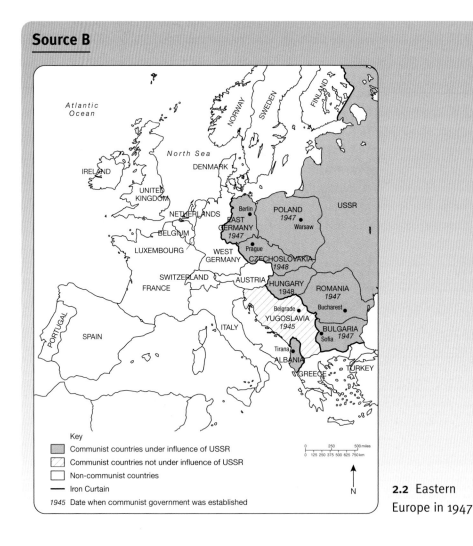

Key

▨ Communist countries under influence of USSR

▨ Communist countries not under influence of USSR

☐ Non-communist countries

— Iron Curtain

1945 Date when communist government was established

2.2 Eastern Europe in 1947

Stage 4: the Truman Doctrine and the Marshall Plan, 1947

By 1947 US foreign policy was to change decisively away from a conciliatory approach towards the Soviet Union, as advocated by Roosevelt, to one that was much more militant. The change was to be embodied in the Truman Doctrine and the Marshall Plan.

The pressure on the US government to adopt a more hard-line approach had been building since the end of 1945. Kennan's 'Long Telegram' and Churchill's Iron Curtain speech of 1946 had encouraged this move. So too did the actions of the Soviet Union. Further evidence of what the West saw as Soviet expansion was revealed by events in Greece in 1947. Since 1944 there had been a civil war in Greece between the monarchists and the communists. After the defeat of Nazi Germany the Greek royal government had been restored to power with the help of the British despite resistance from the communists who were strong in the countryside. Stalin seems to have kept to his agreement made with Churchill in 1942 that Greece was an area of British influence and did nothing to directly help the Greek communists, although the communist governments of Yugoslavia and Albania did send aid. Nonetheless, the West became convinced that this was another sign of Soviet expansion. Firm action was needed, and this was something the British were finding hard to sustain.

By 1947 the draining impact of the Second World War was being felt. The British government owed £3,000 million in debts incurred during the war against Germany. The British economy was in a state of crisis, made worse by the severe winter weather of 1946–47. The British government was forced to admit that it could no longer sustain its overseas commitments. In February 1947 they warned the USA that they could not maintain troops in Greece. Faced with the prospect of a British withdrawal leading to a communist takeover in another country of key strategic importance, the US president issued the **Truman Doctrine**.

In March 1947 Truman issued a statement that declared that 'it must be the policy of the United States to support free peoples who are resisting subjugation by armed minorities or by outside pressures' (see Source G, page 33). The Truman Doctrine, as it became known, was a response to the situation in Greece, but it was clear to all that it was designed to have wider application. Truman saw a straightforward choice between two alternatives: communism and democracy. Wherever communist forces were attempting to overthrow a democratically elected government the USA would take action. In practice Truman was prepared to support any government providing it was anti-communist.

American aid and military advisers were sent to support the royalist government in Greece, and the communist insurrection there was defeated. To Stalin this was evidence of American imperialism, a view reinforced by the launching of the **Marshall Plan**.

In the spring of 1947 George Marshall, the new American Secretary of State, travelled through Western Europe and was shocked by the devastation and economic suffering he witnessed. He recognised that economic support and assistance were desperately needed and the result was the launching of the Marshall Plan. The plan committed large sums of American financial assistance to Europe. It was, according to Churchill, 'the most unselfish act in history'. While providing much needed aid for economic recovery and reconstruction, the motives behind Marshall aid

Definitions

Truman Doctrine

A policy statement issued by the American president in 1947. It stated that the USA would aid any country or government under attack by armed minorities. It was aimed at preventing the spread of communism. It was used to send aid and military advisers to Greece to help the monarchist government against the communists.

Marshall Plan

A plan to provide American financial support to war-torn Europe. It was drawn up by George C. Marshall, the US Secretary of State, in 1947. All countries in Europe were eligible for Marshall aid, but the conditions attached made it impossible for the communist states of Eastern Europe to apply. Over 17 billion dollars were provided to Europe, and by 1952 Western Europe's economy was experiencing sustained growth.

Definitions

Dollar imperialism

A term used by Molotov to describe Marshall aid. He saw the financial aid as a mechanism by which the USA would gain control over Europe and exploit it for America's economic interests.

Cominform

An organisation controlled by the USSR, set up in 1947 to coordinate communist parties throughout Europe. Its propaganda was virulently anti-American.

Comecon

An organisation controlled by the USSR, set up in 1949 to coordinate the economies of communist countries. It was largely a reaction to the Marshall Plan. Economic aid was limited, but the organisation was able to ensure that a Stalinist state-owned economy was imposed on the countries of Eastern Europe.

Discussion point

How can Source C be used to show why the USA took an interest in European affairs after the Second World War?

were more than merely humanitarian. There were concerns that unless the economies of Europe recovered there would be a danger of economic recession in the USA. Without financial assistance Europe would not be able to act as a market for American goods. In addition to this economic motive there was also a political consideration. The Americans saw poverty as the ideal breeding ground for communism. A prosperous Europe was less likely to fall for its attractions.

In theory Marshall aid was available for any European country to apply for, but in practice it went to Western Europe only. The conditions attached to receiving the aid – providing economic records and opening up their economy to American capitalist interests – were such that it was impossible for communist states to do so without a fundamental change to their system. The Soviet Union viewed Marshall aid as nothing more than an attack on communism. Molotov condemned it as foreign interference in the states of Europe and labelled the plan **dollar imperialism**. Under Soviet pressure the countries of Eastern Europe declined the offer of financial aid.

The USSR effectively declared war on the Marshall Plan by tightening their hold over Eastern Europe through the setting up of **Cominform** in 1947, an organisation to coordinate communist parties and groups throughout Europe, and **Comecon** in 1949, an organisation that provided economic assistance to the countries of Eastern Europe. Thus the Truman Doctrine and Marshall aid had resulted in a Soviet response that made the division of Europe more entrenched.

The chances of future agreement between the two superpowers were now negligible. The hopes of 1945 had been swept away by a series of actions that revealed the mutual mistrust between two competing systems.

Source C

2.3 Devastation caused by the Second World War in Dresden, 1945

The actions of the Soviet Union (September 1945 to 1948)

1945

2 September	VJ Day: end of Second World War
11 November	Communists win rigged elections in Yugoslavia
18 November	Communists win rigged elections in Bulgaria
20 November	USSR refuses to remove Red Army from northern Iran

1946

2 January	King Zog of Albania deposed by Communists
15–18 February	Soviet spy ring uncovered in Canada
26 May	Communists head a coalition government in Czechoslovakia
10 September	Greek communists start civil war against royalists

1947

10 July	USSR forces Poland and Czechoslovakia to turn down Marshall aid
31 August	Communists win rigged elections in Hungary
23 September	Cominform established

1948

19–25 February	Communist *coup d'état* in Czechoslovakia
1 April	USSR starts to interfere with Western traffic to Berlin
24 June	USSR starts full blockade of all surface routes to West Berlin

SKILLS BUILDER

Look at the timeline of Soviet actions between September 1945 and 1948. What do these actions suggest about the motives of Soviet foreign policy?

Stage 5: the Czechoslovakian Crisis, 1948

The year 1948 saw a sequence of events that seemed to the West to be evidence of the aggressive and expansionist policy of Stalin towards Europe. At the beginning of the year Czechoslovakia was the only remaining democratic country in Eastern Europe. Elections were due in May during which the communists were expected to do badly. The failure of Czechoslovakia to receive Marshall aid was blamed on communists in the coalition government. Before the election was held the communists staged a **coup d'état**. The police force was taken over by the communists and purged of non-communist personnel. Representatives of political parties other than the communists were removed from government in February. The only remaining non-communist in the government, Jan Masaryk, suffered defenestration: he was thrown from a window, probably by members of the security police, and died from his injuries. President Beneš was forced to resign, replaced by the communist Gottwald. The Czech communists had taken over the country with little bloodshed and without direct help from the Soviet Union.

The Czechoslovakian crisis was of psychological significance for the West. In addition to increasing the fear of communist expansion, it played on

Definition

Coup d'état

A violent or illegal takeover of government.

Questions

1 How might the events in Czechoslovakia in 1948 have affected the attitude of the West towards the USSR?

2 The communist takeover of Czechoslovakia was in many ways similar to the communist takeover of the other Eastern European countries. So why did the West protest so much more over Czechoslovakia?

feelings of guilt, particularly in Britain, because nothing had been done to prevent Hitler taking Czechoslovakia in 1938–39. Ten years later there was again little the West could do to thwart the stamp of oppression on a country that might have provided a valuable bridge between East and West.

Stage 6: the Berlin Blockade, 1948–49

The Cold War in Europe was to reach its first major crisis with the Berlin Blockade of 1948–49. Although disappointed with the increase in Soviet influence in countries such as Romania, Bulgaria and other parts of Eastern Europe, the West could eventually 'forget' them, but Germany was different. Here the troops of both sides stood directly opposite each other: they could not avoid one another. The so-called German problem would not go away because the arrangements agreed at the conferences at Yalta and Potsdam were temporary. At some time the long-term future of Germany would have to be settled. The Berlin Blockade was one of the Soviet Union's most drastic attempts to influence this future.

Source D

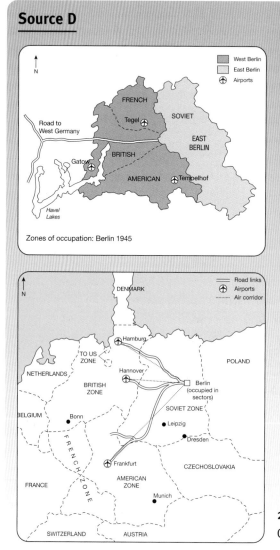

Zones of occupation: Berlin 1945

2.4 The division of Berlin and Germany after 1945

Causes of the Berlin Blockade

- The seeds of the dispute had been laid by the arrangements for the city agreed at the Yalta and Potsdam conferences in 1945. Germany and its capital city Berlin were to be divided each into four zones to be administered on a temporary basis by the wartime allies (see map, page 30).

- The Western zones, run by Britain, America and France, benefited from an influx of Marshall aid. The Eastern zone was run by the USSR, which plundered it for resources, taken as reparations for war damage caused during the Second World War. As East Germany was denied access to Marshall funds, the living conditions there remained low and were slow to recover. By 1948 the difference in living standards between West and East Germany had become embarrassingly obvious. It was in Berlin that this difference was brought into sharp focus. West Berlin had become an island of prosperous capitalism in a sea of communism.

- The Council of Foreign Ministers, which had been attempting to agree a system of administration for Berlin, broke up without agreement in December 1947. No future date for talks was agreed.

- In February 1948 the USA, Britain and France began talks on the administration of Western Germany. This led to the decision to establish a separate West German state in June.

- The Western powers decided to introduce a new currency in their zones, including West Berlin. The new Deutsche Mark would, it was hoped, provide economic stability and aid recovery. It was a symbol of the growing prosperity of the Western sectors compared with the East. For Stalin this was the last straw.

- On 24 June 1948 Stalin took action. All road, rail and canal links with West Berlin were severed.

Results

The West responded to the blockade by organising an airlift of supplies into Berlin. All food and fuel supplies for over 2 million Berliners were flown into the city. It was an expensive operation executed with impressive organisational skill. Despite constant shortages, the city was able to survive. By May 1949 Stalin was forced to concede defeat and lifted the blockade. The actions of the West had been successful, and it was an important boost to morale after the events in Czechoslovakia.

The Berlin crisis had illustrated the need for a more coordinated approach by the West in order to prepare for Soviet aggression. In April 1949 the United States opened talks with Canada and the countries of Western Europe with the aim of committing itself to a military alliance. The result was the setting up of the North Atlantic Treaty Organization (**NATO**). This was an enlargement of the Brussels Treaty of 1948, which had been signed by Britain, France, Belgium, the Netherlands and Luxembourg to establish military cooperation in the event of war. The significance of NATO was

Questions

1 The issue of Berlin was to highlight the different attitudes of the superpowers to post-war Germany.
a) Why did the United States not fear a revived Germany after 1945?
b) Why, in contrast, did the USSR fear a German revival?
2 What were the possible motives behind Stalin's actions in blockading Berlin?

Definition

NATO

The North Atlantic Treaty Organization, a military alliance of the USA, Canada and most of Western Europe. Set up in 1949, it was an organisation to defend the West during the Cold War.

Definition

Isolationism

A policy of keeping out of conflicts in foreign affairs and not getting involved in military alliances. After the First World War the USA adopted a policy of isolationism towards Europe. The British feared the USA would return to isolationism after the Second World War.

that it involved the United States in a military alliance in peacetime and, therefore, made it clear to the Soviet Union that there would be no return to **isolationism**. The guiding principle of NATO was that an attack on one of its members would be seen as an attack on all. A NATO command was set up to coordinate the defence of its members. Thus NATO was a defensive organisation to protect the West and its interests. Stalin viewed the creation of NATO as a deliberately provocative action, but he was able to enhance the capability of the Soviet Union by breaking the American nuclear monopoly. The Soviet Union exploded its first atomic bomb in August 1949, earlier than the West had expected. Despite this increase in Soviet power, the Berlin crisis and the formation of NATO had taken the initiative in Cold War relations away from the USSR.

Another significant result of the Berlin crisis was the end to any hope of an agreement between East and West over Germany. The temporary division of the country, laid down at Yalta and Potsdam, was now to become a more permanent feature. In August 1949 the three western zones of Germany joined together to become the Federal Republic of Germany (commonly known as West Germany). In response, the Russian zone became the German Democratic Republic (East Germany) in October. As capitalism flourished in West Germany, communism was imposed upon East Germany. It was a division that was to last for 40 years.

Source E

2.5 West Berliners watch US aircraft bringing in supplies to the city, 1949

Discussion point

Explain how the information in Source E can be used to highlight both US and Soviet attitudes towards Berlin in 1948–49.

The Berlin crisis of 1948–49 had marked the first major flashpoint of the Cold War. Relations between the USA and the USSR, former allies against Nazi Germany, had reached such a low position of distrust and suspicion that it would be difficult to have any meaningful dialogue let alone agreement. Conflict and tension were to remain constant features of East–West relations for another 40 years with important consequences for Europe and the rest of the world.

Key confrontation: Churchill and the Iron Curtain speech – what was its significance?

Source F

Extract from Churchill's Iron Curtain speech, 1946

An iron curtain has descended across the continent. Behind that line lie all the capitals of the ancient states of Central and Eastern Europe. All these famous cities, and the populations around them, lie in the Soviet sphere, and all are subject in one form or another, not only to Soviet influence, but to a very high and increasing measure of control from Moscow. The Russian-dominated Polish Government has been encouraged to make enormous and wrongful inroads upon Germany, and mass expulsions of millions of Germans on a scale grievous and undreamed of are now taking place. The Communist parties, which were very small in all these Eastern States of Europe, have been raised to leadership and power far beyond their numbers, and are seeking everywhere to obtain totalitarian control. Police governments are prevailing in nearly every case, and so far, except in Czechoslovakia, there is no true democracy.

From what I have seen of our Russian friends during the war, I am convinced that there is nothing they admire so much as strength . . . If the Western Democracies stand together in strict adherence to the principles of the United Nations Charter, their influence for furthering those principles will be immense and no one is likely to molest them. If however they become divided then indeed catastrophe may overwhelm us all.

SKILLS BUILDER

Discuss the significance of Churchill's Iron Curtain speech.(You should comment on how important you think Churchill's speech was in changing US foreign policy towards Europe and the Soviet Union.)

Key confrontation: the Truman Doctrine – a turning point in the development of the Cold War?

Source G

An extract from the Truman Doctrine

At the present moment in world history nearly every nation must choose between alternative ways of life. One way of life is based upon the will of the majority, and is distinguished by free institutions, representative government, free elections, guarantees of individual liberty, freedom of speech and religion, and freedom from political oppression. The second way of life is based upon the will of a minority forcibly imposed upon a majority. It relies upon terror and oppression, a controlled press and radio, fixed elections, and the suppression of personal freedoms.

I believe that it must be the policy of the United States to support free peoples who are resisting attempted subjugation by armed minorities or by outside pressures. I believe that we must assist free peoples to work out their own destinies in their own way. I believe that our help should be primarily through economic and financial aid which is essential to economic stability and orderly political processes.

Source H

A Soviet response to the Truman Doctrine and Marshall Plan

The so-called Truman Doctrine and the Marshall Plan are particularly glaring examples of the manner in which the principles of the United Nations are violated . . .

As the experience of the past few months has shown, the proclamation of this doctrine meant that the United States government has moved towards a direct renunciation of the principles of international collaboration and concerted action by the great powers and towards attempts to impose its will on other independent states, while at the same time obviously using the economic resources distributed as relief to individual needy nations as an instrument of political pressure.

. . . the implementation of the Marshall Plan will mean placing European countries under the economic and political control of the United States . . .

From a speech to the UN General Assembly given by Andrei Vyshinsky,
the Soviet Deputy Foreign Minister (September 1947)

SKILLS BUILDER

1 To what extent does Source H support the view that the Truman Doctrine was a response to the situation in Greece in 1947?

2 By reference to Sources G and H, and your own knowledge, explain how the Truman Doctrine and the Marshall Plan of 1947 contributed to the development of the Cold War.

Key confrontation: the Berlin Blockade, 1948–49

Source I

Stalin was engaged in what George Kennan called a 'kind of squeeze play'. He wanted to force the Western powers either to give up their moves towards a separate West German state, or to relinquish West Berlin . . . in a meeting with Yugoslav and Bulgarian communist leaders, Stalin had stressed that Germany would remain divided: 'The West will make West Germany their own, and we shall turn Eastern Germany into our own state'.

Soviet policy had another, more general, purpose. Soviet leaders regarded relations with the West as a war of nerves, and were determined to show that they would not be intimidated.

From David Holloway, *Stalin and the Bomb*, in M. Leffler & D. Painter (ed.),
Origins of the Cold War, published by Routledge (2005)

Source J

From Russia's perspective the blockade was a legitimate response to the West's unilateral decision to unify the three western occupation zones . . . including to institute a new currency in the western zones.

Detesting the Soviet government, most Americans by 1948 did not seek to understand its viewpoint, much less to find merit in it.

Truman was determined to stay in Berlin . . . Ordinary Germans, Britons and Americans – including the tens of thousands of industrial workers, coal miners, military personnel, and labourers who loaded and unloaded the planes – deserve much of the credit for the airlift's success. Stalin also showed restraint by not ordering Soviet forces to shoot down the planes while they were flying over the Russian zone.

From R. B. Levering & V. Botzenhart-Viehe,
The American Perspective in R. Levering et al. (ed.),
in *The Origins of the Cold War*,
published by Rowman & Littlefield (2001)

Source K

. . . the establishment of a West German state was rightly perceived in Moscow as a complete break with the Yalta-Potsdam agreements . . . In analysing these events for the Kremlin, the Soviet Foreign Ministry concluded that 'the western powers are transforming Germany into their stronghold . . . directed against the Soviet Union'. Desperate to forestall such developments, the Kremlin decided to counterattack by using the most tangible advantage it still held in Germany: control over the geographic space between the western zones and Berlin.

. . . Stalin's hardball tactics, which he pursued too long, proved to be counterproductive. Instead of blocking the implementation of the Western plan for Germany, the Berlin blockade accelerated it.

From V. Pechatnov & C.E. Edmondson,
The Russian Perspective in R. Levering et al. (ed.), in
The Origins of the Cold War, published by
Rowman & Littlefield (2001)

SKILLS BUILDER

Sources I, J and K give different interpretations on the causes and results of the Berlin blockade.

1 Summarize the interpretation that each source gives of the causes of the blockade in no more than 5 words.

2 What phrases or words would you quote from each source to illustrate their view?

3 State one way in which the three sources agree.

4 State one way in which they disagree.

Why did Cold War conflict extend to the Far East 1950–53?

American satisfaction at the lifting of the Berlin Blockade in May 1949 was soon overshadowed by events elsewhere that showed that the USA could not take its lead in the Cold War for granted. In August American nuclear supremacy came to a halt with the announcement that the USSR had developed its own atomic bomb. Worse was to follow in October 1949 when Mao Zedong proclaimed that the People's Republic of China was now established. Communism had spread to cover the largest country in the

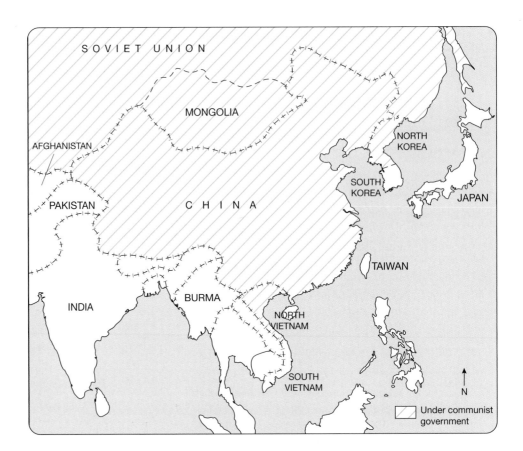

2.7 Communist states in the Far East, 1954

world. The tide seemed to be turning in favour of the forces of world communism, with the focus now on the Far East. It was inevitable that US foreign policy would change to respond to this perception.

1 Events in China

China had been in a state of civil war since the 1920s. The Nationalists (Guomindang), led by Chiang Kai Shek, had faced fierce opposition from the Chinese communists organised by Mao Zedong. In 1945, at the end of the Second World War, the defeat of Japan had left much of China without any form of control. The Communists were successful in quickly gaining a hold over these areas and by 1949 were strong enough to push the Nationalists out of mainland China. Chiang Kai Shek and the remnants of his party fled to the island of Taiwan. Mao's declaration of a Communist People's Republic of China in October sent shock waves across America. But these events were hardly surprising.

Why did the Communists win?

- The Nationalists had been corrupt and out of touch with the needs of the majority of Chinese people.

- In comparison the Communists had gained a reputation for addressing the needs of the bulk of the population. In the areas under their control they had raised production and given peasants control over the land. They were said to 'practise what they preach'.

- The impact of the Second World War had seriously weakened the Nationalists' hold over China. The Japanese invasion had been geared towards taking control of the coastal areas of China, which had been held by the Nationalists. The Communists had tended to hold inland areas, often mountainous regions, which the Japanese were less interested in.

- Yet back in America the Communist takeover of China was seen as evidence of Stalin's work in spreading world communism.

- It was also viewed as the result of the failure of the USA to send enough support to the Nationalists. China had a special place in the hearts of American politicians. Since the nineteenth century the USA had seen itself as the guardian of China against the worst excesses of European imperialism.

There was a sense that the guardian had failed in its role and with such a large country under communist rule, the forces of freedom and capitalism seemed, to many Americans, to be under threat.

2 Korea

With China now in communist hands, the American government became more concerned about other possible victims of communist aggression. These concerns were soon realised in Korea. The Korean peninsula had been temporarily divided at the end of the Second World War, but attempts to secure unification peacefully had failed due to deep divisions between political groups in the north and south of the country. Any possibility of progress towards peaceful unification collapsed when the communist forces of North Korea invaded the capitalist South in 1950. American politicians concluded that this was further evidence of Stalin's attempts to spread communism. Bordering both China and the Soviet Union, North Korea was considered to be under the direction of both Moscow and Beijing. The USA intervened in the Korean War in force, under the auspices of the United Nations. Although Stalin avoided direct involvement in the war, Communist China sent substantial military aid to North Korea.

3 Vietnam

Vietnam had been part of French Indochina until it had been seized by the Japanese during the Second World War. After 1945 the French tried to regain control over its former colonies. The USA was strongly opposed to imperialism and had been very critical of the overseas empires ruled by European powers. But after the Second World War, the countries of Europe no longer had the resources to run vast empires. This posed a serious dilemma for the USA. If France did not regain control over Indochina, what would take its place? In Vietnam the forces of nationalism and communism were combined by the Vietminh, led by the communist Ho Chi Minh. Geographically positioned south of China, Vietnam was well placed to receive assistance from Mao's communists after 1949.

4 The missile gap

Faced with a threat from world communism directed by Stalin and Mao, the USA tried to rely on a measure of security gained through superiority in military weaponry. Between 1945 and 1949 the USA was the only nuclear power. This security was shattered in August 1949 when the Soviet Union announced it had developed an atomic bomb. This was much quicker than the West had thought possible. In 1952 the USA developed the more powerful hydrogen bomb, but the Soviet Union was able, partly with the help of information gained through its spy networks, to produce its own less than a year later. This led to concerns in the US government that the USSR would match and overtake the West in its nuclear and conventional military capability. Thus China's fall to communism focused the minds of the US government on how best to meet the threat posed by world communism.

5 The Red Scare and McCarthyism

The eagerness and determination of the US government to stand up to the threat of communism in the Far East was to play a key role in the process that saw Cold War tensions imposed on events that were more local in their origins. The hardening of US foreign policy towards the threat of Soviet world domination was in part a response to the vulnerability felt by many Americans who feared the spread of communism at home.

Blame for America's failure to match the USSR led some Americans to look for enemy agents at home. Anti-communist feeling was high in the early 1950s, leading to a wave of hysteria generated by a fear that the USA was being undermined by the enemy within.

The Communist Party in the USA was never very large. At its height, membership was no more than 100,000. Yet suspicions that there were communist spies within the American government and administration gained momentum during the 1940s.

This anti-communist hysteria proved to be a useful opportunity for Republican Senator Joseph McCarthy to revive his political career. In 1950 McCarthy accused many who worked for the government of being communists and therefore disloyal to the United States. McCarthy had no evidence to support his claims, but thousands of Americans were willing to believe him. In 1954 McCarthy was revealed as a liar and a crook by defence lawyer Joseph Welch. Nonetheless, anti-communist views remained embedded in US society and they were to play a part in adding to the pressure for hardening the stance of US foreign policy against communism. This was known as **McCarthyism**.

It is tempting to see the spreading of Cold War tensions to the Far East as due to the forces of communism encroaching into Asia. The establishment of the People's Republic of China in 1949, the outbreak of the Korean War in 1950 and the spreading of communism into Indochina after 1945 were viewed by the Americans as evidence of this. Yet this is only part of an adequate explanation for the extension of the Cold War.

Definition

McCarthyism

The wave of anti-communist feeling that spread through the USA in the early 1950s. It is sometimes referred to as the Red Scare and was encouraged by sections of the Republican Party, most notably by Joseph McCarthy. The movement aimed to remove communist sympathisers from all sections of American life, including members of Truman's government who were seen as soft on communism.

The events of this period were to prompt a more aggressive response from the USA, who showed, by their response to the Korean War, that they were willing to take military action against what they perceived as the spread of communism. The implementation of the recommendations of the report NSC-68 (see below) became a reality because they were to find justification in the actions of North Korea in 1950.

Yet the spread of communism in the Far East was only in part due to the strengths of communism. The takeover of China by the Communists had its roots in nationalist sentiment aimed at overthrowing foreigners who had exploited their country for their own ends. The conflicts in Korea and Indochina were in essence civil wars in which nationalism played a significant part. In Korea it was a conflict over the direction of a reunified country that would reclaim its independence after the Second World War; in Indochina it was a nationalist response to the old colonial power.

The rise of communist groups was aided by the unique circumstances prevailing at the time. As in Europe, the end of the Second World War had left a power vacuum in the Far East. In Korea the defeat of Japan and the subsequent occupation by the wartime allies had left the future of the country uncertain. In Vietnam the power vacuum was further complicated by the French attempt to restore old-style European imperialism to the region, an attempt that seemed unlikely to succeed. It was these circumstances, more than a Soviet planned programme to expand communism, that were to provide the uncertainty that was to aid greatly the success of groups that had an attachment to communism.

Questions

1 Explain the role played by each of the following in extending the Cold War to the Far East between 1949 and 1953:
   a) the aggressive nature of communist groups
   b) the growth of nationalism in the Far East
   c) the defeat of Japan in 1945
   d) the decline of European imperialism.
2 Which of these factors was the most important? Explain your choice.
3 What lessons should the USA have learnt from the communist victory in China?

Case study: NSC-68

The early 1950s was a period when many Americans believed they were losing the Cold War. This feeling of vulnerability was to have a significant impact on US foreign policy.

In 1950 President Truman asked the National Security Council to produce a report on US Cold War policy. The result was a document known as NSC-68. This report was to reveal the impact of American insecurities on policy.

Source L

NSC-68 United States Objectives and Programs for National Security NSC 68

The Soviet Union is animated by a new fanatic faith, antithetical to our own, and seeks to impose its absolute authority over the rest of the world. Conflict has, therefore, become endemic and is waged, on the part of the Soviet Union, by violent or non-violent methods in accordance with the dictates of expediency. With the development of increasingly terrifying weapons of mass destruction, every individual faces the ever-present possibility of annihilation should the conflict enter the phase of total war.

On the one hand, the people of the world yearn for relief from the anxiety arising from the risk of atomic war. On the other hand, any substantial further extension of the area under the domination of the Kremlin would raise the possibility that no coalition adequate to confront the Kremlin with greater strength could be assembled. It is in this context that the United States and its citizens in the ascendancy of their strength stand in their deepest peril.

Recommendations

- The United States must have substantially increased general air, ground, and sea strength, atomic capabilities, and air and civilian defenses to deter war and to provide reasonable assurance.
- The United States must develop a level of military readiness which can be maintained as long as necessary as a deterrent to Soviet aggression and as a source of encouragement to nations resisting Soviet political aggression, and as an adequate basis for immediate military commitments and for rapid mobilization should war prove unavoidable.
- The internal security of the United States against dangers of sabotage, subversion, and espionage must be assured.
- Our economic potential, including the strengthening of our peacetime economy must be maximized.
- We must strengthen the orientation toward the United States of the non-Soviet nations; and help such of those nations as are able and willing to make an important contribution to US security, to increase their economic and political stability and their military capability.
- Place the maximum strain on the Soviet structure of power and particularly on the relationships between Moscow and the satellite countries.
- Keep the US public fully informed and cognizant of the threats to our national security so that it will be prepared to support the measures which we must accordingly adopt.

Our position as the center of power in the free world places a heavy responsibility upon the United States for leadership. We must organize and enlist the energies and resources of the free world in a positive program for peace which will frustrate the Kremlin design for world domination.

From the report NSC-68 (issued in April 1950 by the National Security Council)

The report saw the world in **bipolar** terms, highlighting the division of the world into two superpowers in conflict with each other. This situation had been brought about because of the aims of the USSR.

NSC-68 made recommendations for the direction of US foreign policy that marked a change from the earlier policy of containment. Containment had accepted the existence of the Soviet Union and focused on containing communism within its existing borders. The new emphasis was to be on '**roll back**', the view that communism needed to be confronted and pushed back to safeguard the free world. This was, therefore, the basis of a more aggressive American foreign policy.

Nonetheless, there was no guarantee that the government would adopt its own recommendations. The increased level of military commitment would require a large boost in taxation to pay for it. As the report itself acknowledged, the US public needed to be 'fully informed and cognizant of the threats' to US security, otherwise it would not accept the increased commitment. What stopped the report becoming just another piece of paper was the start of the Korean War in June 1950. As Dean Acheson, the **Secretary of State**, stated: 'Korea came along and saved us.'

Key confrontation: the Korean War 1950–53

Source M

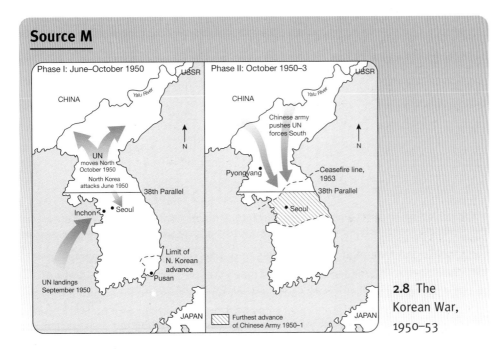

2.8 The Korean War, 1950–53

When the forces of North Korea invaded the South on 25 June 1950, the United Nations called for help for the victim of aggression. The United States was quick to secure a commitment from 16 countries to send troops under the UN banner to help South Korea. Among those who sent troops were Britain, Canada, Turkey and the Philippines, but the vast majority of

Definitions

Bipolar

The idea of the world being divided into two power blocs: those of communism, centred on the USSR, and the West, centred on the USA.

Roll back

The policy of pushing back the frontiers of communism and liberating states where communism had been imposed by force. It was a term that gained currency in the 1950s and marked a more assertive US stance than that of containment, which had dominated American government thinking since 1945.

Secretary of State

The head of the department of the US government that conducts foreign policy.

the troops sent were American. The USA sent over 260,000 troops to Korea. The UN forces were led by the staunchly anti-communist American **General Douglas MacArthur**.

The vigour with which America honoured its promise to South Korea was a reflection of the speed at which South Korea was collapsing. By early September 1950 South Korean forces had been pushed back to Pusan and seemed unlikely to hold out for much longer. On 15 September, under the leadership of General Douglas MacArthur, American marines landed at Inchon. During Operation Chromite, 261 ships landed UN troops almost unopposed. This relieved the pressure on Pusan and within days the South Koreans were able to push North Korea's army back towards the 38th parallel.

The failure of Stalin to aid North Korea or send them large amounts of military supplies (Soviet shipments to North Korea actually declined during the war) provided Truman with confidence that the war could be limited to the peninsula. By early September 1950 the South had been saved from North Korea's forces. The original aims of the intervention had been achieved.

On 30 September South Korean forces crossed the 38th parallel and entered the North. The US government now talked about a 'thrust north'. As the UN voted its agreement American forces were already crossing the border. MacArthur began a rapid advance northwards, capturing the capital of the North, Pyongyang, in October.

Truman's decision to authorise the invasion of the North marked a shift from the policy of containment towards one of attempting to roll back

Biography

General Douglas MacArthur (1880–1964)

A highly competent US general who led the UN forces sent to help South Korea expel the invasion by the North. He had been Commander of the Allied Forces in the Pacific during the Second World War. In 1945 he supervised the occupation of Japan after its surrender. During the Korean War he organised the landings of marines at Inchon, which saved South Korea from collapse. He then carried the campaign against North Korea across the 38th parallel without waiting for authorisation from Truman. Fiercely anti-communist, MacArthur wanted to roll back communism in Korea and China and use nuclear weapons if necessary. His outspokenness led to his dismissal by President Truman in 1951. However, MacArthur and his approach to the war remained popular. He launched a campaign against Truman and gained support from McCarthy, who claimed that Truman's advisers had persuaded him to dismiss the general when he was drunk: 'Most of the tragic things are done at 1.30 and 2 o'clock in the morning when they've had time to get the President cheerful.'

communism from the Korean peninsula. In a directive from the US Joint Chiefs of Staff in September 1950, MacArthur was instructed: 'Your military objective is the destruction of the North Korean armed forces. In attaining this objective, you are authorised to conduct military operations, including amphibious and airborne landings or ground operations north of the 38th Parallel in Korea.' The change to roll back should not, however, be taken as evidence that the US government had always intended to pursue such a policy. It had emerged from the military situation in Korea. The success of the UN forces in pushing back North Korea had presented the USA with an opportunity to weaken communism in Asia.

By November UN forces under MacArthur had marched onwards towards the Yalu River, which marked Korea's border with China. The Chinese became increasingly concerned and decided to send troops and supplies into North Korea. On 27 November 1950 Chinese forces poured over the border into North Korea. A force of about 200,000 joined 150,000 North Korean troops, and the UN forces were pushed into a rapid retreat. The result was panic in Washington as Truman contemplated America's next move. MacArthur recommended using atomic bombs along the border to cut off supplies from China. Truman's more cautious approach predominated. The divergence in approach led to the General's dismissal in April 1951.

The intervention of China on the side of North Korea and their subsequent military success in driving the US army south to back beyond the 38th parallel was to lead to a further re-evaluation of American war aims. Instead of rolling back communism, the priority of the USA at the beginning of 1951 was to drive the communist armies north of the 38th parallel, an aim that was to last for the remainder of the war.

The nature of US military involvement was to be crucial for the South. The USA provided a total of nearly 6 million soldiers for Korea during the 37 months of the war. Of these over 33,000 were killed in action. America provided the firepower of tanks and artillery. They also provided air cover. US air power was to play a significant role in the war. The use of napalm bombs to devastate much of North Korea was so effective that many people in the North took to living underground.

One key aspect of military technology that was raised by US intervention in the war was the use of the nuclear bomb. The US military had considered using nuclear weapons to halt the initial North Korean drive to Pusan in July 1950. The entry of China into the war raised the issue again. As early as November 1950 Truman had told a press conference that 'it is one of our weapons'. US intervention had been important in widening the range of weaponry available for use in the war and with it there was greater potential for destruction.

In early 1951 the communist forces pushed south of Seoul. There were now 400,000 Chinese troops in Korea – a vast number, so there were logistical difficulties in keeping them supplied adequately. Tens of thousands of porters carried equipment on their backs from the Chinese border to the front line over 200 miles away.

To break the stalemate, MacArthur renewed his call for atomic bombs to be used against China. MacArthur's warmongering was beginning to cause tension between himself and Truman. His demands and attitude amounted to insubordination. Truman sacked the general in April 1951, and he was replaced by General Matthew Ridgway. Under Ridgway the stalemate continued, as did heavy bombing of the North by air and sea. In July 1951 both sides were ready to open peace talks at a teahouse at Kaesong.

The peace talks at Kaesong took place while heavy fighting continued, and they soon broke down. They were to resume later in the year at Panmunjon, but progress towards an agreement was slow. On 27 July 1953 an armistice was finally agreed. China, North Korea and the USA signed the ceasefire. South Korea refused to do so but had little alternative other than to accept it.

SKILLS BUILDER

1 Use the maps (Source M, page 41) to describe the sequence of events during the Korean War.

2 How did the USA and China get involved in the Korean War?

3 Why was the Korean War such a key confrontation in the early Cold War?

China's entry into the war

Reasons

- As the UN forces got closer to the Yalu River the Chinese became increasingly concerned about their own security.
- There was alarm at the USA's new desire to roll back communism.
- MacArthur talked openly about the prospects of restoring Chiang Kai Shek's nationalists to mainland China.
- North Korea had provided 145,000 Korean volunteers for Mao's communists in the Chinese Civil War. The favour was now to be returned.
- Stalin had requested that Mao send troops to support North Korea.
- Mao may also have seen the war as an opportunity to replace Soviet influence over North Korea with that of China.

Discussion point

If you were to ask the soldiers shown in Source N why they were fighting in Korea, what do you think their answer would be?

Source N

2.9 American troops in Korea

Unit summary

What have you learned in this unit?

During the period 1944 to 1953 the Cold War developed between the superpowers. The Second World War had resulted in the devastation of much of Europe as well as leaving a legacy of mistrust and suspicion amongst those on the winning side who now faced the task of reconstructing the continent. As events unfolded, the key personalities of Truman and Stalin found it harder to come to agreement. The Truman Doctrine of 1947 saw the point of no return after which any meaningful cooperation between the superpowers seemed unlikely. Stalin's tightening hold over Eastern Europe was becoming deeply distasteful to the West and by the end of 1948 Stalin had upset the West further by blockading the western sector of Berlin. After 1949 the Cold War became focused on the Far East as the rise of communism in China and instability in Korea and Indochina provided the West with evidence that the forces of world communism were on the march and needed to be stopped.

What skills have you used in this unit?

You have been introduced to the key events that led to the emergence of the Cold War between the superpowers during the years 1944 to 1953. You will have understood the sequence of events and how they played a part in the process of deteriorating relations. This understanding will be crucial for the work in the next unit where you will be studying the differing interpretations that have been put forward to explain why the Cold War developed.

Exam style questions

This unit has been concerned with setting the context for one of the key controversies of this topic. It is, therefore, useful for you to reinforce your understanding of the content in readiness for the evaluation of interpretations regarding the causes of the emergence and development of the Cold War that you will consider in the next unit.

The questions centred on this controversy will appear in Section B of the exam. They will ask you to use two or three sources and your own knowledge to make a judgement on an interpretation. For example:

- How far do you agree with the view that the development of the Cold War in the period 1945–50 was the result of Stalin's foreign policy?

To answer this question you will need to examine the role played by Stalin's foreign policy in causing the deterioration in superpower relations in the period 1945–50 and assess its responsibility alongside other factors such as Truman's foreign policy. Interpretations, such as the one given in this question, require you to use the sources you are presented with in the exam and your own knowledge. You will be examining examples of sources by historians in the next unit. To help you assess these by using your own knowledge, use the material you have covered in this unit to identify evidence that could be used to support the following:

(i) evidence that Stalin's actions caused superpower relations to deteriorate

(ii) evidence that Truman's actions led to a deterioration in relations

- Who should carry the most responsibility for the development of the Cold War?

- What other factors were responsible for the development of the Cold War?

Exam tips

The most effective answers to questions have a clear line of argument that gives a reasoned judgement in response to the question asked. Weaker answers tend to outline an argument by giving an assertion in the introduction but failing to support it by detailed evidence.

A useful strategy for planning answers is to use the following process:

- What is the point I wish to make?
- What evidence supports this point?
- Explain how this evidence relates to the point.

Thus, each paragraph covers: 1) Assertion; 2) Illustration; 3) Explanation.

RESEARCH TOPIC

Other key personalities: Molotov and Bevin

A lot of attention is given to Roosevelt, Truman, Stalin, Churchill and Attlee as the key individuals in the events of the early Cold War. Other individuals require consideration. Your task is to research the role of two of these lesser individuals: Vyacheslav Molotov and Ernest Bevin. Try to find out:

- what their positions were

- how much influence they had on the leaders of their respective countries.

3 Why did the Cold War between the superpowers emerge in the years to 1953?

What is this unit about?

This unit focuses on the key historical controversy of why the Cold War developed between the superpowers in the years 1944 to 1953. In the last unit you have looked at the events that saw the emergence of the Cold War; this unit builds upon that knowledge by examining the ways in which historians have debated the significance of the factors that produced these events. The relative importance of the causes that led to the Cold War has been a highly contentious issue, and this unit seeks to help you explore the differing interpretations offered by historians. Ultimately, this will enable you to assess and evaluate these interpretations and present convincing arguments of your own. In this unit you will:

- consider the different interpretations of the role the USA played in the development of the Cold War
- examine differing views of Stalin's foreign policy and its role in shaping events during the development of the Cold War
- explore the arguments that have been offered for explaining why the Cold War extended to the Far East in the period 1950–53
- assess and evaluate historical interpretations on the causes of the Cold War
- examine the historical debates that exist over the key confrontations between the superpowers during this period: the Iron Curtain speech; the Truman Doctrine; the Berlin Blockade; the Korean War.

Key questions

- How and why have historians' interpretations of the causes of the Cold War differed?
- How valid are these different interpretations in seeking to explain the causes of the Cold War?

Introduction

These sources highlight one of the key issues related to the historical controversy concerning why a Cold War developed between the superpowers after 1944. Both sides tended to blame the other for causing the deterioration in international relations. The attitude of the USA was that the Soviet government, and Stalin in particular, could not be trusted. In turn the Soviet government was highly suspicious of the intentions of the USA and the West. Because the Cold War lasted until the 1990s most historians have been influenced by the prevailing attitudes within the society they were writing in at that time. Even today those attitudes have an impact on the historians of the Cold War. This has made the historical debate on this controversy both lively and difficult to resolve. Approaches have tried to move away from 'who' was to blame to 'what' was to blame but have found it very challenging to find a stance that deals with the issue objectively. The issue of what causes conflict, and how best to deal with it, is one that the modern world is still struggling with. How we view the policies of governments today in dealing with war and the threat of international terrorism reflects on our views of why the conflict of the Cold War emerged.

Discussion points

- Who does Source A blame for causing Cold War tension? Explain the message of the cartoonist.
- Who does Source B blame? What techniques is the cartoonist using to convey his message?

Source A

" WHO'S NEXT TO BE LIBERATED FROM FREEDOM, COMRADE ?"

3.1 A British cartoon, 2 March 1948

Source B

3.2 Soviet cartoon, 1950

How far was the USA responsible for the Cold War?

One of the key issues of historical debate concerns the role that US foreign policy, especially that of Truman, played in the development of the Cold War. The Truman Doctrine and Marshall aid marked a more strident stance against the USSR and as such led to a deterioration in relations that made negotiation and compromise with Stalin extremely difficult. Although the Truman Doctrine of 1947 can be seen as an important turning point, not all historians see it as marking the point of no return. Thus it is important to place the Truman Doctrine within its wider context.

- For those historians, such as Arthur Schlesinger, who see the Cold War as an ideological conflict between communism and capitalism, the origins of the Cold War lie in the Bolshevik Revolution of 1917, when for the first time there were states representing both ideologies. The events of 1947 are, therefore, part of a sequence that had deeper roots than the immediate situation presented to Truman in this year. Truman's response was directed by the pressures that had built up over the preceding decades.

- If the view is taken that the Cold War developed when both the USA and the USSR played a major world role and came into conflict with each other, then the key moment in the development of the Cold War would be 1945. This marks the end of wartime cooperation as the Second World War drew to an end and the issue of the post-war settlement for Europe became impossible to avoid. **Revisionist historians**, such as William A. Williams in *The Tragedy of American Diplomacy* (1959), emphasise the importance of the decision of the USA to play a major world role after the Second World War as a key factor in the emergence of Cold War conflict.

- Yet for those historians who see compromise and negotiation as still possible in the years immediately following the end of the Second World War, the start of the Cold War can be placed in 1947. This approach has found favour with **post-revisionist historians**, such as J. R. Starobin, who focus on the breakdown of the mechanics of diplomacy. Contemporaries, such as General Lucius Clay, argued that an accommodation with the USSR was possible in 1945. But by the end of 1947 the Truman Doctrine and the Marshall Plan, and the tightening of Soviet control over Eastern Europe, had made any chance of a post-war settlement through negotiation and compromise between the superpowers impossible. Thus, the Cold War can be argued to have begun properly in 1947, the point of no return.

Critics of Truman have often pointed to the change from Roosevelt's policy of compromise and negotiation to Truman's more aggressive 'Iron Fist' approach as playing a large part in responsibility for the development of the Cold War. This view is, perhaps, too simplistic. Truman's approach was not just a reflection of his personality and insecurities, although these certainly played a part; it was also a reaction to a perception that Roosevelt's approach had failed to prevent Stalin manipulating events and agreements for his own benefit. The failure of the USSR to hold free and fair elections in Eastern Europe, as agreed at the Yalta and Potsdam conferences, was seen as symptomatic of Stalin's attitude to the West.

Definitions

Revisionist historians

Those historians who challenged the traditional view that Stalin was responsible for the development of the Cold War. They have tended to be more critical of US policies, seeing the actions of the US government as playing an important role in escalating conflict.

Post-revisionist historians

Those historians who were critical of both the traditional and revisionist approaches to the Cold War. They sought to move away from the issue of who was to blame to one of looking at the process by which conflict developed. This approach tended to see Cold War conflict emerging from a complex series of interactions between the superpowers where mistrust and suspicion caused relations to deteriorate.

In defence of Truman's approach, it could be argued that he was making a necessary response to the view that many in the US administration were taking towards Stalin's government. Truman was well aware of the pressure to stand up to a Soviet leader who could not be trusted and who was likely to use expansion in Europe to strengthen his position within the USSR. These views were articulated by George Kennan, the Deputy Chief of Mission in the US Embassy in Moscow, in his 'Long Telegram' of 1946.

Source C

At the bottom of the Kremlin's neurotic view of world affairs is traditional and instinctive Russian sense of insecurity . . . For this reason they have always feared foreign penetration, feared direct contact between the Western world and their own . . . And they have learned to seek security only in patient but deadly struggle for total destruction of rival powers, never in compacts and compromises with it . . . this is only the steady advance of uneasy Russian nationalism, a centuries-old movement in which conceptions of offence and defence are inextricably confused. But in new guise of international Marxism, with its honeyed promises to a desperate and war-torn outside world, it is more dangerous and insidious than ever before.

From George Kennan's 'Long Telegram' (22 February 1946)

Some historians, such as John Lewis Gaddis, have seen Truman's approach to the Soviets as a necessary response to the actions of Stalin in going against the spirit of the wartime agreements and tightening the hold of the USSR over Eastern Europe. The USA were traditionally seen as the protectors of the free world during the Cold War. Truman, worried that previous US policy had been too 'soft' on Stalin, resorted to a more hard-line approach than Roosevelt. 'Unless Russia is faced with an iron fist and strong language, another war is in the making,' Truman was to observe in 1946.

Faced with these beliefs, Truman's approach could also be said to have strengthened the West's defence against Soviet encroachment in Europe. Yet it was an approach that hardened the existing divisions in superpower rivalry and therefore was an important factor in the development of the Cold War.

Historians of the Cold War have argued that Truman's foreign policy was not merely the result of political pressures. The role of economic pressures on the American government has been long debated. Writers from the political Left, such as T. J. McCormick in *America's Half-Century* (1989), have been keen to highlight the power of big business and the military–industrial sector in pushing the US government towards Cold War confrontation as a way of protecting the economic interests of capitalism at a time when post-war disruption threatened an economic crisis.

Thus both political and economic pressures were steering Truman's foreign policy away from the direction taken by Roosevelt. Negotiation and

3.3 US President Harry S. Truman

compromise were no longer seen as productive methods of dealing with the USSR. Ignoring the USSR's security needs, Truman aimed to limit Soviet power and influence. Yet his actions were to be seen by Stalin as provocative and in their turn prompted the USSR to further actions designed to strengthen its own position in the growing superpower conflict. Thus extracting the role played by Truman's policies in this 'tit for tat' process has been difficult and the cause of much debate.

How do historians differ in their views of US responsibility for the development of the Cold War?

Source D

An historian explains how the 'Riga Axioms' developed

During the 1920s, a new 'Soviet Service' developed in the State Department. It was anti-Bolshevik and opposed to diplomatic recognition of the USSR. Cohesive, with a strongly articulated sense of identity, this group advocated a policy of sophisticated anticommunism in an **axiomatic** form. Its outlook was based on personal experience, assessment, study and pessimism. As US leaders attempted, after World War II, to analyse Soviet policy and select an appropriate American course, this group's position provided one end of the spectrum of the debate. Eventually its axioms triumphed.

The USA maintained an observation post in the American mission in the Baltic port city of Riga, which was, through the interwar years, the capital of the independent republic of Latvia. It was in this mission during the 1920s that much of the research on the Soviet Union was conducted, personnel trained, and fundamental attitudes formed and nurtured; and it was from the mission that there issued constant warnings against the international menace.

Robert F. Kelley, who became the chief of the (Russian) Division in 1926 and directed the creation of the Soviet Service, was the guiding force . . . he had special influence on those he referred to as 'my boys', the young State Department officers who went through a study program in Russian language, culture and history that he initiated in 1928. He insisted that the two officers chosen for it each year emerge with a background similar to that 'of a well-educated Russian of the old, pre-Revolutionary school'. It was not only the education that shaped the outlook of these young officers; their first contacts with Russians were the white refugees. They became friends and identified with these anticommunist but highly cultured Russian émigrés . . . This left the Americans with an attitude toward the Soviet Union compounded of fascination and distaste, which continued through the decades.

From Daniel Yergin, *Shattered Peace* (published in 1990)

Definition

Axiomatic

Based on a principle that is considered to be a self-evident truth.

Source E

By the end of 1945 most American and British leaders had come round – some reluctantly, others eagerly – to a **dispositional** explanation of Stalin's behaviour. Further efforts to negotiate or compromise with him were likely to fail, or so it seemed, because success would require that he cease to be what he was. One could only resolve henceforth to hold the line, remain true to one's principles, and wait for the passage of time to bring a better world. Such at least was the view of George Kennan, whose top secret 'long telegram' from Moscow of 22 February 1946, would shape American policy over the next half century . . . Nor was 'containment' just an American strategy: Frank Roberts, the British *charge d'affaires* in the Soviet capital, was dispatching similar arguments to London even as former prime minister Winston Churchill, speaking at Fulton, Missouri, was introducing the term 'iron curtain' to the world.

From John Lewis Gaddis, *We Now Know* (published in 1997)

Definition

Dispositional

Refers to an explanation of an individual's actions based on natural inclination and temperament.

Source F

In November 1946, the mid-term congressional elections were a resounding success for the Republicans as they gained control of the Senate and House of Representatives for the first time since 1928. After the elections, Truman and his Democratic advisers met and decided that he would have to take definite steps if he was to have any chance of winning the 1948 presidential election. One such step was to make it clear to the American people that Truman strongly opposed Soviet actions in Eastern Europe and the Far East.

It could therefore be argued that the Truman Doctrine was an attempt to talk up the threat from the Soviet Union. In the months leading up to the elections of 1948, the administration took additional steps to show its commitment to contain communist expansion both within the USA and externally. In spring 1947, Truman created the Federal Employee Loyalty Programme, which gave government security officials authorisation to screen 2 million employees of the federal government for any hint of communist sympathies.

From Christine Bragg, *Vietnam, Korea and US Foreign Policy* (published in 2005)

Questions

1 What does each of the Sources D, E and F tell us about the reasons why the US government was so hostile to the USSR?
2 For each Source D, E and F, using your knowledge draw up an analysis of the value of each interpretation. In order to do this make lists of points about the source under the following headings:
   a) What does the source say? How does the language and tone of the source reflect its message and what does it suggest about its perspective?
   b) What information from your own knowledge supports the view of the source?
   c) What information could be used to argue against the view given in the source?

What were Stalin's motives for Soviet expansion?

Historians seeking to explain the development of the Cold War have often focused on the role of Stalin and his foreign policy. There seems little doubt that Stalin's foreign policy was designed to expand Soviet influence, as evidenced by the course of events after 1945. The debate has been over the motives behind this expansion. Was Stalin aiming to spread communism worldwide or were his aims more defensive, limited to creating a buffer zone in Eastern Europe to safeguard the USSR against attack from the West?

During the Cold War the West regarded Stalin's foreign policy as provocative and expansionist. Its aggressive nature was singled out as the prime cause of the Cold War. The actions of the USA and the West were therefore reactions, prompted by aggressive Soviet actions and designed to safeguard the free world. This view does, however, take a rather simplistic approach towards Stalin's possible motives. An examination of Soviet foreign policy in this period shows a more complicated picture where mistrust as well as a lack of understanding led to a misrepresentation of Stalin's motives for expanding Soviet influence in Eastern Europe.

Source G

3.4 Soviet poster of Joseph Stalin from the late 1940s

Discussion points

- What image of Stalin is Source G trying to convey?
- Why might this image be politically useful to the Soviet government within the context of the emergence of the Cold War in the late 1940s?

Definition

Permanent Revolution

The name of the policy vigorously promoted by Trotsky, who saw the need to spread world revolution as the priority after the Bolshevik Revolution of 1917. Trotsky argued that without world revolution the revolution in Russia would not survive.

1 Spreading world revolution

On coming to power in 1917 the Bolsheviks envisaged a wave of revolution in the rest of the world, which would lead to the collapse of the imperialist, capitalist nations. These hopes were to be quickly dashed. Yet many communists continued to believe that the only way to ensure the survival of the Communist Revolution in the USSR was to spread communism throughout the world. Trotsky's call for **Permanent Revolution** in the 1920s represented this attitude. This was the belief that without a world revolution the Bolshevik revolution in Russia would not survive because conflict between capitalism and communism was inevitable. Although

Stalin argued against Trotsky, it was largely a difference of priority and personality. To Stalin the USSR needed to be strengthened before it could engage in the pursuit of world revolution. Thus Stalin was not against expanding communism; in fact, his ideological beliefs would have steered him in this direction. It was merely a matter of priority at the time. By 1945 the international situation had been transformed. Was it now time to spread the revolution?

Evidence of Stalin spreading world communism

- The Comintern was seen in the West as tangible evidence of the USSR's continuing desire to spread revolution. Comintern, or the Third International, was an organisation to facilitate contacts between communist groups throughout the world. The Soviet government controlled its activities, and from 1919 to 1926 its chairman was Zinoviev, a leading member of the Communist Party. Comintern encouraged communist groups to stir up unrest across Europe, including in Britain and Germany. These actions were not forgotten, even though the organisation was dissolved in 1943. The establishment of Cominform at a conference in Sklarska Poreba, Poland, in September 1947 seemed to resurrect Soviet attempts to coordinate communist parties across Europe.

- The defeat of Nazi Germany in 1945 gave Stalin the opportunity to spread communism throughout Eastern Europe. The Red Army controlled large areas of Eastern Europe at the end of the Second World War and was in a position to enforce Soviet policy. To the West, the imposition of communist governments on Eastern Europe, the civil war in Greece, where communist guerrillas were attempting to remove the monarchists, the communist takeover of Czechoslovakia in 1948 and the Soviet blockade of Berlin in 1948–49 were all seen as evidence of Stalin's intention to spread communism.

To many politicians in the West it was this view of Soviet foreign policy as expansionist and aggressive that seemed the most credible. It was a view supported and developed by George Kennan in his 'Long Telegram' of 1946 and in subsequent articles such as 'The Sources of Soviet Conduct' (1947). To Kennan Soviet foreign policy was viewed as the product of the **totalitarian** nature of the USSR. He presented an analysis of Soviet foreign policy driven by notions of class struggle on a world scale and the need of the Soviet government to present its people with a perceived foreign threat that would mobilise the population in order to secure its own position. This view has been highly influential and has been the basis of many works by historians in the West on the Cold War.

2 Traditional Russian expansionism

Some Western historians, such as Samuel Sharp and F. Schuman, have seen Stalin's foreign policy as driven by a more traditional Russian expansionism similar to that of the Tsars than by the primary aim of spreading communism. Thus Stalin was merely acting like a 'Red Tsar', using

Definition

Totalitarianism

A concept used to explain the nature of the dictatorships that had emerged in the 1930s. It focused on a political system by which total control was gained over the economic, social and political life of a nation. It highlighted the use of propaganda and terror as methods of social control. The concept was developed by political scientists in the USA and was used to describe Nazi Germany, Fascist Italy and Stalinist Russia.

expansionism to build up the power of the Russian Empire. According to this view, any Russian leader, whether communist or not, would have undertaken the same policies of expansion. The opportunities presented after 1945 were too great to ignore.

In the 1920s the West had used the countries of Eastern Europe as a *cordon sanitaire*, a barrier to prevent the spread of communism. The USSR had resented this and welcomed the opportunity to use Eastern Europe for its own benefit after 1945.

Many of Stalin's gains from the Second World War were concerned with the recovery of territories lost under the Treaty of Brest-Litovsk in 1918: parts of Poland, the Baltic States and Bessarabia. Thus Stalin was, in this respect, seeking to regain control of areas that had been part of the Tsarist empire.

3 Defensive actions to create a buffer zone against attack from the West

The view of Stalin as an expansionist for whatever motives needs to be challenged. More recent studies, such as John Lewis Gaddis's *The Cold War* (2005), have explored the nature of Soviet foreign policy without resort to the rather simplistic notions of communist aggression favoured by earlier writers. Rather than seeking to expand, the underlying motive of Stalin's foreign policy would appear to have been more defensive. Soviet foreign policy must be seen within the context of Western hostility to the USSR, which had existed since its inception. Soviet weakness in 1945, caused by exhaustion due to the war effort, made the USSR concerned to protect its borders. The sheer scale of Soviet losses in the war, which are almost impossible to comprehend, produced a sense of insecurity. The war had resulted in the deaths of over 20 million Soviet citizens, the highest of any of the countries involved in the war. The human cost was also to be measured in the numbers of widows, orphans and invalids. In addition there was an enormous economic cost, with over 25 million people left homeless and losses in factories and farms amounting to one-third of the country's wealth.

The extension of Soviet control to Eastern Europe can be seen as a defensive measure: the creation of a buffer zone to protect the Soviet Union from invasion from the West. In this respect Stalin's foreign policy should be seen as the product of Soviet weakness rather than its strength.

After 1945 Stalin was determined to ensure that the countries of Eastern Europe were friendly to the Soviet Union. This would not be an easy task. Poland was traditionally hostile towards Russia and had spurned Soviet offers of help against Nazi Germany in 1939. The refusal of the Red Army to help the Warsaw rising of 1944 and the revelation of the Soviet massacre of Poles in the Katyn Forest intensified this hostility between the neighbouring states. Hungary, Romania and Bulgaria had all sided with Nazi Germany during the Second World War. In this situation, allowing the peoples of Eastern Europe free democracy was unlikely to produce governments friendly to the USSR.

Yet even Stalin was prepared initially to make some accommodation to the West's demands for broad-based coalition governments to be established in Eastern Europe. It was only later in 1947 that Stalin insisted on communist regimes on the Stalinist model as a response to a more hard-line American policy towards the USSR. This seemed to be the only way to guarantee pro-Soviet governments. To the USSR a buffer zone of satellite states in Eastern Europe was essential, and US foreign policy moves after 1945 seemed to confirm the West's determination to undermine communism.

4 The role of personality

Biographies of Stalin have been useful in highlighting how Soviet foreign policy after 1945 was a reflection of Stalin's own personality. Even more specialist histories, such as Geoffrey Roberts's *Stalin's Wars* (2006), have drawn attention to the role of personality. Rather than painting a picture of Stalin as an aggressive expansionist, these studies reveal him to have been cautious and more concerned with defence. Stalin's experiences had taught him to trust no one and to proceed with vigilance – an approach he was to use in domestic politics as well as international relations. The Nazi–Soviet Pact of 1939 was an acknowledgement of the weakness of the USSR. Stalin's inability to direct events forced him into signing what was a non-aggression pact with Nazi Germany, a regime based on a hatred of communism. The subsequent invasion of the USSR by Nazi Germany in 1941 had a profound impact on Stalin. Despite an avalanche of intelligence sources telling him that an invasion was imminent, Stalin refused to believe that Hitler would break the agreement. His shock at the invasion led him to suffer a breakdown, and he was to remain highly suspicious of the promises of others thereafter.

There is plenty of evidence that can be used to support this interpretation of Stalin as a cautious leader. During the Greek crisis Stalin kept his word to Churchill, given at their meeting in Moscow in 1944, that the USSR did not consider Greece part of its sphere of influence, and so he refused to send help to the communists fighting to remove the Greek monarchy. Tito, the communist leader of Yugoslavia, did send help, to the embarrassment of Stalin. The USSR may have been pleased to see the communist coup in Czechoslovakia, but it played no active role in the events. The Soviet blockade of West Berlin in 1948 was more provocative but again revealed Stalin's wariness. No action was taken against American and British planes that airlifted supplies into the city during the blockade. Stalin recognised that if war was provoked, the superior military might and nuclear monopoly of the USA would decide the outcome.

Thus Soviet foreign policy under Stalin can be seen in many ways as a reflection of its leader's cautious personality.

The simplistic view of Stalin as an aggressive communist pursuing expansion at every opportunity is now rejected by historians, but this does not mean that historians are in agreement about the nature of his foreign policy. A more complex picture of Soviet foreign policy has emerged.

SKILLS BUILDER

1 How can the following events be used as evidence EITHER of Stalin's aggressive policy of spreading world revolution OR of the defensive actions of a Soviet state threatened by a hostile world?

   a) the imposition of Stalinist style communist governments in Eastern Europe

   b) the creation of Cominform and Comecon

   c) the Berlin Blockade.

   Which of the two explanations of Soviet actions do you find the most convincing?

2 How convincing do you find the interpretation that Stalin's foreign policy was a continuation of traditional Russian expansionism?

3 What evidence could be used to support the interpretation that Soviet foreign policy in the period 1945–50 reflected Stalin's cautious personality?

4 What evidence might you use to challenge this interpretation?

Source exercise: interpretations of Stalin and the Berlin Blockade

Source H

The view of an East German historian

This currency provocation was however only one part of a crisis planned and prepared by the most aggressive circles in Washington, with the aim of presenting the American Cold War strategy behind a smoke screen of anti-Soviet propaganda . . . The self-blockade of the Western occupation powers hit the West Berlin population with especial hardness in the winter months of 1948–49. The people were starving and freezing.

From the first official East German history of Berlin (1961)

Source I

In April 1948 the Western Powers announced that they intended to reform the West German economy, in order to place it on a viable footing and so enable its recovery . . . This was closely followed by the announcement of an intention to establish a new West German state. The Russians perceived this to be a thinly veiled attempt to reconstitute Germany as a military power that would yet again spearhead a future invasion of the Soviet Union.

. . . Stalin ordered that land access to Berlin was to be denied, and by June 1948 the divided city had been blockaded. Stalin's ultimate objective was to make the presence of the Western Allies in Berlin untenable, so that they would be forced to leave and give control of the whole city to the Russians.

From David Stone, *Wars of the Cold War: Campaigns and Conflicts 1945–1990* (published in 2004)

SKILLS BUILDER

1 How far does Source H give a complete and reliable view of the causes of the Berlin Blockade?

2 How and why does Source I give a different interpretation of the causes of the Berlin Blockade to that offered by Source H?

3 To what extent does Source J agree with the view of Stalin's motives for the Berlin Blockade given in Source I?

Source J

Defensive it may have been, but the offensive character of this (The Blockade of Berlin) and the other measures Stalin took in response to the Marshall Plan wound up increasing, not decreasing, the Soviet Union's security problems . . . The Berlin blockade convinced the European recipients of American economic assistance that they needed military protection as well: that led them to request the creation of a North Atlantic Treaty Organisation, which committed the United States for the first time ever to the peacetime defense of Western Europe. By the time Stalin grudgingly lifted the Berlin blockade in May 1949, the North Atlantic Treaty had been signed in Washington and the Federal Republic of Germany had been proclaimed in Bonn – another result that Stalin had not wanted . . . And there were no signs whatever of the disagreements among capitalists that Stalin's ideological illusions had led him to expect. His strategy for gaining control of postwar Europe lay in ruins, and he had largely himself to blame.

From John Lewis Gaddis, *The Cold War* (published in 2005)

Historiographical debate: what caused the Cold War?

The study of the origins of the Cold War has produced much historical writing and many different schools of thought. Many of these approaches have focused on the role of key individuals such as Stalin and Truman and their foreign policies in the development of the Cold War. More recent approaches, since the 1980s, have widened the debate further by examining the processes that brought about the Cold War. This has moved the debate away from 'who' was responsible to 'what' led to the Cold War. The main approaches are as follows.

1 The orthodox school

This school of historians sees the Cold War as the product of the aggressive and expansionist foreign policy of Stalin and the USSR. The Soviet government was seen as fundamentally hostile to the West, only cooperating with the West when it was necessary. This orthodox view, as it became known, was outlined by George Kennan in his highly influential 'Long Telegram' (1946). President Truman used it to justify the need for an 'Iron Fist' approach in dealing with the USSR. This was, in itself, a criticism of the more moderate line taken by Roosevelt in dealing with Stalin.

This analysis was adopted by the majority of American and Western European politicians and scholars and dominated historical thinking in the West until the 1970s. It has been presented by historians such as W. H. McNeill in *America, Britain and Russia: Their Co-operation and Conflict 1941–46* (1953), H. Feis in *Churchill-Roosevelt-Stalin: The War They Waged and the Peace They Sought* (1957) and A. Schlesinger, *Origins of the Cold War* (1967). Schlesinger wrote, 'The intransigence of Leninist ideology, the sinister dynamics of a totalitarian society, and the madness of Stalin . . .

made it hard for the West to accept the thesis that Russia was moved only by a desire to protect its security and would be satisfied by the control of Eastern Europe.' The language used in this statement clearly shows the influence of the totalitarian view of the Stalinist regime that was so dominant in the West after 1945.

The views of the orthodox school were clearly a product of the attitudes in the West at the time of the development of the Cold War and provided a useful justification for American foreign policy and its stand against Soviet actions. As such, the orthodox view has been criticised for ignoring or failing to understand the legitimate defensive needs of the Soviet Union in its rush to lay the blame for the Cold War at Stalin's feet. Nonetheless, Soviet behaviour throughout the Cold War was often seen to prove the validity of this perspective.

2 The revisionist school

This school sees the Cold War as the result of the provocative actions of the USA rather than those of the Soviet Union. This approach stresses the defensive aspect of Stalin's foreign policy when faced with an aggressive USA attempting to gain economic dominance over Europe. Henry A. Wallace, Secretary of Commerce in Truman's administration, argued in favour of greater cooperation with the USSR as the best means of safeguarding American trade abroad. These views are also presented in *The Tragedy of American Diplomacy* (1959) by William A. Williams, and in the 1960s by G. Kolko and G. Alperowitz. They represented the emergence of the 'New Left', writers who were influenced by the failures of US foreign policy in Vietnam. Their views were more critical of the USA and the American system.

3 The post-revisionist school

This school includes a range of historians who have sought to move away from the tendency to blame one side or the other for the breakdown in relations and to approach the topic from a more objective standpoint. The generation of writers emerging in the mid-1970s was more removed from the events of the early Cold War and therefore able to approach the topic in a more detached manner. Instead of trying to decide which side should be blamed for the development of the Cold War, the post-revisionists have attempted to examine in detail the issues involved and to bring out the full complexity of decision-making that led to the deterioration in relations. Thus there has been a move away from a mono-causal explanation, involving the identification of a single cause of the Cold War, to examining a wider range of factors. This approach underlies works such as *Shattered Peace: The Origins of the Cold War and the National Security State* (1980) by D. Yergin and *We Now Know* (1997) by J. L. Gaddis.

The post-revisionists have attempted to examine in detail the complexity of Soviet decision-making and show that there were more determinants of

Soviet foreign policy than just Stalin. This has led to renewed attention to the USSR's security needs. J. R. Starobin emphasises the destabilising impact of the Second World War, 'which had outmoded earlier ideological and political premises'. This theme was developed further by J. L. Gaddis in *Russia, the Soviet Union and the United States* (1990).

Yet many post-revisionist approaches have also concluded that within the context of a wide range of factors and pressures pushing the superpowers into conflict, Stalin is still to blame for the Cold War. This is the judgement of the leading historians of the so-called 'new Cold War history': V. Zubok and C. Pleshakov (*Inside the Kremlin's Cold War*); V. Mastny (*The Cold War and Soviet Insecurity*); and J. L. Gaddis.

Since the 1980s there has been a re-emergence of interpretations that stress the role played by Western European governments in the development of superpower tension. David Reynolds in *Origins of the Cold War in Europe* (1994) has drawn attention to the pressure exerted on the USA by Europe to play a larger role in containing the USSR. Many Western European politicians feared an American return to isolationism, which would leave a war-weary and economically devastated continent vulnerable to Soviet expansion. Churchill's Iron Curtain speech can be seen within this context.

The increase in the availability of sources on domestic politics in the USSR has encouraged an examination of foreign policy within the context of internal affairs, with some commentators seeing foreign policy as driven by domestic concerns. In *A History of Twentieth Century Russia* (1997) R. Service stressed the importance of 'dynamic internal processes' in explaining Soviet foreign policy. After 1945 the threat of capitalism to the USSR was used to justify the power of the Party and its leadership. T. Dunmore, in *Soviet Politics 1945–53* (1984), has shown how the rivalry between Zhdanov and Malenkov in the Soviet leadership resulted in a more hard-line approach to the West.

4 Soviet historiography

Soviet historiography was based on the standard Marxist line that conflict was inevitable given the hostility of capitalism towards the USSR, which was seen as the bastion of communism. Soviet writers highlighted the actions of Soviet foreign policy as attempts to safeguard the Revolution against the aggressive capitalist powers in the West. In Molotov's own account, *Problems of Foreign Policy* (1949), the USA was accused of attempting to enslave Europe economically 'to the rule and arbitrary will of strong and enriched foreign firms, banks and industrial companies'. In the *Official History of the USSR* (1959) B. Ponomaryov described the Truman Doctrine as a smokescreen for American expansion and Marshall aid as a tool of American power and influence. It was not until Gorbachev's refusal to support unpopular communist regimes in Eastern Europe at the end of the 1980s that Soviet writers could be critical of Soviet dominance over the Eastern Bloc.

5 Russian writers since 1991

The collapse of the Soviet Union has produced some interesting reassessment of Stalin's foreign policy. In *The Rise and Fall of the Soviet Empire* (1998) D. Volkogonov has emphasised the role of Comintern as a puppet organisation of the Soviet government to spread revolution. To Volkogonov Stalin's foreign policy aims were 'based on the twin pillars of Communist internationalism and Soviet great-power status'. This challenges the view that Soviet foreign policy was merely defensive. Volkogonov's work is valuable because of his inside knowledge of decision-making in the USSR. His career within the Soviet army made him highly conscious of foreign policy issues. Yet as a disillusioned communist caught up in the collapse of the USSR, Volkogonov represents a strand of thinking that is highly critical of the communist past.

Historical writing on the development of the Cold War has come a long way since the early views presented during the initial period of the Cold War. There is now a much more diverse range of viewpoints. The trend away from 'who' was responsible for the Cold War to 'what' caused the Cold War has highlighted the complexity of the situation and the interaction between factors, for example that of leaders such as Stalin and Truman with the context within which they were making decisions. By this process the course of events can be seen as more strongly determined by the pressures that were exerted on leaders rather than the leaders' personalities exerting an influence on events.

Source exercise: why did a Cold War emerge between the superpowers after 1945?

Source K

Russian leaders clearly recognized their dilemma, and realised that rehabilitation and military security were the points upon which its resolution had to hinge. But American policy offered the Russians no real choice on those key issues. Particularly after the atomic bomb was created and used, the attitude of the United States left the Soviets with but one real option: either acquiesce in American proposals or be confronted with American power and hostility. It was the decision of the United States to employ its new and awesome power in keeping with the traditional Open Door Policy which crystallized the cold war.

. . . The United States never formulated and offered the Soviet Union a settlement based on other, less grandiose, terms . . . The popular idea that Soviet leaders emerged from the war ready to do aggressive battle against the United States is simply not borne out by the evidence.

. . . Kennan's analysis spawned a vast literature which treated Stalin as no more than a psychotic . . . Having argued that they had to create imaginary foreign dangers in order to stay in power at home, Kennan concluded with a policy recommendation to create a very serious (and from the Soviet point of view, mortal) outside challenge to their authority.

From William A. Williams, *The Tragedy of American Diplomacy* (published in 1959)

Source L

There has been too much of a tendency to assume that all that happened was of a single piece, foreordained and determined. But how world leaders perceived their interests and acted on those perceptions counted for a very great deal.

The Soviet outlook was not the only significant ideological factor involved in the development of the global antagonism. There was also the American ideology – the ideas and outlook that US leaders brought to international affairs, their world set. The understanding American leaders had of events and possibilities controlled their own actions and reactions in the dialectic of confrontation.

From Daniel Yergin, *Shattered Peace*
(published in 1990)

Source M

Stalin had certain characteristics that set him off from all others in authority at the time the Cold War began. He alone pursued personal security by depriving everyone else of it . . . He alone had transformed his country into an extension of himself: no Western leader could have succeeded at such a feat, and none attempted it. He alone saw war and revolution as acceptable means with which to pursue ultimate ends: no Western leader associated violence with progress to the extent that he did.

Did Stalin seek a Cold War? The question is a little like asking: 'Does a fish seek water?' Suspicion, distrust, and an abiding cynicism were not only his preferred but his necessary environment: he could not function apart from it.

From John Lewis Gaddis, *We Now Know*
(published in 1997)

Source N

The issue of the inevitability of the conflict forces us to pose the question: who were the enemies? If we may assume that Washington and Moscow played the paramount roles in unleashing the 'Cold War', the East–West conflict more broadly speaking was mainly the outcome of a failure to achieve a lasting peace settlement in Europe. To this failure, however, numerous international actors contributed. In fact, the immediate post-war period was only to a limited extent bipolar. If in the communist world the Soviet Union was still the undisputed 'Fatherland of Socialism', in the Western camp both Britain and France had still, at least in theory, the role of 'great powers'. Neither should one forget the influence exerted by the European context itself – by the German question and by the smaller states – on the chain of events that marked the failure of the wartime 'Grand Alliance'. We therefore have to look more closely at a broad European international context in order to understand the origins of the Cold War.

From 'Reflections on the Origins of the Cold War', an article by Antonio Varsori, in Odd Arne Westad (ed.), *Reviewing the Cold War* (published in 2000)

SKILLS BUILDER

1 What is the argument given by each source K to N as to the cause of the Cold War?

2 For each source, list evidence from your own knowledge that could be used to (a) support and (b) challenge the argument presented.

3 Using Sources K to N, and your own knowledge, how far do you accept the view of Source K that it was American foreign policy that 'crystallized the Cold War'?

Exam tip

Just because a historian gives a viewpoint does not make it true!

All viewpoints and opinions need to be tested for validity. How can you do this?

- The background of the author and date of publication need to be considered. How might this background influence the sources that they have used and the interpretations they have drawn from them?
- Use your own knowledge to test the validity of the interpretation. Good answers are able to place a source firmly into its context and relate the interpretation it gives to the events they describe.
- Don't be frightened of disagreeing with a historian's view. Remember, two historians rarely agree. What is important is that you explain why you disagree by reference to precise and specific evidence.

How have historians differed in their views on the extension of the Cold War to the Far East in the period 1949–53?

The key event in the extension of the Cold War to the Far East was the Korean War, which threatened to escalate a local war into a major international conflict. Historians have been interested in debating whether the invasion of South Korea by the North in June 1950 was the product of the Communist Bloc, newly strengthened by China, attempting to expand its power. The Korean War also involved military intervention by the USA, and the reasons for this more assertive American approach have also been the subject of much debate.

Historiographical debate: what caused the Korean War?

The exact sequence of events that saw the start of the war in Korea have, in themselves, been the source of some debate. The North claimed it had been attacked by the forces of South Korea, who had begun by shelling an area on the Ongjin Peninsula on 23 June and had invaded the town of Haeju. This view was counter to that accepted by the West, which was that the North had, on 25 June 1950, sent its army across the 38th parallel on the Ongjin Peninsula in order to seize the South. The seizure of Haeju by South Korea's 17th Regiment has often been used to support the North's claim that the South had started the war. The historian Bruce Cumings has pointed out that the 17th Regiment was a crack unit made up of soldiers from the North who hated communism and were keen to resist attack. The capture of Haeju was therefore more likely to have been due to their initial success in combating an invasion from the North rather than the event that started the war. Yet the debate over who made the first move can detract from the context within which the invasion took place.

There is little debate over the long-term causes of tension in Korea. The country had been annexed by Japan in 1910 but had a long history of independence. When Japan surrendered at the end of the Second World

War, Korea was to be occupied by the military forces of the USSR and the USA. The 38th parallel was set as the dividing line between the Soviet occupied North and the USA in the South.

This arrangement was not intended to be permanent, but it would oversee the country until elections could be organised by the United Nations. The UN committee to oversee these elections, UNTCOK, was dominated by the USA and its allies, so North Koreans and the USSR refused to cooperate with its activities.

After elections were held in the south in 1948 the Republic of Korea was formally established under the government of the staunchly anti-communist Syngman Rhee. Rhee had a limited base of support, made up largely of middle class business interests and landowners, and faced several rebellions against his rule by remnants of the left-wing People's Committees, which had been established in the South after 1945.

In the North the communists established the Democratic People's Republic of Korea led by the popular Kim Il Sung. Kim was a hero of the resistance to Japanese rule.

In 1949 the USA and the USSR withdrew their troops from Korea as previously agreed. The government of South Korea was now dangerously exposed.

Where historians are in disagreement is over the factors that sparked off the war from this instability and produced the resulting escalation in the conflict.

1 Traditional or orthodox view

Traditional assessments of the origins of the war, such as David Rees in *Korea: the Limited War* (1964), place responsibility on the North, which was acting under instructions from Stalin to spread communism.

Traditional interpretations have supported US involvement in the war, viewing Truman's argument that the principle of deterring aggression as sincerely held and paramount. This principle enabled the USA to give its intervention in Korea the seemingly noble motive of helping the victims of aggression. UN involvement had been important as a mechanism for securing firm support for US military intervention in the war under the aegis of acting in the interests of the wider principles of upholding democracy and peace against aggression. Syngman Rhee's regime in South Korea was hardly a model of freedom and democracy, but the US government was willing to overlook this fact because of Rhee's anti-communist credentials. The use of the UN also gave the action of the USA in Korea the publicity it needed to sway other countries into supporting its action.

Events at the beginning of the war had forced the issue. The South Korean army was disintegrating rapidly under the assault of the North's People's Army. The urgency of the military situation in Korea required a swift and direct response. What made the USA so keen to get involved was their perception of the forces of world communism acting together to expand their influence. America had not always been so keen to intervene in the affairs of other states, but in the context of the Cold War US involvement in Korea was seen as imperative. In American eyes there was little doubt that the war had been started by the North under Stalin's orders. Revisionist historians believe that it was this perception by the US government, determined by their experience of, and attitudes to, communism during the development of the Cold War in Europe since 1945, that was the key factor in pushing them into the war.

The struggle for supremacy between the forces of capitalism and communism had been dramatically transformed by the communist takeover of China in 1949. There was now a large communist state in Asia, which was not only considered to be a puppet of the Soviet Union but also a base for future communist expansion throughout the region. From China communism was ideally placed to spread into neighbouring Indochina and Korea. In the wider context of the Cold War, it had delivered a substantial blow against the USA. The stakes were, therefore, raised when the Korean War broke out the following year. The USA were determined to halt the inexorable advance of world communism.

2 Revisionist views

The view that the Korean War was the result of expansionist and aggressive actions by the forces of world communism has been challenged by those historians, such as Kathryn Weathersby, who see Stalin as having been too cautious to risk an escalation of conflict with the USA. This is supported by Khrushchev's memoirs, which state that Kim Il Sung, the North Korean leader, had informed Stalin of his decision to invade the South, but the Soviet leader had advised him 'to think it over . . . Stalin had his doubts'. These memoirs are not an altogether reliable source, but they do confirm the prudence Stalin took elsewhere with his foreign policy. Soviet archives opened up to historians in the 1990s support Khrushchev's assessment on this occasion.

Weathersby, in *Korea 1949–50, To Attack or Not to Attack? Stalin, Kim Il Sung and the Prelude to War* (1995) argues that Stalin played the role of facilitator rather than originator of the war. The minutes of a meeting between Stalin and Kim Il Sung in March 1949 reveal that Stalin gave the impression that he did not approve of an invasion by North Korea – he certainly avoided making any commitment of troops to support such an occurrence. Yet by April 1950 Stalin was to offer more encouragement. He informed Kim Il Sung that there had been 'a significant strengthening of the socialist camp in the East: the victory of the Chinese revolution, the signing of an alliance between the USSR and the People's Republic of China, and the USSR's acquisition of an atomic bomb.' As Stalin concluded: 'The South Korean regime was determined to launch an attack on the North sooner or later and it was important to forestall this aggression.'

The Chinese leader Mao was also to offer support to Kim, and the North Koreans were effective at playing off the two communist leaders to their own advantage. The exact role played by Stalin, therefore, continues to attract discussion.

3 The 'local/international factors' approach

The works of Bruce Cumings, especially *The Origins of the Korean War* (1981), have focused on the Korean conflict as a local war that drew in the superpowers. In this respect he highlights the US policy of containment as a factor in escalating a civil war into a Cold War conflict. William Stueck, in *Rethinking the Korean War* (2002), argues that the Korean War was a civil war moulded by the attitudes and actions of the USA, Soviet Union and China. This linkage of civil war and international conflict remains the subject of debate.

4 The significance of domestic pressures on Truman's foreign policy

This has also received consideration by historians. They have highlighted how the forceful response by the USA to the situation in Korea was in part the result of domestic pressures placed on Truman. The Republicans accused Truman of being too 'soft' on communism and attempted to discredit his entire foreign policy. He was blamed for the loss of China. The McCarthy witch-hunt against those in the American establishment suspected of harbouring communist sympathies was evidence of the force of public concerns about Truman's approach. Within the US establishment there was pressure for firm, direct action against communism from hawks in the air force, such as Vandenberg and Finletter, who wanted to attack North Korea at the start of hostilities. When the Korean War began Truman was under immense pressure to show he would not capitulate to communist aggression once again. The internal politics of the USA impelled Truman to take a tougher stance when the Korean War started.

The debate continues between historians over the relative importance of international and domestic factors driving Truman to intervene in the war in Korea. What is clear is that these factors produced a hardening of American attitudes towards foreign policy and the methods that should be used in combating the spread of communism. American belief in the domino theory seemed to be confirmed by the events in the Far East: if one country was allowed to fall to communism, others would follow. The fall of China to communism now put Korea at risk. The barrier against communism had to be shored up by direct and forceful action. Truman used this argument to justify sending US troops to Korea: 'If we let Korea down, the Soviets will keep right on going and swallow up one piece of Asia after another.' It was this approach that was to play a significant role in extending the Cold War to the Far East.

Source exercise

Source O

The reasons are controversial, even today. Partly because we lacked access for years even to the most rudimentary North Korean, Soviet and Chinese sources, but partly also because of the improbable juxtaposition of circumstances that produced the Korean War in the first place, its origins have been shrouded in an unusually bewildering array of officially sponsored myths and tortured historical interpretations. So simple a matter as whose troops crossed the 38th parallel first, on the morning of 25 June 1950, remained for years the subject of intense argument – let alone the question of for what purpose. The most prominent American historian of this conflict (Bruce Cumings), having devoted well over a decade and some 1,500 pages to studying its origins, could conclude as late as 1990 that 'no-one and everyone' was responsible . . .

From John Lewis Gaddis, *We Now Know* (published in 1997)

Source P

According to the later memoirs of Nikita Khrushchev, *Khrushchev Remembers*, Kim Il Sung conceived the plan of invading South Korea during 1949, and journeyed twice to Moscow to obtain Stalin's approval and promise of military aid. Kim did indeed visit the Soviet capital several times in 1949.

But the precise timing may have been left, in circumstances still unclear, to Premier Kim. A successful invasion of South Korea would solve the unification problem on Communist terms. It would also present the Soviet Union with considerable strategic gains in North East Asia. There can be little doubt that Moscow both knew of, and provided the resources to North Korea for the invasion . . .

From David Rees, *A Short History of Modern Korea* (published in 1988)

Source Q

The planners in Pyongyang (the North Korean capital) were almost certainly lured into the attack of 25 June 1950 by a misreading of the mood in Washington. It seemed that the Americans had accepted, however grudgingly, the communist victory in China and, from the pronouncements of numerous eminent politicians and service chiefs, that they would also accept the subjugation of the Republic of Korea, now that American troops had been withdrawn. On 12 January 1950, when Dean Acheson made his notorious National Press Club address in Washington defining American Far Eastern policy, he added that there was no longer an intention to guarantee any areas on the Asiatic mainland against military attack.

Kim Il Sung was encouraged by these pronouncements.

From M. Hickey, *Korean War: The West Confronts Communism, 1950–53* (published in 1999)

Source R

The superpowers had superimposed their rivalry upon a civil war that would have existed in any event. Both Kim and Rhee were determined to unify the country on their respective terms . . . Both sides had been conducting raids across the parallel for some time prior to the outbreak of hostilities. Neither Korean leader could mount a full-scale invasion on his own, though: each would need to persuade his superpower sponsor to provide the necessary equipment and support. The question boiled down, then, to whether the Soviet Union or the United States would sanction an attempt to reunify Korea by military means. The evidence now confirms that, after three repeated attempts, Kim got a green light from Stalin early in 1950, while all Rhee received from Washington were yellow lights shading over into red.

From John Lewis Gaddis, *We Now Know* (published in 1997)

SKILLS BUILDER

1 Look at Source O. What problems face the historian studying the causes of the Korean War?

2 According to the historian Bruce Cumings 'no one and everyone was responsible' for causing the Korean War. Make a list of the possible culprits. For each state a motive.

3 How far does the interpretation of the causes of the Korean War offered by Source P differ from that of Source Q?

4 To what extent does Source Q agree with the view offered by Source R of the reasons for the Korean War?

Exam tips

When assessing the value of interpretations offered by sources it is important to look for areas of agreement and disagreement.

Although no two historians are likely to agree, often the disagreement is over a matter of emphasis rather than being directly opposed.

The language used by the authors of sources can therefore be crucial in identifying these subtle differences. How the policies of individual leaders such as Stalin and Kim are described can give indications of the view of the author.

In your answers you should maker close reference to the sources, quote short phrases and discuss them.

Remember that words are precision instruments! They are carefully chosen by the author. Your task is to explain what lies behind them.

Unit summary

What have you learned in this unit?

The issue of why the Cold War emerged between the superpowers in the years 1944 to 1953 has led to a wide range of historiography. Historians have engaged in an often heated debate over who or what was responsible for the deterioration in superpower relations. The roles of Truman and Stalin and their foreign policies have attracted particular attention, as have the reasons leading to the extension of the Cold War to the Far East after 1949. Viewpoints on the Cold War have also changed through time as new archival material has been released. The collapse of the Soviet Union in 1991 has led to the opening up of archives that have helped clarify some issues but raised others.

As is often the case in history, judgements can only be provisional. Many official sources relating to the foreign policy of the USSR continue to be undisclosed 'in the interests of national security'. The debate over the development of the Cold War is certain to remain an area of interest and controversy.

What skills have you used in this unit?

You have examined the ways in which historians have debated the issue of what factors led to the emergence of the Cold War between the superpowers during the years 1944 to 1953. You will also have understood why historians have offered differing interpretations and how the factors influencing historians themselves have changed. This understanding has enabled you to assess the validity of these interpretations and offer clear, reasoned judgements on them. As a result you can present your own interpretations with conviction and confidence.

Exam style questions

The questions centred on this controversy will appear in Section B of the exam. They will ask you to use two or three sources and your own knowledge to make a judgement on an interpretation. An example is given below.

Source S

It is difficult to say what would have happened if the West had responded positively to Stalin's last initiative on the German question [a call for a neutral, united Germany]. It might have led to German reunification some time in the 1950s and to a considerable easing of cold war tensions in Europe. On the other hand, it might have led to greater uncertainty and instability as there was no guarantee Germany would have remained neutral or disarmed for long. As western diplomats and politicians often pointed out to the Soviets in the 1950s, there were advantages for Moscow in West Germany's inclusion in the western bloc. As the old saying has it: NATO was established to keep the Americans in, the Russians out, and the Germans down! But this sanguine perspective was not shared by Stalin or by his successors as Soviet leader, whose view of the German question was formed by their experience of the Great Patriotic War and by their continuing dread of the re-emergence of a powerful and aggressive Germany.

Even as the cold war raged, the idea of a revival of the Grand Alliance to contain Germany still had its allure in Moscow, not least for Stalin who had been very reluctant to relinquish the project of postwar co-operation with the west. In January 1949 Stalin responded positively to a question from an American journalist about whether he would be prepared to meet Truman to discuss a 'peace pact' – an American-Soviet non-aggression agreement.

In Europe Stalin sought peace and a resolution of the German question. In military competition with the United States his policies were reactive and restrained. Although on occasion he rattled his sabres, he talked constantly and consistently about peaceful coexistence with capitalism. The one exception to this pattern of restraint was the Korean War of 1950–53.

From Geoffrey Roberts, *Stalin's Wars* (published in 2006)

Source T

Stalin's goal was not to restore a balance of power in Europe, but rather to dominate that continent as thoroughly as Hitler had sought to do. He acknowledged, in a wistful but revealing comment in 1947, that 'had Churchill delayed opening the second front in northern France by a year, the Red Army would have come to Paris'. Unlike Hitler, however, Stalin followed no fixed timetable . . . Nor would he write off diplomacy in securing his objective . . .

Stalin's was, therefore, a grand vision: the peacefully accomplished but historically determined domination of Europe.

From John Lewis Gaddis, *The Cold War*
(published in 2005)

Source U

It is tempting to lay total blame for the Cold War on the delusions of Stalin and his lieutenants. A closer look at the Cold War from the Soviet side reveals, however, that they were not the only culprits in the conflict. We cannot disregard other complex factors, such as the crass nature of power politics, choices of US and British policy-makers, and the deeper causes of hostility and mistrust between dictatorship and democracy in an uncertain world. Stalin, notwithstanding his reputation as a ruthless tyrant, was not prepared to take a course of unbridled unilateral expansionism after World War II. He wanted to avoid confrontation with the West. He was even ready to see cooperation with the Western powers as a preferable way of building his influence and solving contentious international issues. Thus, the Cold War was not his choice or his brainchild.

From Vladislav Zubok and Constantine Pleshakov,
Inside the Kremlin's Cold War (published in 1996)

- Use Sources S, T and U and your own knowledge. How far do you agree with the view that Stalin's foreign policy was a major contributing factor to the emergence of the Cold War in the period 1945–50?

Exam tips

Note the instruction 'use Sources S, T and U *and* your own knowledge'. This is not a choice.

Weaker answers will tend to discuss the sources first and deal with own knowledge separately. It is much more effective to integrate your own knowledge with the sources. For example:

- Use your own knowledge to explain phrases in the source.
- Use own knowledge to place the source into its context, i.e. to clarify what it is saying and the circumstances that it is about.
- Own knowledge should be used to test the validity of the interpretation in the source.

For Source S you should use your own knowledge to assess the validity of the statement that Stalin's policies were 'reactive and restrained'. If you find evidence that agrees with this view, then your answer to the question is likely to be different to what your answer would have been if you had disagreed.

Note that you will be asked to refer to at least two sources in your answer. These sources will be deliberately chosen to remind you that there is more than one interpretation of the issue and that you are dealing with a historical debate. Your answer should therefore engage in this debate and give a reasoned judgement on the interpretation of the issue highlighted in the question.

RESEARCH TOPIC

Compiling an annotated bibliography

Research the material available on the Cold War and compile a list of works by historians relevant to this topic.

Once you have compiled your list, choose two of the books from your bibliography and find out the following about them:

- the background of the author

- the perspective of the book

- the focus of the book (i.e. the content it covers)

- how the book is useful to you

- any possible limitations of the book for your purpose.

This exercise will help you to develop the way in which you think about the works you read. As you go through the course you are likely to come across other works that you can add to your annotated bibliography.

4 What impact did the post-Stalin thaw have on superpower relations 1953–62?

This unit focuses on the thaw in Cold War relations between the superpowers that developed after the death of Stalin in 1953. It will give you an understanding of the ways in which Soviet foreign policy changed under Stalin's successors and the response of the US government to these changes in the years to 1962. This will allow you to assess the degree of change brought about by the 'Thaw'. In this unit you will:

- examine the impact of Stalin's death on international relations
- discover the reasons for the policy of Peaceful Coexistence
- assess the ways in which US politicians responded to the new Soviet foreign policy
- use sources to consider the impact of individuals on international relations
- examine the key confrontations between the superpowers during this period: the Hungarian Uprising of 1956, the Berlin crisis of 1958–62
- assess the achievements against the limitations of the 'Thaw'.

Key questions

- How, and for what reasons, did the Soviet foreign policy of Peaceful Coexistence develop?
- How, and with what success, did US foreign policy respond to Khrushchev's policy of Peaceful Coexistence?

Timeline

1953	
5 March	Death of Stalin
17 June	Rising of workers in East Berlin
26 June	Beria removed from Soviet leadership
27 July	Ceasefire agreed in Korea
12 September	Khrushchev becomes First Secretary of the Soviet Communist Party
1955	
May	Warsaw Pact established
	USSR signs agreement recognising independence of Austria
July	Geneva Summit (Khrushchev and Eisenhower)

1956	
February	Khrushchev delivers his 'secret speech' criticising Stalin
November	Soviet troops invade Hungary
1958	
November	Start of second Berlin crisis: Khrushchev asks West to leave Berlin
1960	
May	U-2 spy plane shot down over USSR
	Paris Summit between Eisenhower and Khrushchev abandoned
1961	
January	Kennedy becomes US President
12 April	Yuri Gagarin becomes first man in space
June	Vienna Summit (Kennedy and Khrushchev)
August	Berlin Wall erected

Introduction

Source A

4.1 Stand-off at Checkpoint Charlie, October 27 1961

Discussion point

- What is going on in this photograph?
- What do you think had led to this situation?
- Why was this situation so dangerous?

The stand-off between the superpowers, shown in the photo, was solved after 16 hours when a Soviet tank started its engine and pulled back five metres. An American tank then followed, also pulling back a mere five metres. This continued until all the tanks had withdrawn.

The period that followed the death of Stalin in 1953 was to see a general improvement in superpower relations. The change in Soviet leadership was to produce a policy of 'Peaceful Coexistence'. At the same time Truman's successors, Eisenhower and Kennedy, were to make their own mark on US foreign policy, seeking to respond effectively to the new Soviet policy while retaining US superiority in the Cold War. The result of these changes was to usher in a so-called 'Thaw' in Cold War relations that was to last until 1962. Nonetheless, as the photograph – taken in Berlin in 1961 – shows, this period was to see alarmingly swift changes from moments of conciliation to dangerous confrontation.

What impact did the death of Stalin have on international relations?

On the evening on 1 March 1953 Stalin was discovered in his Kremlin rooms. He was lying on the carpet in his pyjamas soaked in his own urine. He had suffered a stroke. His death followed four days later.

Stalin's death was met with great relief in the West where he was seen as the dominant factor in the development of the Cold War. With Stalin now gone, the dynamics of Cold War relations were likely to be different. Liberal historians of the Cold War, who have emphasised the role of personality, have seen Stalin's death as a determining factor in the development of the 'Thaw'. Yet it was unlikely that Stalin was the only influence on the direction of Soviet foreign policy in the early 1950s. Historians have argued over the extent of Stalin's ability to retain control over Soviet foreign policy in his final years. Revisionist studies have drawn attention to the loss of Stalin's power and examined his position within the structures of the Party leadership. W. McCagg's *Stalin Embattled 1943–48* (1978) presents an image of Stalin as only one player in a complex political game, and one whose power had been undermined by the growth in power of groups both inside and, in the case of the army, outside the Party. This **structuralist view** has been supported by W. Hahn in *Post-war Soviet Politics 1945–53: The Fall of Zhdanov and the Defeat of Moderation* (1982) and T. Dunmore's *Soviet Politics 1945–53* (1984). These studies examine the political manoeuvring among the leadership to show the conflict that existed, thus challenging the view that Stalin was able to dominate affairs. It is a view that finds support in comments by Stalin's daughter, Svetlana Alliluyeva, in *Twenty Letters to a Friend* (1967): 'All-powerful as he was, he was impotent in the face of the frightful system that had grown up around him like a huge honeycomb and he was helpless either to destroy it or bring it under control.'

Whether or not it was Stalin who controlled Soviet foreign policy in his final years, the initiative was running away from the Soviet Union in 1948–49. The failure of the Soviet blockade of Berlin, the formation of NATO and the defection of Yugoslavia from Cominform were all failures for Stalin's foreign policy. Thus his death in 1953 provided an opportunity for the new Soviet leadership to change its approach to the West.

Definition

Structuralist view

Approach to explaining historical change that stresses the importance of structures and organisations in influencing the behaviour of individuals and leading to events occurring. Thus individuals matter less in the process of historical change than the structures that produce the circumstances within which they operate.

Change had also occurred at the head of the US government. Two months before Stalin's death Dwight Eisenhower had become the American president. Due to his military background many Americans had voted for Eisenhower expecting him to be tough on communism. Yet the new president was aware that excessive military spending could jeopardise economic prosperity. Eisenhower's 'New Look' policy, therefore, reflected a change towards greater conciliation where it was in US interests, allowing military spending to be reduced.

Thus 1953 saw a change in the conduct of the Cold War. By this time the earlier fluidity in Cold War positioning had been largely settled. The boundaries of each superpower's sphere of influence had been established and accepted, albeit rather reluctantly. In this respect the circumstances of 1953 demanded different policies to work within this greater stability. This switch in policy was promoted by the change in leadership on both sides.

How, and for what reasons, did the Soviet foreign policy of 'Peaceful Coexistence' develop?

The precarious, hostile stand-off between the superpowers, which had been symbolised by the harsh words and hard-line approach of both Stalin and Truman, changed after 1953. There was a move, albeit rather hesitant, towards establishing a dialogue between the superpowers. On the Soviet side this was to lead to the adoption of a policy that became known as 'Peaceful Coexistence'. In the new Soviet leadership **Malenkov** (see page 79) had used this term in 1952, but under **Khrushchev** (see page 79) it was developed into a fully formed policy. As Khrushchev accepted the Marxist belief that the downfall of capitalism was inevitable, Peaceful Coexistence was the best way of conducting relations in the meantime. Thus the class struggle would continue but by different means. With nuclear war too dangerous to contemplate, the two systems would have to accept the existence of each other in the short term. As Khrushchev was to make clear, 'There are only two ways – either Peaceful Coexistence or the most destructive war in History. There is no third way.'

Peaceful Coexistence was encouraged by the new change in Soviet leadership, yet it was not merely the result of a change of personnel. There were factors relating to the wider context within which international relations were operating that pushed both sides towards seeking some degree of accommodation with each other.

The consolidation of positions

The fact that by 1949 the division of Europe into two armed camps had been established and consolidated was to give relations between East and West a degree of stability. The Iron Curtain was now a defined line marking the border between the different spheres of influence. The insecurity of the second half of the 1940s had been caused by both sides attempting to mark out their areas of dominance. By 1949 the division of Europe had become entrenched. The American military commitment to NATO was an indication of the strength of their attitude towards defending Europe from the spread of communism. The Warsaw Pact of 1955 symbolised what had been evident for some time: the willingness on the part of the USSR to protect the Eastern Bloc from the perceived evils of American imperialism. The USA and the USSR were forced to accept the resulting division of Europe and to eye each other across an established dividing line. With their positions in Europe more secure, the superpowers were more willing to attempt negotiation.

The military and economic context

The development of nuclear capability by both sides had made the Cold War potentially very dangerous. By 1955 both sides were in possession of the hydrogen bomb, whose destructive capability was far greater than that of the atomic bomb dropped on Hiroshima. On 1 March 1954 the USA tested a lithium bomb in American waters. The impact of radioactive fallout from the test killed a Japanese fisherman 82 miles away. The stakes for mankind were becoming increasingly high. It was to have a sobering effect on the superpowers.

With the development of nuclear weapons both sides took action to ensure they did not fall behind in their capacity to wage war. The ensuing arms race involved committing large sums of money to military expenditure. In 1950 the USA had 298 atomic bombs; by 1955 this figure had risen to 2,422. The vast sums of money required to try to stay ahead in this arms race were to seriously unbalance the economy of the Soviet Union. Approximately one-third of the Soviet economy was geared to the military sector. This arms race was to divert much needed money from social reforms and more productive sectors of the economy in both countries.

The death of Stalin

The impact of Stalin's death was to be felt both within and outside the USSR. The Soviet leadership was to go through another period of rivalry, as it had done after the death of Lenin in 1924. This time the rivals included Beria, Malenkov and Khrushchev. Lavrenti Beria was the sinister sexual predator in charge of the secret police. His control over the apparatus of terror was a constant concern of his rivals who hoped to outmanoeuvre him. Georgi Malenkov had risen during the last years of Stalin's rule. His skills as an administrator had made him a leading figure in the **Politburo**, despite being the butt of jokes about his large hips that had resulted in his nickname 'Melanie'. The eventual victor in the power struggle was Nikita Khrushchev, a leading Politburo member after being brought back to Moscow by Stalin in 1949. Clumsy and impulsive, Khrushchev was prepared to take high risks. This approach allowed him to outmanoeuvre his opponents by the summer of 1957.

Beria

The death of Stalin in 1953, probably hastened by medical neglect on the part of his associates in the Politburo, provided the opportunity for his successors to try a different approach to dealing with the West. In the immediate aftermath of Stalin's death it was unclear to the West who was in charge of Soviet foreign policy. Within the Soviet Politburo **Lavrenti Beria** (see page 78), the long-serving head of the secret police, took the initiative and offered the West a proposal for a reunified, neutral Germany, arguing that 'All we want is a peaceful Germany and it makes no difference to us whether or not it is socialist.' This statement caused great concern to the East German government. The new Soviet leadership seemed prepared to abandon East Germany to capitalism. Walter Ulbricht, the East German leader, had already started a programme of Soviet-style industrialisation in order to impose socialism on his country. Part of this programme involved the introduction of longer working hours and price increases. The workers of the so-called workers' republic protested. The uprising of June 1953 started when workers on the prestigious building projects on Stalinallee, East Berlin, downed tools and protested at the new economic measures introduced by the government. In a largely spontaneous action, strikes spread across East Germany. Soviet troops were needed to restore order, leading to the arrest of 25,000 people of whom 400 were executed.

These developments in East Germany were to deliver a blow to Beria's foreign policy initiative and seriously undermined his attempt to gain the leadership of the USSR. East Germany may have been merely the artificial by-product of Cold War tension between the superpowers, but without the agreement of the West for a unified Germany to be neutral the USSR had little choice but to ensure the survival of this 'temporary' state.

Beria's motives for his German initiative may have been to distance himself from Stalin's policies or merely to impress his colleagues in the Politburo, but on both of these counts he failed. Beria's association with the less pleasant aspects of Stalin's policies was too much for the other members of the Politburo and he was arrested within months. Absurdly accused of being a British agent he was later executed.

4.2 Malenkov (front left) and Beria (front right) carrying Stalin's coffin, 1953

Malenkov's 'New Course'

With the removal of Beria, Soviet foreign policy fell into the control of Georgi Malenkov, who with Khrushchev and Bulganin formed a collective leadership. Despite this change, the softer tone towards the West was maintained and even further developed.

Malenkov was able and intelligent and recognised the limitations of a hard-line approach of confrontation towards the West. He decided to embark on a 'New Course'. Malenkov believed that war between capitalism and communism was no longer inevitable and therefore resources could be directed away from arms and heavy industry towards consumer goods and raising living standards in the USSR. This approach did not mark an end of conflict between capitalism and communism, merely a belief that as the collapse of capitalism was inevitable, there was no need to engage in war to ensure its demise. The advent of the nuclear age made war a risky strategy; there were other, safer methods that could be used to defend communism while waiting for the inevitable collapse of the world capitalist system. Malenkov's 'New Course' was criticised by Khrushchev during his struggle for power, yet after Malenkov was removed from the position of Prime Minister in 1955, Khrushchev was to adopt and develop the 'New Course' into a policy of 'Peaceful Coexistence'.

By the summer of 1957 Khrushchev was the established leader of the USSR. He had successfully outmanoeuvred his rivals Beria and Malenkov. At the 20th Party Congress in 1956 Khrushchev had delivered a secret speech highly critical of features of Stalin's rule. It was clear that the new leader wanted to detach himself from key aspects of Stalinism; at home, Khrushchev's approach became known as **De-Stalinisation**. Nonetheless, the impact of this struggle for power on Soviet foreign policy was very limited. All three Soviet leaders had since Stalin's death recognised the military and economic pressures that made continued confrontation with the West a dangerous and expensive option. Beria had made the tentative first moves, and despite his failure, both Malenkov and Khrushchev were to build on his thinking. The continuity between Malenkov's foreign policy and that of Khrushchev is highlighted by the fact that the name associated with Khrushchev's policy – Peaceful Coexistence – had already been used by Malenkov to describe his own approach.

Definition

De-Stalinisation

The attempt by Khrushchev, the Soviet leader, to move away from the policies of Stalin. Khrushchev criticised Stalin's use of terror and his economic policies of concentrating on heavy industry and forced collectivisation in agriculture. Khrushchev's actions encouraged those in Eastern Europe who wanted reform to push for change. In 1956, the Soviet response to attempts in Hungary to introduce liberal measures showed that there were limits to De-Stalinisation. It would not be allowed to threaten the security of the Socialist Bloc.

SKILLS BUILDER

1 Define the term 'Peaceful Coexistence'.

2 To what extent was the policy of Peaceful Coexistence a reflection of changing personalities in the Soviet leadership?

Biography

Lavrenti Beria (1899–1953)

As head of the secret police, he was Stalin's chief henchman from 1938 until 1953. He was a sinister master of intrigue and a sexual predator who picked up women from the streets for his own pleasure. Despite his association with Stalin's apparatus of terror, there are indications that Beria would have introduced some liberal reforms if he had become Stalin's successor: he initiated the release of 1 million prisoners from the labour camps. He was to underestimate Khrushchev during the power struggle and was outmanoeuvred by the 'moon-faced idiot'. He was arrested and shot in 1953.

Biography

Georgi Malenkov (1902–88)

Malenkov rose through the ranks of the Communist Party under Stalin to become a Politburo member in 1946. On Stalin's death he held the positions of Prime Minister and head of the Party. His foreign policy was known as the 'New Course', and this encouraged better relations with the West. Within the Politburo he was outmanoeuvred by Khrushchev in 1957 and dismissed. He was then sent to Kazakhstan to run a hydroelectric plant but his active political career was over.

Biography

Nikita Khrushchev (1894–1971)

Khrushchev emerged as leader of the Soviet Union after the death of Stalin in 1953. Although he was a committed communist, Khrushchev wanted to move away from the brutal policies of Stalin. He criticised Stalin's policies during a congress of the Soviet Communist Party in 1956 and encouraged De-Stalinisation. In international relations Khrushchev adopted a softer tone towards the West than Stalin had. He believed that the superpowers should accept each other's existence and put forward the idea of 'Peaceful Coexistence'. Yet when Soviet power was under attack, Khrushchev made threats to the West. His language was often colourful and undiplomatic. The Soviet climbdown during the Cuban Missile Crisis of 1962 was a personal embarrassment from which he never recovered. He was sacked by the Soviet Politburo in 1964 and died quietly in retirement in 1971.

Investigation: Khrushchev and Peaceful Coexistence

Source B

In his more reasonable, pragmatic incarnation, he [Khrushchev] conclusively ended Stalin's reign of terror. He allowed new Soviet elites to emerge and consolidate into a permanent strata of the political hierarchy. And he recognised the bipolarity of the nuclear world, as a source of new opportunities for Soviet foreign policy, but also as an ultimate constraint.

At the same time . . . his fiery and uncultivated persona, greatly aggravated the Cold War in the late 1950s and early 1960s . . . [leading] to the brink of war during the Cuban missile crisis.

From Vladislav Zubok and Constantine Pleshakov, *Inside the Kremlin's Cold War*, published by Harvard University Press (1996)

Source C

Whilst we need not accept the assumption that a change of leadership in the USSR in 1953 was enough to signal a transformation in superpower relations and the Cold War, we do need to recognise that the new Soviet leadership did manage to signal a shift in foreign policy . . . [this] could be seen to reflect the concern of the new Soviet leadership over the consequences of military conflict with the West. These concerns were encapsulated in the idea of 'peaceful coexistence'.

From Richard Saull, *The Cold War and After*, published by Pluto Press (2007)

SKILLS BUILDER

1 How far does Source B agree with the view of Source C that Khrushchev brought about a change in Soviet foreign policy?

2 Which of these interpretations do you find the most convincing?

3 How would the US government in the 1950s have viewed Khrushchev's desire for 'Peaceful Coexistence'?

What was the immediate impact of Khrushchev's policy of Peaceful Coexistence?

The new Soviet leadership under Khrushchev led to several new developments that gave hope to the West that accommodation and agreement could be reached between the superpowers. The more conciliatory line adopted by the Soviet leadership in the immediate period following the death of Stalin had already produced a cease-fire in the Korean War in 1953. Under Khrushchev further agreement was possible.

1 The Austrian State Treaty, 1955

In 1945 Austria had been dealt with by arrangements similar to those for Germany and Berlin. It was divided into zones of occupation. Austria seemed likely to suffer the same fate as Germany in the sense that this division would become a more permanent arrangement. Negotiations on the long-term future of Austria had ground to a halt as common ground between the two superpowers seemed impossible to find. The USSR used their zone as a source of economic resources to be used for their own benefit. The US pumped in Marshall Aid and secretly rearmed the western zone. By 1954 Khrushchev was in a position to over ride the more obstinate approach of Molotov and decided that Austrian neutrality was better than permanent division. This echoed Khrushchev's approach to the status of Finland. He was also hoped that Soviet concessions here would convince the West that the USSR were serious about negotiating on matters of importance that they wished to resolve in their favour. The Austrian State Treaty of 1955 was the result.

Under the Treaty, both the US and the USSR would withdraw its armed forces from Austria in return for agreeing its neutrality. The influence of both superpowers in Austria was reduced but so was a potential source of tension and conflict. Khrushchev regarded the Treaty as a sign of a more mature approach to international relations, stating that he had swapped 'boy pants for adult trousers'.

2 Soviet withdrawal from Finland, 1956

The USSR had an interest in Finland, its neighbour and enemy during the Second World War. Under the Finnish-Soviet Peace Treaty, signed in Paris in 1947, the terms of the armistice signed in 1944 were largely confirmed. Finland was to pay $300 million in reparations to the USSR and lose land along its border to the Soviet Union. In addition the USSR was given a 50-year lease to the Porkkala region.

By the autumn of 1955 Khrushchev was ready to withdraw the Soviet presence from Porkkala. He saw no reason to retain Soviet influence in a non-communist country and considered Porkkala to be of little strategic use and more of a burden than an asset. Molotov had tried to over-rule the decision to withdraw at a meeting of the Central Committee of the Communist Party but had been defeated. In 1956 Porkkala was returned

SKILLS BUILDER

How far do the agreements over Austria and Finland in 1955–56 show that Khrushchev had changed the nature of superpower relations?

to Finland. During the late 1950s and 1960s Finland followed a more neutral position with regards the superpowers but the USSR was still able to exercise some influence when they felt their interests were threatened. In 1962 it forced the withdrawal of a candidate for president of Finland.

To what extent did the foreign policy of Eisenhower and Dulles differ from that of Truman?

Change in the Soviet leadership was accompanied by a change in the American presidency. Yet at face value the change in American leadership seemed much less likely to promote a thaw in superpower relations.

Dwight Eisenhower had won the presidential election of 1952 on a platform that was highly critical of Truman's foreign policy for failing to stand firm against communism. No less hostile to communism than Truman, Eisenhower was, however, to present a different style and approach towards the USSR. He was also ably supported by his Secretary of State, **John Foster Dulles**. During the election of 1952 Dulles had talked of 'rolling back' communism and of the 'liberation' of the states of Eastern Europe from the evils of communism. The appointment of Dulles seemed to signal a more hard-line approach to the USSR than Truman.

Biographies

Dwight Eisenhower (1890–1969)

Eisenhower was the US general who was Supreme Commander of the Normandy landings in the Second World War. He became first Supreme Commander of NATO in 1950 and then Republican presidential candidate in 1952, and President from 1953 to 1961.

John Foster Dulles (1888–1959)

Dulles was an American lawyer who gained foreign policy experience at Versailles in 1919. He became Eisenhower's Secretary of State in 1953. Staunchly anti-communist and known for his tough speaking, he retired in April 1959 and died of cancer the following month.

Definitions

New Look

The name of Eisenhower's foreign policy that took a hard line against communism based on an increased role for nuclear weapons to further containment.

Massive retaliation

A phrase popularised by Dulles, Eisenhower's Secretary of State. It implied the use, or at least the threat, of nuclear action against any aggressive move by the Communist Bloc.

The foreign policy approach adopted by Eisenhower was known as the 'New Look'. This 'New Look' was a hard-line approach to foreign policy that won much support in the USA. Its key features were:

- the belief that the Soviet Union and its communist allies were pursuing expansionist policies
- the use of military means to contain communism
- a policy of 'massive retaliation' against communist aggression: this had been advocated by Dulles during the election campaign of 1952, and it

implied a much greater role for the use of nuclear weapons than envisaged by Truman

- the policy of **brinkmanship** in the use of nuclear weapons: Dulles explained that 'the ability to get to the verge without getting into war is the necessary art. If you cannot master it, you inevitably get into war. If you try to run away from it, if you are scared to go to the brink, you are lost'

- the increased use of covert operations within countries that would destabilise the forces of communism. Truman had always felt uneasy about using these methods. This new attitude was helped by the closer relationship between the Secretary of State, John Foster Dulles, and the CIA, now headed by his brother, Allen Dulles.

The 'New Look' seemed unlikely to produce compromise and conciliation, yet in practice there were pressures that made the USA willing to reach an understanding with the new Soviet leadership.

- As a military man Eisenhower was aware of the destructive force of nuclear weapons. Like the new Soviet leadership in 1953, he was keen to avoid the prospect of nuclear annihilation.

- In private, both Eisenhower and Dulles were cautious and their actions were based on a reasoned approach to the situation they faced. Eisenhower was very conscious of the growth of power and influence of the military-industrial complex within the USA. He was also aware that economic resources that could help improve living standards were being diverted into arms production. The huge expansion of America's armed forces that had taken place during the Korean War was in danger of distorting and unbalancing the US economy. By 1954 over 12 per cent of America's GNP was spent on armaments. With the growth in expensive nuclear missiles, this problem was unlikely to go away unless some sort of agreement could be reached with the USSR. Eisenhower's 'New Look' was designed in part to save money on conventional arms by relying on fewer but more powerful nuclear weapons. To coin the phrase used at the time, it would provide 'more bang for the buck'.

- Eisenhower was a much more confident politician than Truman. He was a war hero of the Second World War and had served as Commander-in-Chief for NATO. Eisenhower's credentials in the fight against communism were difficult to fault. He was, therefore, more immune from the constant attacks by Joseph McCarthy of being 'soft' on communism than Truman had been. Eisenhower had the self-confidence gained from his military career to pursue his own policies and was a firm believer in the benefits of personal face-to-face diplomacy. Thus, the public rhetoric of hard-line anti-communism did not always translate into practical policy-making.

- By 1958 data provided by U-2 spy planes meant that Eisenhower was confident that the USA had nuclear superiority over the Soviet Union. He was therefore more willing to negotiate with the USSR now he knew it was from a position of strength.

Thus, from the early 1950s the US government under Eisenhower was facing many of the same pressures as the USSR. These pressures, coupled with the changes in leadership since 1952, had pushed the superpowers towards reaching an accommodation with each other. The result was the so-called 'Thaw'. It was to be a hesitant and delicate process but the trend was there.

SKILLS BUILDER

1 In what ways did the 'New Look' mark a change from the conclusions of NSC-68?

2 In what ways was the 'New Look' similar to the foreign policy pursued by Truman?

3 How far would you accept the view that the foreign policy of Eisenhower and Dulles was based on empty rhetoric?

Investigation: the influence of Dulles on US foreign policy

Source D

In March 1955 the Chinese Communists attacked the islands of Quemoy and Matsu which, although they were just off the Chinese mainland, were occupied by Chiang Kai-Shek's troops. As the Chinese began to bombard Quemoy and Matsu, the Eisenhower administration seriously considered dropping nuclear weapons on the mainland. Dulles threatened to use 'new and powerful weapons of precision, which can utterly destroy military targets' – in other words, tactical atomic bombs. The Chinese gave way and the Dulles policy of Brinkmanship, going to the brink of war to force the enemy to retreat, was triumphant.

From Hugh Higgins, *The Cold War*, published by Heinemann (1974)

Source F

For Dulles the key to Soviet communism was that it was based on 'an atheistic Godless premise' from which everything else flowed. Not only did this make compromise difficult, but it also meant that conciliatory moves by Moscow were dismissed as propaganda gestures or as evidence of Soviet weakness.

From M. Bowker and P. Williams, *Superpower Détente: A Reappraisal*, published by Sage (1988)

Source E

Dulles combined amazing energy and strong moral convictions – 'there is no way to solve the great perplexing international problems except by bringing to bear on them the force of Christianity,' he insisted. His objectives were magnificent; his strategy was grandiose. Instead of waiting for the communist powers to make a move and then 'containing' them, the United States should put more emphasis on nuclear bombs and less on conventional weapons.

Despite his determination, energy, and high ideals, Dulles failed to make the United States a more effective force in world affairs. Most of Dulles's other schemes were quite unrealistic. 'Unleashing' Chiang Kai-shek against the Chinese communists would have been like matching a Pekingese against a tiger. 'Liberating' Russia's European satellites would have involved a third world war. Above all, massive retaliation made little sense when the Soviet Union possessed nuclear weapons as powerful as those of the United States . . . the only threat behind massive retaliation was the threat of human extinction.

From John Garraty, *The American Nation*, published by HarperCollins (1991)

1 Sources D and E give two differing interpretations of the effectiveness of Dulles's foreign policy. Using these sources and your own knowledge, give your own reasoned assessment of the principles behind Dulles's foreign policy.
2 Using Source F and your own knowledge, what factors would (a) promote and (b) restrict the influence that Dulles would have on Eisenhower?

What impact did Kennedy have on US foreign policy?

Eisenhower had been aware of the limitations of the policy of 'massive retaliation'. He had discussed with his advisers in 1954 the futility of winning a nuclear war that might leave most of the world devastated. Yet by relying on a strategy that placed its emphasis on the use of nuclear weapons this seemed a possibility. This dilemma was to lead to his successors re-evaluating US foreign policy.

When John F. Kennedy became President in 1961, a new foreign policy approach was developed that became known as 'Flexible Response'. It marked a move away from the emphasis on nuclear weapons to an approach that relied on developing a wider range of strategies to meet the threat of communism: from conventional armed forces to covert actions and economic aid. Nuclear weapons would still be used, but they would now be seen as one of a range of methods that could be utilised to combat the spread of communism.

'Flexible Response' was a reaction to the perception of many in the US government that the communist forces were using a more diverse set of approaches to spread their influence, especially in the developing countries of the so-called Third World. 'Flexible Response' would give the US President a choice of options: as Kennedy stated in July 1961, 'We intend to have a wider choice than humiliation or all-out nuclear war.'

Economic aid would be targeted at removing poverty and the economic conditions that provided a breeding ground for communism. Over $20 billion was given to Latin America to promote land reforms for the poor.

Covert methods had been used by Eisenhower but were to be enlarged in scope and ambition under Kennedy. CIA involvement in attempts to remove Fidel Castro, the new communist leader of Cuba, gathered pace leading to the fiasco of the Bay of Pigs affair in 1961.

The expansion of conventional forces was inevitable under the policy of 'Flexible Response'. The cuts in expenditure introduced by Eisenhower were reversed by Kennedy. The army grew from 2.5 million in 1960 to 2.7 million in 1964. Resources were also used to develop special forces such as the Green Berets, who were to be deployed against communist guerrilla forces in Vietnam.

At the same time as developing these strategies, Kennedy, like Eisenhower, was willing to engage the Soviet leaders in negotiations where they seemed appropriate.

SKILLS BUILDER

1 In what ways did 'Flexible Response' differ from Eisenhower's foreign policy?
2 What were the similarities between 'Flexible Response' and the 'New Look'?
3 How far would you agree with the view that Kennedy's approach to the USSR marked a return to that adopted by Truman?

Key debate: What, if anything, were the achievements of the 'Thaw'?

The 'Thaw' in superpower relations that developed after 1953 resulted in a series of summits between Eisenhower and Khrushchev. These summits became part of the so-called 'Geneva Spirit'. After the years of mud-slinging, the fact that the two most powerful leaders in the world were talking to each other was a significant step forward, even if what was achieved was rather limited.

Key developments

- An armistice was concluded in 1953 that brought the fighting in the Korean War to an end. The war had produced a stalemate since 1951 and the peace talks that had been going on had been protracted. The change in leadership in both the USA and the USSR gave these talks the impetus needed to reach a conclusion. The new Soviet leadership put pressure on North Korea's Kim Il Sung to agree to a ceasefire.

- At the Berlin Foreign Ministers' conference of January 1954 Molotov, the Soviet representative, called for the creation of an all-German government out of those in West and East Germany to begin the move towards reunification. The West opposed this proposal, arguing that free elections must be held *before* the creation of a German government not afterwards. Molotov's proposal was rejected.

- At the *Geneva Conference* of April 1954 a settlement was reached that allowed the French to withdraw its forces from Indochina. Despite reservations on the part of Dulles over the wisdom of the settlement, the agreement was endorsed by all involved. Dulles was concerned that the agreement confirmed communism in North Vietnam, and he walked out of the conference before it had finished. His verbal endorsement was given reluctantly.

- In early 1955 the USSR agreed to the reunification of Austria, which, like Germany, had been divided into zones of occupation in 1945. The USSR was prepared to accept a united Austria providing it remained neutral.

- The *Geneva Summit* of July 1955, the first summit meeting of Soviet and American leaders since Potsdam in 1945, was attended by Eisenhower, Khrushchev, Eden (GB) and Faure (France). Hopes were high that the new 'Geneva Spirit' of cooperation would produce results. The issue of German reunification was raised again. Khrushchev was prepared to allow a united Germany providing it was neutral. This issue was now complicated by the admission of West Germany into NATO in May. The USA saw West Germany, due to its geographical position, as central to the defence of Western Europe. Khrushchev replied to this with a suggestion that both NATO and the Warsaw Pact be dismantled and replaced by a new system of collective security. The West was not prepared to agree to this but was willing to look at proposals for a limit on arms. Eisenhower surprised Khrushchev by calling for an 'Open Skies' agreement whereby spy planes would be allowed to fly over each other's territory in order to verify arms agreements. Khrushchev did not accept this offer.

Definition

Warsaw Pact

The organisation set up in 1955 to coordinate the military forces of the Soviet Bloc in Eastern Europe. The organisation was established by the Treaty of Friendship, Cooperation and Mutual Aid, signed in Warsaw, the Polish capital. It was a response to the entry of West Germany into NATO the previous week. The pact was dominated by the USSR and was a useful vehicle for facilitating the deployment of their troops in Eastern Europe. The pact was not without tensions, and Albania left the organisation in 1968. Romania also distanced itself from the pact in the 1970s. The organisation was formally disbanded in 1991.

- The only agreement to come out of the Geneva summit was one on cultural exchanges of scientists, musicians and artists between the USA and the USSR.
- Khrushchev accepted an invitation to visit the USA in September 1959. The visit was generally a success, although there were tensions. When Khrushchev was denied access to Disneyland on health and safety grounds, he accused the US government of hiding rocket launching pads there. Khrushchev also caused a diplomatic incident when he boasted, 'We will bury you.' He was talking about the USSR's plans to overtake the US economy but, in a nuclear age, his choice of words was unfortunate.
- A summit meeting between Eisenhower and Khrushchev at Paris in May 1960 collapsed when an American U-2 spy plane was shot down over Soviet airspace. The pilot, Gary Powers, had ejected and was caught by the Russians who, to the embarrassment of the US government, put him on trial.
- A summit between Kennedy and Khrushchev was arranged for Vienna on 3 June 1961. Although an improvement on the Paris Summit of 1960 that had had cancelled in the wake of the U-2 incident, nothing was agreed. Khrushchev felt he had been able to dominate the young and relatively inexperienced Kennedy.
- The so-called 'Geneva Spirit' did not prevent crises from developing. The Hungarian Uprising of 1956 and the Berlin crisis of 1958–62 were to show how fragile superpower relations remained. Nonetheless, the fact that each side recognised the other's sphere of influence removed the likelihood of an intervention that could have provoked war.
- 'Peaceful Coexistence' also had an effect on relations within the Communist Bloc. One success for Khrushchev was an improvement in relations with communist Yugoslavia, although he had to agree to the request of Tito, the Yugoslav leader, to dissolve Cominform. Perhaps more serious for communist unity was the split with China. Mao, the Chinese communist leader, had not been consulted about De-Stalinisation and was pursuing Stalinist policies within China. Mao's resentment led to a breach in relations with the USSR that was to complicate the Cold War.
- Military coordination of the Communist Bloc in eastern Europe was strengthened by the establishment of the **Warsaw Pact** in 1955.
- Both superpowers failed to reduce military expenditure in any meaningful way. Under Eisenhower the 'New Look' policy had brought about some cuts in spending, as the number of costly ground troops was reduced after the Korean War, but these were to be reversed under Kennedy's 'Flexible Response' approach. In the Soviet Union a lot of resources were diverted to the development of a space programme that was seen to have military applications. The vast sums of money did at least bear some dividends. In October 1957 the Soviet Union launched the first ever space satellite, Sputnik. The 'beep, beep, beep' signal emitted from Sputnik caused dismay in the USA. As the historian Harold Evans has stated, 'It suggested that communism had mastered the universe.' In 1961 the Soviet Union was the first country to put a man into space. Yuri Gagarin orbited the earth in Vostok I. The USA became determined to be the first to put a man on the moon.

Source G

4.3 An evening reception in July 1955, held during the Geneva Summit. The guests include (front left) Soviet leader Nikita Khrushchev, (second from left) British Prime Minister Sir Anthony Eden and (right) American President Dwight D Eisenhower and his wife Mamie

Source H

Khrushchev gives his view of the meeting

At the end of the Geneva meeting we prepared a joint statement setting forth the position of the four delegations. This statement was formulated in such a way as to leave each delegation with the possibility of interpreting it in its own way. The wording was the result of various compromises which allowed us all to sign. We didn't want to disperse without having anything to show for the meeting. On the other hand none of us wanted any point in the statement to be interpreted as a concession in principle or policy to the other side.

We returned to Moscow from Geneva knowing that we hadn't achieved any concrete results. But we were encouraged, realizing now that our enemies probably feared us as much as we feared them. They rattled their sabres and tried to pressure us into agreements which were more profitable for them than for us because they were frightened of us. As a result of our own showing in Geneva, our enemies now realized that we were able to resist their pressure and see through their tricks . . . The Geneva meeting was an important breakthrough for us on the diplomatic front. We had established ourselves as able to hold our own in the international arena.

From N. Khrushchev, *Khrushchev Remembers* (published in 1971)

Source I

Eisenhower's assessment of the Geneva Summit, 1955

It had been held in a cordial atmosphere, which represented a sharp departure from the vitriolic recriminations which characterised so many meetings in the past . . . People had been given a glowing picture of hope and, though it was badly blurred by the Soviets, at least the outlines of the picture remained.

From Eisenhower's memoirs

Questions

1 Study Source G. Explain why Eisenhower and Khrushchev were attending this summit meeting together.
2 Study Sources H and I. How and why do Eisenhower and Khrushchev give differing assessments of the achievements of the Geneva Summit of 1955?
3 What evidence would you use to support the view that the 'Thaw' failed to achieve anything of substance?
4 What evidence would you use to support the view that the 'Thaw' was successful?
5 How far would you accept the judgement that the 'Thaw' 'produced meaningful dialogue between the superpowers but nothing of substance'?
6 'The superpowers tendency to veer between conciliation and confrontation in the period 1953 to 1961 was a reflection of the personalities of their leaders.' To what extent would you agree with this view?

What do the Hungarian Rising of 1956 and the Berlin crisis of 1958–62 tell us about the nature of superpower relations during the Thaw?

Despite the fact that the superpowers had made steps towards an improvement in relations, the period 1956–62 saw the development of a series of important crises that revealed the superficial nature of the Thaw. These crises were also important in highlighting the need for some form of rules by which conflict should take place and therefore be limited. These themes can be illustrated by an examination of the Hungarian Uprising of 1956 and the Berlin crisis of 1958–62, which led to the building of the Berlin Wall.

The Hungarian Rising, 1956

The events in Hungary in 1956 showed the vulnerability of the Soviet sphere of influence that had been built up after the Second World War. The calls for liberalisation within Hungary were encouraged by Khrushchev's policy of De-Stalinisation and demonstrated the impact that changes within the Soviet Union could have on its satellite states.

De-Stalinisation encouraged reform by criticising Stalin's system of terror and by Khrushchev's suggestion that there could be more than one road towards socialism. In the Soviet Union's satellite states of Eastern Europe De-Stalinisation led to calls by the general public for a liberalisation by its regimes.

Khrushchev's secret speech denouncing Stalin had caused shock throughout Eastern Europe – in Poland Boleslaw Bierut, the party leader, had a heart attack and died after reading the speech. In the summer of 1956 workers' protests in Poland forced the Polish Communist Party to elect yet another new leader, Wladyslaw Gomulka, and introduce a series of moderate reforms.

Encouraged by the Polish example, Hungarian reformers started demonstrations in order to put pressure on the government. Khrushchev sensed the danger in a wave of disturbances sweeping through Eastern Europe. The Hungarian leader Matyas Rakosi, a staunch Stalinist, was informed by the Soviets that he was 'ill' and needed 'treatment' in Moscow. Gerö, Rakosi's replacement could not control the increasingly violent demonstrations.

Soviet troops stationed in Budapest, the Hungarian capital, were forced to leave the city. Under Soviet pressure Gerö was replaced by the more moderate **Nagy**, who the Soviet leadership hoped would be more acceptable to the reformers. Nagy's attempts to introduce moderate reforms, known as the New Course, failed to satisfy the increasing demands of popular opinion. In order to keep a hold on events Nagy gave in to demands to introduce multi-party democracy and to leave the Warsaw Pact. These measures were too much for the USSR. Soviet forces were sent into Hungary and a new government under Kadar was established.

Biography

Imre Nagy (1896–1956)

Leader of the Hungarian Communist Party, Nagy had spent several years in the USSR before returning to Hungary after the Second World War. He had been critical of Stalin's style of leadership and economic policies. He became leader of the Hungarian government in 1956 and introduced reforms. His proposal to take Hungary out of the Warsaw Pact led to a Soviet invasion of the country. Nagy was removed and replaced by the more hard-line Kadar. Nagy was seized by Soviet forces and taken to Romania. He was later executed.

Order was restored but at the loss of over 35,000 lives, including that of Nagy, who was executed. The Soviet Bloc remained intact, but the resulting bitterness and resentment was to be long-lasting.

Results

- Despite a degree of liberalisation within the USSR, the subsequent actions of the USSR in Hungary indicated that there were limits to the independence of the Eastern Bloc countries.

- The Soviet response to calls for reform was to invade Hungary and restore a government of its own liking. These actions showed a willingness on the part of the USSR to maintain a tight hold over its sphere of influence in Eastern Europe.

- The Warsaw Pact, which had been created the previous year, had helped Soviet dominance, and the organisation ensured that other Eastern Bloc countries contributed to the Soviet straitjacket over the region.

- The reaction of the West was important in establishing some of the rules of the Cold War. Statements of condemnation were issued by the West, but they made little attempt to intervene in a crisis that was seen as within the Soviet sphere of influence.

Source J

The Hungarian uprising, from its beginning to its bloody suppression, was an occurrence that inspired in our nation feelings of sympathy and admiration for the rebels, anger and disgust for their Soviet oppressors.

An expedition across neutral Austria, Titoist Yugoslavia or Communist Czechoslovakia, was out of the question. The fact was that Hungary could not be reached by any United Nations or United States units without traversing such territory. Unless the major nations of Europe would, without delay, ally themselves spontaneously with us, we could do nothing. Sending United States troops alone into Hungary through hostile or neutral territory would have involved us in general war.

From D. Eisenhower, *Mandate for Change*, published by Heinemann (1963)

Source K

(Eisenhower) . . . behaved like a spectator without any direct interest in the outcome of the Hungarian Revolution and its abject failure to extort any price from Moscow, diplomatic, economic, military. There were no diplomatic notes, no pressure, no offers to mediate. Nothing.

From Henry Kissinger, *Diplomacy*, published by Simon & Schuster (1994)

SKILLS BUILDER

Sources J and K give two differing assessments of the reaction of the US government to the Hungarian Rising. How valid are these assessments? Give reasons for your answer.

Berlin, 1958–62

While West Germany underwent an 'economic miracle' in the 1950s, East Germany struggled to present itself as a meaningful independent state. The failure of the East German government to win over its own people was shown by the growing exodus across the 'Iron Curtain' into the increasingly prosperous, and capitalist, West Berlin.

By 1958 Khrushchev had decided that firmer action was needed to shore up the Eastern Bloc, and he issued an ultimatum to the West that called for the removal of all occupying forces from Berlin. Khrushchev wanted Berlin to become a free city with the existence of East Germany recognised formally by the West. The West were unwilling to give up West Berlin because of its immense propaganda value in undermining the Socialist Bloc. Thus, Khrushchev's ultimatum resulted in another crisis over Berlin. It was only after Eisenhower invited Khrushchev to visit the USA that he dropped the ultimatum. This highlighted the role of personal diplomacy between the individual leaders of the two superpowers in reducing international tension.

SKILLS BUILDER

What does Source L tell us about the possible motives behind Khrushchev's Berlin ultimatum of 1958?

Source L

The crisis was triggered off in November 1958 by Khrushchev's famous ultimatum to the Western powers. Contending that the Western Allies had forfeited the right to remain in Berlin because of violations of the Potsdam Agreement, he demanded that West Berlin become a free, demilitarised city, possibly under the auspices of the United Nations and that access to the city would have to be negotiated with the GDR . . .

His challenge to the West was undoubtedly influenced by the boost to his confidence from his country's technological achievements, notably the Sputnik, and from a widespread – though erroneous – belief in the Soviet Union's superiority in missile capability over the USA. The time therefore seemed appropriate for a bold initiative to wrest concessions from the West by applying pressure on one of its exposed nerves, West Berlin, or, as Khrushchev put it, to make the West scream by squeezing on West Berlin, the 'testicles of the West'.

From M. Dennis, *The Rise and Fall of the German Democratic Republic* (published in 2000)

Biography

Walter Ulbricht (1893–1973)

Ulbricht was the communist leader of East Germany from 1949 to 1971. A hard-line Stalinist, Ulbricht had received his political education in Moscow during the Second World War.

The ultimatum was renewed in June 1961, when Khrushchev met Eisenhower's successor, Kennedy, at the Vienna Summit. When Kennedy made clear his intention not to relinquish West Berlin, Khrushchev finally gave his approval to the East German government's request to build the Berlin Wall.

The Berlin Wall, 1961

Khrushchev had been using the **German Democratic Republic** as a bargaining tool with the West. Whether Khrushchev really would have relinquished a hold over East Germany in return for a neutral unified Germany is uncertain. Yet once it was clear that this tactic was unlikely to produce results, Khrushchev was willing to agree to the solution proposed by the East German government for shoring up the Communist Bloc. It was a solution that was to give physical meaning to the phrase 'Iron Curtain'.

To stem the exodus of its own people, the East German government closed the main frontier between East and West Germany in 1958 but it was still possible to move from East Germany into West Berlin. The continuing loss of population threatened the survival of East Germany as a separate country. The solution to this problem was the building of the **Berlin Wall**. **Walter Ulbricht**, the East German leader, had wanted this solution for some time but had been overruled by Khrushchev. As the situation grew more desperate, Khrushchev changed his mind, and in August 'security constructions of the border' were built in a military-style operation.

The Berlin Wall was a huge concrete structure over three metres high. Referred to in the West as the 'Wall of Shame', the East German government preferred to call it the 'anti-fascist protective barrier'. It was to be a physical symbol of a divided continent. With a secure border established between itself and the West, East Germany was stabilised. The flood of refugees was halted, although about 5,000 people risked their lives escaping over, through or under the Berlin Wall. Not all were lucky: 191 people died in the process. East Germany became notorious as the country whose population had to be penned in to stop them escaping. It was not a good advert for communism.

Source M

4.4 Berliners at the newly-constructed Berlin Wall, 1961

Definitions

German Democratic Republic (GDR)

The official name of the communist state established in 1949 in the former Soviet zone of Germany. It is commonly referred to as East Germany, sometimes known by its initials GDR, or in German DDR.

Berlin Wall

Built in 1961 to halt the flood of refugees escaping from communist East Germany into capitalist West Berlin. This huge concrete structure became the ultimate symbol of the East–West divide. The order to build the Wall was given by Ulbricht, the East German leader, and was implemented by Erich Honecker, who later became East Germany's leader. The East German government referred to the Wall as the 'anti-fascist protective barrier' and avoided calling it a wall. In the 1980s Honecker occasionally referred to it as the 'so-called wall', just as West German newspapers usually referred to East Germany as the 'so-called DDR', indicating that they did not accept its existence.

Source N

At the Warsaw Pact summit in Moscow at the end of March (1961) Ulbricht (the East German leader) had tried to persuade his alliance colleagues of the necessity of a guarded barbed wire along the Soviet zone border . . . Ulbricht left Moscow without approval for his plan.

The number of refugees fleeing to the west was growing by the month – in January 1961 10,000 had left, in July 30,000. Half the refugees were young, skilled people under twenty-five – those East Germany could least afford to lose. About 2.7 million East Germans had left for West Germany since 1949. Sometime between the end of April and the end of July Khrushchev must have dropped his opposition to the project.

From Anne McElvoy, *The Saddled Cow* (published in 1993)

Source P

. . . speeches were prepared in the East on how peace in Europe had been 'saved' by this extraordinary measure.

The Americans moved tanks right up to the new frontier but the statesmen of the West barely moved at all. Many were on holiday. Walter Ulbricht kept his head down . . . He was now literally immured with one of the unhappiest populations in Europe.

From M. Simmons, *The Unloved Country* (published in 1989)

Source O

The Berlin question caught fire at the Kennedy–Khrushchev summit in Vienna in June 1961. During the heated exchanges, Khrushchev insisted that all of Berlin was on GDR territory and even threatened war if the USA refused to compromise. Kennedy made it clear that the USA would not back down

Khrushchev apparently continued to hope until the last moment that the problem of the GDR and Berlin could be resolved through diplomatic pressure. A barrier would torpedo this strategy and it would expose the political bankruptcy of socialism. On the other hand, as the Kremlin could not allow a key ally to disintegrate, Khrushchev let it be known in late July that he was not unsympathetic to Ulbricht's request for a barrier. On 13 August 1961, with **Honecker** in charge of the operation, makeshift barbed wire fencing and wooden barriers severed the sectoral border in Berlin. The prefabricated concrete blocks soon followed.

From M. Dennis, *The Rise and Fall of the German Democratic Republic* (published in 2000)

Source Q

Kennedy gives his verdict on the Berlin Wall

It's not a very nice solution but a wall is a hell of a lot better than a war.

As quoted in John Lewis Gaddis, *The Cold War* (published in 2005)

Biography

Erich Honecker (1912–94)

Honecker carried out Ulbricht's order to build the Berlin Wall in 1961. A member of the East German Politburo from 1950, he later served as Communist leader of East Germany from 1971 to 1989.

SKILLS BUILDER

1 How does Source M highlight the function and impact of the Berlin Wall?

2 Using Sources N and O, discuss the importance of both internal and external factors in leading to the East German government's decision to go ahead with the building of the Berlin Wall.

3 How far would you agree with the view that both the Hungarian Rising of 1956 and the Berlin Wall revealed the strengths as well as the weaknesses of the Communist Bloc?

4 Study Sources P and Q. In what ways was the response of the West to the building of the Berlin Wall similar to its reaction to the Hungarian Rising of 1956?

Unit summary

What have you learned in this unit?

Despite the rhetoric and tension generated by crises such as those over Hungary in 1956 and Berlin between 1958 and 1962, superpower relations after 1953 also illustrate the growing entrenchment and stability of the spheres of influence created by the superpowers in Europe. Within this context both sides felt secure enough to pursue different approaches to those followed since 1945. Pressures arising from the nuclear arms race and economic concerns pushed both sides towards an accommodation with each other. A change of leadership in both the USA and the USSR promoted different approaches as each new leader tried to impose their own particular stamp on policy. These changes in the conduct of foreign policy were to lead to attempts to establish a framework for improved relations.

As a tentative improvement in superpower relations became evident, commentators started to talk of a 'thaw' in Cold War relations. Tension was, in many ways, reduced and dialogue promoted, but there was little in the way of tangible achievements for both sides by 1955.

Between 1956 and 1962 events in Hungary and Berlin revealed both the potential dangers of crisis and confrontation as well as the rules each side was prepared to adopt in order to stabilise relations during the Cold War.

One particular issue that emerged in this period was the influence of individual personalities on the direction of international relations. The lurch from crisis to crisis was in many respects a consequence of the erratic policy pursued by Khrushchev. The large degree of power vested in the Soviet leader was a product of the political system established in the USSR by Stalin. Thus changes in Soviet foreign policy were strongly influenced by the personal preferences of individual leaders. Khrushchev's De-Stalinisation policy had a marked impact on superpower relations as well as the Soviet Union's control over its satellite states. His changing temperament could also assist the trend towards a 'thaw' in relations, as in his promotion of Peaceful Coexistence, or lead to confrontation, as it did during the Berlin crisis. It is worth noting that when Khrushchev was dismissed as Soviet leader the Politburo accused him of 'hare-brained scheming'; he had become increasingly unpredictable. This unpredictability was to bring the world to the edge of nuclear destruction during the Cuban Missile Crisis of 1962.

What skills have you used in this unit?

You have been able to practise your skills in argument and making a judgement based on reasoning. The exercises in this unit have given you opportunities to reach your own substantiated judgements on the impact of Stalin's death on Soviet foreign policy, the US response to this and resulting events such as the Hungarian Uprising of 1956 and the Berlin crisis of 1958–62.

Exam style questions

This unit covers one of the issues that are assessed in Section A of the examination. The questions in this section are different to those in Section B. They will require you to analyse a historical issue or problem and come to a reasoned judgement. Questions are likely to ask 'how far/to what extent . . .' you agree with a statement or interpretation. For example:

- To what extent was the development of the post-Stalin thaw in superpower relations between 1953 and 1962 the result of Khrushchev's policy of 'Peaceful Coexistence'?

Exam tips

Answers such as these require thoughtful planning before you start to write your answer. You can therefore outline your argument at the beginning, in your introduction, and sustain your argument through the answer. This approach is always better than the 'this is evidence for/this is evidence against/ this is my conclusion' answer because the reasoning will be more likely to be found throughout the answer rather than just at the end.

Nonetheless, a useful planning strategy is to think about the evidence for and the evidence against, but this should form a basis from which you can develop your reasoning rather than replace it.

For the question above, a plan would help you focus on the factors that led to the post-Stalin thaw.

Factor 1: Khrushchev's policy of 'Peaceful Coexistence'.

- It is usually best to start with the factor that is given in the question.
- You need to explain how Peaceful Coexistence brought about a thaw.
- You need to explain how Peaceful Coexistence worked.
- How did the USA respond to Peaceful Coexistence?

Other factors:

- The statement in the question needs discussion. Is it valid to link Peaceful Coexistence to Khrushchev?
- Who else had an input into the policy? The roles of Beria and Malenkov in changing Soviet foreign policy after the death of Stalin need to be examined.
- What changes occurred to US foreign policy that helped the post-Stalin thaw develop?
- How did Eisenhower's approach to the USSR encourage a thaw?
- Was the post-Stalin thaw a response by both sides to the development in nuclear arms and economic realities?

When examining these factors, try to explain how they interlink with each other rather than seeing them as separate and operating in isolation.

RESEARCH TOPIC

The Hungarian Uprising of 1956

This uprising reveals a lot about the how superpower rivalry was conducted as both sides established agreed, if unofficial, rules to the Cold War 'game'.

Your task is to research the Uprising. Aim to find out:

- What caused the uprising?

- What actions the USSR took in Hungary in 1956 and why.

- What the response of the US was to these events and why.

- What were the 'rules' of the Cold War game, as revealed by the Hungarian Uprising?

5 What impact did nuclear weapons have on the conduct of the Cold War 1949–63?

What is this unit about?

This unit focuses on the arms race and its role and impact on superpower relations between 1949 and 1963. This period saw important developments in nuclear technology by both superpowers as the USA and the Soviet Union sought to match each other in their nuclear missile capability. The Cuban Missile Crisis of 1962 was to illustrate the potential dangers of nuclear warfare and was followed by the start of agreements designed to bring some control over the nuclear arms race that had developed. This unit will therefore give you an understanding of the ways in which the conduct of Cold War relations between the superpowers was influenced by developments in nuclear weaponry and the resulting arms race. In this unit you will:

- examine the factors that produced an arms race between the superpowers
- discover the potential dangers caused by the destructive powers of nuclear weapons
- examine the ways in which the arms race developed, with particular emphasis on the types of weapons and delivery methods used
- consider the role of nuclear weapons during the Cuban Missile Crisis of 1962
- assess the impact of the Cuban Missile Crisis on the arms race by examining the agreements that followed immediately from the crisis.

Key questions

- Why and how did an arms race develop between 1949 and 1963?
- What role did nuclear weapons play in the Cuban Missile Crisis and its aftermath?

Timeline

1945	
16 July	First test firing of an atomic bomb by the USA at Alamogordo, New Mexico
6 August	USA drops atomic bomb on Hiroshima
9 August	USA drops atomic bomb on Nagasaki
1946	Failure of the Baruch Plan to limit nuclear weapons
1949	
29 August	USSR tests atomic bomb at Semipalatinsk
1952	
1 November	USA tests hydrogen bomb

1953	
8 August	USSR explodes its first lithium bomb
1954	
1 March	USA explodes a lithium bomb
1955	USA develops first intercontinental bombers
1956	USSR develops TU20 Bear (intercontinental bomber)
1957	USSR develops first ICBM (intercontinental ballistic missile)
5 October	USSR launches Sputnik, first space satellite
November	Sputnik II is launched Gaither Report warns President Eisenhower of missile gap
1959	Fidel Castro leads revolution in Cuba.
1960	
July	USA launches Polaris, first submarine-launched ballistic missile
1961	
April	USSR puts first man (Yuri Gagarin) into space Bay of Pigs invasion
1962	
October	Cuban Missile Crisis
1963	
June	'Hot line' telephone link is established Test Ban Treaty is signed

Introduction

Source A

If Britain were ever faced with an immediate threat of nuclear war, a booklet would be distributed to every household as part of a public information campaign that would include announcements on television and radio and in the press. The following are extracts from the booklet compiled in May 1980.

If Britain is attacked by nuclear bombs or by missiles, we do not know what targets will be chosen or how severe the assault will be.

If nuclear weapons are used on a large scale, those of us living in the country areas might be exposed to as great a risk as those in the towns. The radioactive dust, falling where the wind blows it, will bring the most widespread dangers of all. No part of the United Kingdom can be considered safe from both the direct effects of the weapons and the resultant fall-out.

The dangers which you and your family will face in this situation can be reduced if you do as this booklet describes.

Read this booklet with care
Your life and the lives of your family may depend upon it
Do as it advises
Keep it safely at hand

Plan a Fall-out Room and Inner Refuge

The first priority is to provide shelter within your home against radioactive fall-out. Your best protection is to make a fall-out room and build an inner refuge within it.

First, the Fall-out Room

Because of the threat of radiation you and your family may need to live in this room for fourteen days after an attack, almost without leaving it at all. So you must make it as safe as you can, and equip it for your survival. Choose the place furthest from the outside walls and from the roof, or which has the smallest amount of outside wall. The further you can get, within your home, from the radioactive dust that is on or around it, the safer you will be.

Now the Inner Refuge

Still greater protection is necessary in the fall-out room, particularly for the first two days and nights after an attack, when the radiation dangers could be critical. To provide this you should build an inner refuge.

Here are some ideas:

Make a 'lean-to' with sloping doors taken from rooms above or strong boards rested against an inner wall. Prevent them from slipping by fixing a length of wood along the floor. Build further protection of bags or boxes of earth or sand – or books, or even clothing – on the slope of your refuge, and anchor these also against slipping. Partly close the two open ends with boxes of earth or sand, or heavy furniture.

Protect and survive

Issued by the Home Office (1980)

These instructions were issued by the British government in 1980 and were themselves a revision of similar guidelines produced in the 1950s. Each government had drawn up its own contingency plans in case of nuclear attack. In the 1950s the US government had launched an educational information programme – the so-called 'Duck and Cover' campaign – to raise awareness of procedures to adopt in case of attack. These preparations highlight the fact that for much of the duration of the Cold War the threat of nuclear attack and its consequent devastation was real and taken seriously by governments, even if the general population remained sceptical about their effectiveness. How the arms race in nuclear weapons developed and its consequences provide the focus of this chapter.

Why did an arms race develop?

'During conflict your armaments help determine your influence; during war they help determine the outcome.'

While this statement is not necessarily true, it is often believed and therefore helps explain why an arms race occurred during the Cold War. It was to be driven by the national vulnerabilities of the superpowers and the political and personal insecurities of their leaders. In order to keep ahead of the opposition, each side decided to apply the possibilities of science to weaponry that would bolster their own prestige and reputation. Where the reality of weapon development lagged behind expectation the difference could be made up by public boasting of supposed capability. Such boasting, even when not believed, fed the insecurities of the other side to the point where a response that required an additional increase in arms became unavoidable. Thus the actions of both sides fed into an upward spiral of weapon development that constituted an arms race.

Arms races had developed before in history, for example in the years immediately preceding the First World War, but the arms race of the Cold War was different in terms of the destructive power that it was now possible to unleash. The purpose of weapons was usually to fight wars; nuclear weapons were developed to make the prospect of war so horrifying that war would be avoided. It was, therefore, an insurance against the actions of the enemy.

The great Prussian military strategist, Carl von Clausewitz, writing in the nineteenth century, warned against unlimited violence. War is, according to Clausewitz, 'a continuation of political activity by other means'. Thus war should never be considered the goal in itself, merely one method that could be used if appropriate to achieve political goals. The destructive nature of nuclear weapons made it unlikely that political goals could be secured if they were actually used. As Eisenhower stated in 1954: 'What do you do with the world after you have won a victory in such a catastrophic nuclear war?' This statement explains why no superpower wanted to use nuclear weapons, but the threat of using them could be used to further political goals by putting pressure on their opponent.

Causes of the arms race

- *The growth of international tension.* The build-up of arms by both sides was a response to external factors: the growing hostility between the superpowers after 1945. As the Cold War developed, arms were viewed as necessary to safeguard the interests of East and West. What gave this particular arms race a unique feature was the development of the atomic bomb. The nuclear age increased greatly the destructive power of the weapons available and therefore increased the feeling of vulnerability of the side that failed to keep pace with the new technology. The USA had a monopoly in nuclear warfare from 1945 until the Soviet Union developed its own atomic bomb in 1949. Soviet secrecy, coupled with Stalin and Khrushchev's tactic of boasting about their nuclear capability, helped fuel American concerns that they needed to keep ahead of the USSR. The decision of the USA to develop the hydrogen bomb was prompted by the Soviet challenge over Berlin in 1948–49, the communist takeover of China in 1949 and the outbreak of the Korean War in 1950. This in turn led to a Soviet response to develop its own super bomb. Each power viewed the nuclear capacity of the other with anxiety and became convinced that their nuclear superiority was the only way of guaranteeing their defensive needs. It could also help when trying to gain concessions from your opponent during summits. The arms race became a substitute for war.

- *National and personal considerations.* Keeping ahead in the arms race became a matter of national pride. Both sides saw the competition that the arms race engendered as an opportunity to raise national prestige and secure their reputation in world affairs. This became increasingly important in the 1950s as each side tried to impress the so-called Third World with the supposed benefits of capitalism or communism. Technological achievement became a yardstick by which the relative merits of capitalism and communism could be measured. Coupled with the issue of national reputation was that of the standing of individual political leaders. This is probably best illustrated by Khrushchev, whose constant boasting was a reflection of his own personal insecurities in the position of Soviet leader. In April 1956, during a visit to London, Khrushchev informed the Prime Minister's wife that Soviet missiles could easily reach Britain. Most of Khrushchev's boasts were untrue but his need to strengthen his own position meant that he felt it necessary to develop nuclear weapon technology. He took a particular interest in the Soviet space programme.

American leaders were more susceptible to the pressures of democracy and these often pushed presidents towards increasing arms. At the beginning of Eisenhower's presidency a fear that a 'bomber gap' had developed between the USA and the USSR led to an increase in American defence spending on nuclear arms. Even when the photographs taken by U-2 spy planes revealed that the USSR had no such lead over the USA in nuclear weapons, Eisenhower found it difficult to reduce spending due to continuing public fears of the possibility of Soviet superiority. In 1961 Kennedy's youth and inexperience as US president made him feel vulnerable to Soviet manipulation and as a result he felt it necessary to increase military spending. By 1962 military expenditure reached $50 billion for the first time since the Korean War.

- *Domestic factors.* Because the arms race provided lucrative orders and resources for those sectors of the economy related to the armaments industry, it can be seen as resulting at least in part from the situation within each country rather than external factors. Those groups who benefited from armaments orders gained considerable power and influence. In the USSR the armed forces were able to exert influence within the Soviet government because defence needs were given such a high priority. Any attempt to cut the amount of spending on arms, and therefore threaten the power of the military, was strongly resisted as Khrushchev, the Soviet leader, found out in 1964. In the USA the arms race provided large sums of money to manufacturers, scientists and the armed forces to the extent that it led to the employment of over 30 million American civilians. This **military-industrial complex** was able to wield enormous control over American politics. President Eisenhower had raised his concerns about this development but had been unable to reduce the power of this sector of the economy. In was in the interests of the military-industrial complex to highlight the danger posed by the Soviet Union. The Soviet army, in turn, emphasised the American threat in order to secure resources. Thus both fed off each other in perpetuating the arms race, and with it their power and influence within their own country was maintained.

> **Definition**
>
> **Military-industrial complex**
>
> The term given to the powerful bloc created by links between the armed forces and those sectors of the economy reliant on defence orders. In the USA this included firms such as Lockheed and General Dynamics, which lobbied Congress to ensure arms manufacture continued, and the armed forces, which wanted resources and armaments. In the USSR this term is applied to the Ministry of Defence, the armed forces and those industries involved in the manufacture of military products.

SKILLS BUILDER

As an adviser to either the US government or the Soviet leadership in 1950, write a report arguing the case for committing a vast amount of resources towards the development of a thermo-nuclear bomb.

In your answer refer to the context of 1950 and the events that would influence the attitudes of your country towards your rival. Also discuss the possible consequences of failing to invest resources in this project.

How did the arms race develop between 1949 and 1963?

From the moment the first atomic bomb was dropped on Hiroshima on 6 August 1945 the enormous implications of the atomic bomb were evident for all to see. Yet the destructive power that had been unleashed resulted not in attempts to limit the number and power of nuclear weapons but in a race to develop weapons of even more destructive power with delivery systems that could greatly increase the scope of these bombs.

The bombs

The Americans had been the first to develop the atomic bomb. The first test firing of an atomic bomb on 16 July 1945 at Alamogordo in New Mexico was the culmination of the work of scientists under a programme known as the Manhattan Project. The use of atomic bombs on Hiroshima and Nagasaki brought the Second World War in the Far East to an end but also highlighted the growing mistrust between the USA and the USSR.

The USA had, for the moment, a nuclear monopoly. The attempt by the United Nations to control the atomic bomb through the Baruch Plan of 1946 failed. Some scientists, such as Robert Oppenheimer, who had worked on the atomic bomb project, argued that was unlikely that America's monopoly would last and therefore a mechanism for controlling atomic projects was needed. The Baruch Plan called on America to share its knowledge of nuclear technology but stipulated that no other nation would be allowed to develop atomic weapons. The USSR saw the plan as an attempt to maintain the US monopoly on atomic bombs. The Plan was dropped. The US government was reluctant to share its nuclear secrets but spies were able to get round this anyway. The US nuclear monopoly lasted from 1945 until 1949.

On 29 August 1949 the USSR exploded its own atomic bomb at Semipalatinsk. The Soviet nuclear programme had been helped by spies such as Klaus Fuchs and Ted Hall, but this alone does not explain the speed at which the USSR developed its own bomb. Their programme was headed by Igor Kurchatov, an inspiring and able scientist who was able to secure the resources he needed from his political masters.

With both sides equally matched in terms of possession of the atomic bomb, the race to develop a super bomb commenced. The USA decided to develop a hydrogen bomb, a thousand times more destructive than the atomic bomb. This bomb was tested at Eniwetok in the Pacific on 1 November 1952. The result was a crater in the seabed 60 metres deep and one mile in diameter and a mushroom cloud of radioactive dust that measured 100 miles in diameter.

The American monopoly this time was much shorter. Nine months later the USSR tested their super bomb at Semipalatinsk. The Soviet bomb used lithium rather than hydrogen and did not need to be refrigerated. This made the Soviet super bomb easier to use by deploying a conventional bomber.

On 1 March 1954 the USA tested its own lithium bomb. The thermo-nuclear age had arrived. The race was now on to develop more effective delivery systems.

Source B

5.1 American nuclear weapons test on Eniwetok in the Marshall Islands, 8 May 1951

Discussion point

Why do you think the nuclear test shown in Source B was conducted?

The delivery systems

The USA had invested in the development of aircraft that acted as bombers. By 1955 the USA possessed the first bomber with intercontinental range, the B52 Stratofortress. The USSR replied by developing the TU20 Bear in 1956. Yet the use of conventional aircraft as bombers posed several weaknesses. They were relatively slow and vulnerable to being shot down by anti-aircraft systems. The application of rocket technology was to minimise these issues.

The Russians had pioneered developments in rocket science. The scientist Tsiolkovsky had undertaken research in this area before the First World War. After the defeat of Nazi Germany in 1945 many of its scientists were captured and put to work on the Soviet rocket programme. The Nazis had attempted to use rockets as delivery systems for its bombs, developing the V2 rocket. This expertise was to be invaluable to the Soviets. In 1957 they launched their first rocket in Kazakhstan. It was the first ICBM (intercontinental ballistic missile) capable of carrying a thermo-nuclear bomb.

The success of the Soviet rocket programme was further highlighted by the successful launch of Sputnik, the first ever space satellite, on 5 October 1957. The military application of satellite technology was obvious. Sputnik II followed in November carrying the dog Laika into space. American attempts to emulate the Soviets resulted in failure as their attempt to launch a satellite ended with it rising half a metre into the air before exploding. (It was nicknamed 'Kaputnik'.) In 1961 the Soviet Union became the first nation to put a man into space. Yuri Gagarin orbited the earth in Vostok I and returned to a hero's welcome in the USSR. The Soviet Union made the most of what seemed to be tangible signs of its superior technological achievements.

Nonetheless, many of Khrushchev's boasts about Soviet supremacy in the arms race were not supported by reality. The historian John Lewis Gaddis has termed Khrushchev's approach 'Potemkinism', the process of building just enough capability to provide the illusion that more lies behind it. One deliberate example of this was during the Moscow air show of 1955, when the identifying numbers on planes were painted out so that they could do several flypasts in front of foreign guests to give the illusion that the USSR possessed more of them than they actually did.

The Soviet lead in ICBMs was also less impressive than it seemed. The early missiles were very unreliable and unsuitable for operational use, as Khrushchev knew. By 1960 the USSR only possessed four ICBMs that were functional.

The CIA Gaither Report of 7 November 1957 warned President Eisenhower of a missile gap but he refused to be panicked. He placed his confidence in the supremacy of the US Strategic Air Command (SAC), which coordinated the deployment of B52 bombers in preparation for a nuclear strike. The information provided by the U-2 spy planes soon confirmed the emptiness of Khrushchev's boasts of supremacy. Nonetheless, Eisenhower did increase the allocation of resources for science education and research to ensure the USA kept its lead.

The USA developed the world's first submarine-launched ballistic missile, Polaris, in July 1960. Kennedy ordered the construction of 41 nuclear submarines, expanded the number of Minuteman ICBMs to 1,054 and committed America to landing a man on the moon within ten years. By 1962 the USA had 4,000 missile warheads compared with the Soviet Union's 220 warheads.

These developments completed the advance in delivery systems that by 1960 ranged from bombers to missiles and submarines. Both superpowers were now able to launch nuclear strikes and counter-strikes to produce mutually assured destruction (MAD). An awareness of the possible consequences behind MAD was brought home by the Cuban Missile Crisis of 1962.

SKILLS BUILDER

1 Compile a timeline of the key dates in the development of nuclear weapons and delivery systems.

2 On your timeline indicate which of the superpowers was in the lead for technological supremacy during each stage. If you think there are periods where parity was achieved, indicate this as well.

3 How far would you accept Khrushchev's claim of Soviet supremacy in the arms race in the 1950s?

4 How far do you accept the judgement that by the beginning of 1962 the arms race had made nuclear war unlikely?

Why did the Cuban Missile Crisis occur?

The potential dangers of superpower conflict in the nuclear age were to be demonstrated by the Cuban Missile Crisis of 1962. For the first time during the Cold War the USA and the Soviet Union faced each other in direct conflict. American brinkmanship involved the threat to use nuclear weapons in order to safeguard its interests. In the words of Dean Rusk, the American Secretary of State, the superpowers were 'eyeball to eyeball'. The world waited to see who would be the first to back down.

The origins of this crisis lay in the events that had occurred within Cuba since 1959. The Caribbean island of Cuba had been under US influence since the end of Spanish rule in 1898. This relationship was threatened when the corrupt and brutal regime of Fulgencio Batista was overthrown in 1959 by revolutionaries led by **Fidel Castro** and Che Guevara. As a nationalist, Castro wished to make Cuba independent of American control, and this caused tension to develop between Cuba and the USA. By early 1961 many American economic interests in Cuba had been seized and there was little surprise in the USA when Castro announced his conversion to communism.

The American government had cut off all trade in arms to Cuba after the revolution, and in 1961 the new American President **John F. Kennedy** supported an invasion of Cuba by anti-Castro supporters. The Bay of Pigs invasion consisted of less than 1,500 Cuban exiles, who were supported by the **CIA**. The US government was hopeful that the invasion would lead to a popular uprising against Castro. This was an over-optimistic view: the

Definition

CIA

Central Intelligence Agency: the US agency for collecting information on foreign actions that affect US interests. Its agents work undercover. The CIA has trained and equipped foreign groups in order to depose governments seen as acting against US interests.

Biography

Fidel Castro (b.1926)

Cuban leader since the revolution of 1959, which brought him to power. His revolt against Batista began in 1956 when a group of his supporters landed in Cuba. They were forced to retreat to the Sierra Maestro Mountains from where they built a base to attack Batista. They were able to overthrow Batista in January 1959 and Castro formed a new government. He had been a liberal nationalist wishing to rid Cuba of foreign control but as relations with America deteriorated he was forced to except help from the USSR. Castro converted to communism in 1961 and the revolution developed on communist lines. Despite a US trade embargo since 1960 Castro's government was able to improve the conditions of Cuba's poorest citizens. Cuba's education and medical facilities under Castro have been among the best in the less developed world.

Biography

John F. Kennedy (1917–63)

US President from 1961 to 1963. Born into a rich Boston family, Kennedy had served in the US Navy during the Second World War. A member of the Democratic Party, he was seen as a progressive liberal who represented a younger, more vibrant generation than most American politicians at the time. He was still relatively young and inexperienced when he became President. Conscious of foreign policy failures over the Berlin crisis of 1961 and the Bay of Pigs invasion later in the same year, he decided to stand firm during the Cuban Missile Crisis. In public he used the tactics of brinkmanship, but he was more cautious in private. His stand against Khrushchev over Cuba worked and the Soviet missiles were withdrawn from the island. He did not live long to enjoy his success. He was assassinated in Dallas in 1963.

invasion was a complete disaster. As relations deteriorated, the USA decided to cut its trade in sugar with Cuba, a measure that would have had serious consequences for the Cuban economy. Castro decided to take appropriate action and asked the Soviet Union to purchase Cuban sugar. He also appealed for arms. The USSR was willing to take advantage of the situation and agreed.

In the context of general Cold War tension, a national revolution was transformed into a struggle for superpower supremacy.

Source C

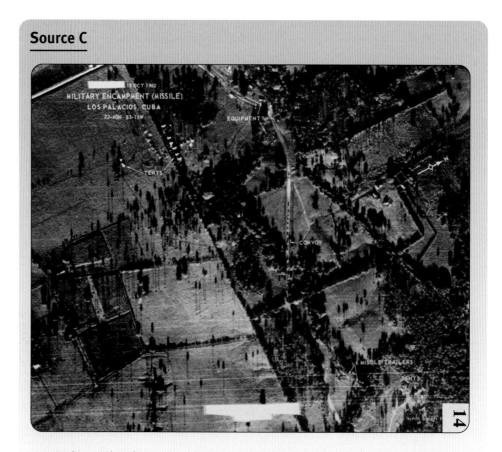

5.2 A photo taken by an American spy plane showing evidence of Soviet bases in Cuba in 1962

Discussion point

What conclusions might the US government have drawn from the evidence shown in Source C?

The Missile Crisis develops, October 1962

Tensions between Cuba and the USA were ignited in October 1962 when American spy planes brought back photos of missile bases under construction in Cuba. The bases were for the installation of Soviet medium-range ballistic missiles, which had a nuclear warhead capable of destroying large cities. Soviet ships carrying military supplies were spotted by intelligence services. They were heading for Cuba. When Kennedy was presented with this information he was horrified. Firm action would need to be taken. The executive committee of the US National Security Council, known as 'ExComm', was called to discuss Kennedy's options.

Why was Kennedy determined to stand firm against Communism during this crisis?

In order to understand why Kennedy was prepared to risk nuclear war over the Cuban Missile Crisis it is necessary to consider the specific influences on US foreign policy in this region.

Source D

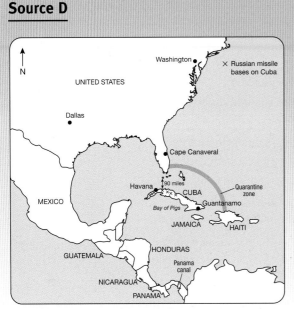

The US government had long considered Latin America (i.e. South and Central America) to be within its sphere of influence. This was known as the Monroe Doctrine, which had been put forward in 1823 and had formed the basis of US foreign policy towards Latin America.

5.3 Central America during the Cuban Missile Crisis, 1962

SKILLS BUILDER

1 Use the information on the map (Source D) to outline how US interests were under threat by Soviet actions in Cuba.

These factors meant that the missile bases were seen as a direct danger to American interests. In addition the crisis posed a threat to Kennedy's own position and reputation as President of the USA.

2 How had the following weakened Kennedy's reputation in international affairs? (You may need to look back at the information in Unit 4):

a) the meeting with **Khrushchev** (see page 109) in Vienna in June 1961
b) the Berlin crisis of 1961
c) the Bay of Pigs invasion, 1961.

3 How might these events have influenced Kennedy's actions during the Cuban Missile Crisis?

On Khrushchev's part there were also reasons why a firm line was needed during the crisis. His own reputation as a Soviet leader able to safeguard the security of the Communist Bloc was on the line. After the Bay of Pigs incident Kennedy organised Operation Mongoose, a series of CIA activities aimed at undermining Castro's government. Over 10,000 Cuban exiles, supported by 400 Americans, were sent in secret to Cuba to blow up railway lines, poison sugar crops and explode bombs in shops and factories.

It was in this context that Castro appealed to Khrushchev for military support. In March 1962 Kennedy had written an article for a leading US newspaper in which he had made clear his belief that he was entitled to use a nuclear strike. Thus when the USSR sent arms to help Castro, Khrushchev considered nuclear missiles a necessary part of the package. He also saw Soviet missiles in Cuba as a reasonable counter-measure to the newly installed American missiles in Turkey, a country with a land border with the USSR.

SKILLS BUILDER

1 Using the evidence of Source E and your own knowledge, how far would you accept the view of NcNamara, that the Missile Crisis was 'primarily a domestic political problem'?

2 How far might Khrushchev's situation be described in the same way?

3 What would be the advantages and disadvantages of each option?

4 What sort of concessions would be acceptable to Kennedy?

Source E

Kennedy meets with his advisers at the start of the crisis

McBundy: What is the impact on the United States of MRBMs* in Cuba? How greatly does this change the strategic balance?

Kennedy: You may say that it doesn't matter if you get blown up by an ICBM flying in from the Soviet Union or one from ninety miles away . . . What difference does it make? They've got enough to blow us up anyway.

McNamara: I don't believe it is primarily a military problem. It's primarily a domestic political problem.

From a meeting of ExComm, as quoted in S. Judges, *Superpower Rivalry* (published in 1994)

*medium range ballistic missiles

5.4 Kennedy with advisers during the Cuban missile crisis

What were Kennedy's options during the crisis?

What gave the crisis its urgency was the belief, by the Americans, that they did not have time on their side. They had to act quickly before the missiles were in place. With Soviet supplies about to arrive in Cuba, a swift response was essential.

Kennedy's advisers considered the options. How could they stop the USSR installing missile bases in Cuba?

Option 1: Dean Rusk, the Secretary of State, urged immediate military action. General Taylor, the chairman of the Joint Chiefs of Staff, called for a 'surgical air strike'.

Option 2: Robert ('Bobby') Kennedy, the President's brother and adviser, preferred an alternative approach put forward by McNamara, the Defense Secretary. He suggested a blockade of Soviet ships going to Cuba.

Kennedy's actions

On 22 October President Kennedy announced a quarantine zone around Cuba. If any Soviet ships entered this zone action would be taken. US forces were placed on high alert: 54 bombers, each with four nuclear warheads, were on standby; 150 intercontinental missiles aimed at the USSR were armed and nuclear Polaris submarines were put to sea. Soviet ships with supplies for Cuba were approaching the quarantine zone. The world waited anxiously.

At 10.25 a.m. the Soviet ships stopped and turned away from Cuba. Dean Rusk announced 'We're eyeball to eyeball and I think the other fellow just blinked.'

The crisis was not yet over. The USA still needed to ensure that Soviet missile bases were removed from Cuba.

Option 1: Follow the view of the US Joint Chiefs of Staff who called for an immediate invasion of Cuba to destroy the missile bases.
Option 2: Accept the terms of a message received from the Soviet leader on 26 October. This message was a long and rambling letter from Khrushchev, which took over twelve hours to be transmitted by cable. In the letter Khrushchev agreed to remove all missiles if the USA agreed never to invade Cuba in the future.
Option 3: Accept the terms of a second letter from Khrushchev received on the 27 October. This letter was more strident in tone and added the demand for the USA to withdraw its missiles from Turkey.

Biography

Nikita Khrushchev (1894–1971)

Leader of the USSR from 1954 until his dismissal in 1964. Khrushchev's approach to the West marked a change from the hard-line aggressive stance of his predecessor Stalin. Khrushchev developed a policy of 'Peaceful Coexistence', an awareness that the two superpowers had to accept each other rather than slide into mutual destruction. It did not, however, mean the USSR would give up promoting communism throughout the world. Khrushchev's actions in foreign affairs appear inconsistent. He sometimes took a hard-line approach, especially in 1956 when he ordered the Soviet invasion of Hungary, but in general he wished to see improved relations with the West. This inconsistency was, perhaps, a reflection of his personality. He had a tendency to react strongly and display anger in public. He caused a storm in 1960 when he banged his shoe on a table at the United Nations. His decision to back down during the Cuban Missile Crisis, despite the opposition of his own armed forces, averted nuclear war.

On his brother's advice Kennedy publicly accepted the first message and ignored the second. It was left to Bobby Kennedy to secretly inform Soviet contacts that missiles would be withdrawn from Turkey. On 28 October Radio Moscow announced that the missile bases were to be 'dismantled and returned to the Soviet Union'. The crisis was over.

What were the results of the Cuban Missile Crisis for superpower relations?

The Cuban Missile Crisis had shown the dangers of the policy of using brinkmanship in an era of nuclear weapons. The Cuban Crisis was in two senses the result of the arms race. First, Khrushchev's action to install nuclear bases in Cuba was a response to US bases in Turkey. In addition, it was the development of increasingly large numbers of nuclear missiles that gave the crisis its potential to be so devastating.

Yet it can be argued that the crisis was less about nuclear missiles than it seemed. Kennedy's actions may have been couched in terms of standing up against the danger of a Soviet nuclear strike on the USA but the driving force behind Kennedy's actions was his need to repair his damaged political reputation. In this respect the crisis was resolved successfully for Kennedy.

The crisis provided Kennedy with a much-needed foreign policy success. He could claim to have removed the potential danger of Soviet nuclear warheads from America's own 'backyard'. He had, however, given an assurance not to remove Castro from Cuba and, despite at least eight assassination attempts on Castro by the CIA, was left with a communist neighbour for the foreseeable future. The agreement to remove US missiles from Turkey was kept secret from the American public until 1968.

Kennedy's threat to use nuclear weapons, if Soviet ships did not return to Russia and the missile bases were not dismantled, was brinkmanship in action. Nonetheless, Kennedy was keen to ensure that opportunities for a peaceful compromise were pursued. The difference between hard-line rhetoric in public and caution and negotiation in private was a vital part of Kennedy's approach.

Khrushchev could claim credit for securing the American promise not to invade Cuba. In his memoirs Khrushchev described it as a great victory, 'a spectacular success without having to fire a shot'. Yet it was he who had backed down. Khrushchev was left humiliated. The Soviet armed forces never forgave him and the crisis was a contributing factor in his dismissal from the post of Soviet leader in 1964.

Despite the use of brinkmanship, both leaders showed restraint during the crisis. Khrushchev took no action when a US spy plane strayed into Soviet air space. Kennedy did not retaliate when one of his spy planes was shot down over Cuba. Yet there was a feeling amongst the superpowers that too much was being left to chance.

The impact that individual leaders could have on international relations was illustrated by the increasingly erratic foreign policy moves of Khrushchev, such as his storming out of the Paris Summit in 1960. The Cuban Missile Crisis was due in part to Khrushchev's tendency to push the limits and test his opponents.

Both Kennedy and Khrushchev were removed from power, although in different circumstances, not long after the events of 1962, but the impact of the Cuban Crisis on superpower relations was to be longer lasting. The dangers of nuclear devastation that were exposed by the crisis led to a recognition that relations had to be improved. And if ideological differences remained too deep to heal tension, then at least rules should be established for the conduct of conflict. The **'hot line' telephone link** and the **Nuclear Test Ban Treaty** of 1963 were the first steps towards the cooperation that developed in the 1970s into **Détente**.

What impact did the arms race have on the nature of Cold War conflict between 1949 and 1963?

During the arms race the dangers inherent in the use of nuclear missiles became increasingly evident. This was to have an impact on the nature of military strategy. The danger of initiating nuclear war restrained both the USA and the USSR from direct, armed confrontation. As John Lewis Gaddis has stated, 'This pattern of tacit cooperation among bitter antagonists could hardly have emerged had it not been for the existence of nuclear weapons.' In this context other strategies had to be deployed.

The concept of the limited war was used to reduce the dangers of escalating conflict to nuclear deployment. Conventional warfare was used during the Cold War but this was played out on immediate territory and was kept localised. The concept of limited war was used to avoid direct confrontation. This concept first emerged during the Korean War of 1950–53 where there was a real threat of the war escalating. The USSR took no direct role in the war and, despite the calls of General McArthur to use nuclear weapons against China, Truman preferred to use military tactics that ensured the war remained limited in scale. Nuclear weapons forced each side to think twice before taking any measure to escalate war.

By the mid-1950s the US government was concerned to develop a strategy that seemed to avoid the dilemma of how to use nuclear weapons. What was the point of having weapons that you were too scared to use? If the USSR believed the threat to use nuclear bombs was based on bluff, their value as a deterrent would be negligible. Under Eisenhower and Dulles the US government developed a strategy of massive retaliation. This was based on the threat of using large numbers of US nuclear bombs against communist aggression. As the USA still had nuclear superiority this would, it was hoped, act as a deterrent. The result of this strategy was the tactic of brinkmanship, of being prepared to go to the brink of nuclear war in order

Definitions

'Hot line' telephone link
A system of direct communication between the leaders of the USA and the USSR. It was set up in 1963 in response to the Cuban Missile Crisis. Its aim was to prevent misunderstanding during a crisis. It was used in 1971 by Nixon and Brezhnev during the war between India and Pakistan.

Nuclear Test Ban Treaty, 1963
A treaty that banned the testing of nuclear weapons above ground and below water. It was signed by the USA, Britain and the Soviet Union and was a measure of the desire to limit nuclear destruction after the Cuban Missile Crisis. Attempts to sign a similar treaty had been rejected by the USSR in 1961. It was, however, only a partial ban: testing underground was permitted. France and China refused to sign the treaty.

Détente
A more permanent relaxation in tension. The term was used to describe the improvement in superpower relations that existed after the Cuban Missile Crisis until the Soviet invasion of Afghanistan in 1979 led to a deterioration in relations.

to stop enemy aggression. It was a risky business, as Kennedy found out during the Cuban Missile Crisis of 1962.

The development of MAD (mutually assured destruction) caused both sides to rethink their strategies. By the early 1960s both superpowers possessed enough nuclear missiles to destroy the other and systems to ensure a counter-strike was possible even after being hit first. Both sides recognised the limitations of this all-or-nothing approach and decided that a more flexible range of responses was needed. This led to the strategy of counterforce, which would use smaller, targeted nuclear missiles to provide the option of using more limited action to achieve more specific objectives.

The arms race also had an impact on conventional arms. If the devastation caused by nuclear weapons was too horrific to contemplate except as a last resort, the importance of conventional arms remained central to military strategy. Attempts to reduce conventional arms were undertaken by Eisenhower and Khrushchev, both of whom saw nuclear weapons as a cheaper alternative. The Korean and Vietnam wars were fought with conventional arms and showed the need to keep a numerical advantage in conventional weaponry. This would allow each side an alternative to the use of nuclear missiles, a strategy Kennedy referred to as 'Flexible Response'.

The arms race was also to have important civilian consequences. The innovation it promoted led to computers and space technology, which were to have significant civilian applications. Yet the vast economic cost of the arms race was to place a significant burden on the populations of the superpowers. Resources that could have been used to develop adequate up-to-date consumer goods were diverted to the military. The civilian sectors of their respective economies were held back, especially in the Soviet Union where the stress on the military sector was to increase the secrecy already present in the Soviet Union. The development of nuclear arms was to become a weapon by which the economic resources of the opponent could be stretched to breaking point.

The fact that nuclear arms were not used during the Cold War does not make them an insignificant part of the conflict: the arms race was one of the chief methods by which conflict took place and was therefore an integral part of the struggle for supremacy. Nuclear arms represented a yardstick of technological superiority that the USA and the USSR saw as central to highlighting the pre-eminence of their political and economic systems.

Investigation: the results of the Cuban Missile Crisis: the hot line and the Test Ban Treaty

Source F

The missile crisis shocked the United States and its allies into realising the precariousness of their own security, for all the diversity upon which it rested . . .

The Soviet–American competition did take on a certain stability, even predictability, after 1962. Neither side would ever again initiate direct challenges to the other's sphere of influence . . . The strategic arms race intensified in the wake of the missile crisis, but it was conducted within an increasingly precise set of rules, codified in formal agreements like the Limited Nuclear Test Ban Treaty of 1963 . . .

From John Lewis Gaddis, *We Now Know* (published in 1997)

Source G

The Partial Test Ban Treaty, 1963

Seeking to achieve the discontinuance of all test explosions of nuclear weapons for all time, determined to continue negotiations to this end, and desiring to put an end to the contamination of man's environment by radioactive substances.

Have agreed as follows:

Each of the Parties to this Treaty undertakes to prohibit, to prevent, and not to carry out any nuclear weapon test explosion . . .

. . . in the atmosphere; beyond its limits, including outer space; or under water, including territorial waters or high seas or . . .

From the terms of the Partial Test Ban Treaty of 1963

Source H

Molotov, in retirement in the 1980s, gives his view of the Test Ban Treaty. Molotov had served as Soviet Foreign Minister until he was dismissed by Khrushchev in 1956

We have signed a nuclear test-ban treaty with the imperialists of America and England, a treaty directed against socialist China. Why bar China from having nuclear weapons? China just shrugged off the ban and developed its own bomb. France disregarded the ban. We proved to be helpless as a newborn babe.

We signed the treaty: peace, peace! But there can be no peace without war.

From F. Chuev, *Molotov Remembers* (published in 1991)

Source I

One cannot know what might have happened if Kennedy and Khrushchev, both of whom had urgent preoccupations of their own – the civil rights crisis in the United States, the agricultural crisis in the Soviet Union – had been free to deal with their foreign affairs bureaucracies. But, if opportunities were lost, they were probably not decisive ones. Both sides needed time to digest the test ban before they would be ready for a next large step. What was lost was a shaping of the atmosphere, a continuation of the momentum, which might have made steps quicker and easier.

Other moves were meanwhile carrying forward the hope of Détente in one way or another. Least heralded but perhaps the most important was the tacit acceptance of reciprocal aerial reconnaissance from space satellites . . .

. . . the so-called hot line – an emergency communications link between the White House and the Kremlin – had been installed over the summer. Then, early in October, Kennedy authorised the sale of surplus wheat to the Soviet Union as 'one more hopeful sign that a more peaceful world is both possible and beneficial to us all' . . . Later in the month the UN, with enthusiastic American and Russian support and much self-congratulation, passed a resolution calling on all states to refrain from 'placing in orbit around the earth any objects carrying nuclear weapons . . .' This resolution . . . represented the bold attempt of the earthlings to keep the nuclear race out of the firmament.

From Arthur M. Schlesinger Jr, *A Thousand Days: John F. Kennedy in the White House* (published in 2002)

SKILLS BUILDER

Using the information in Sources F–I:

a) Draw up a list of points that could be used to support the argument that the Cuban Missile Crisis led to a significant improvement in superpower relations.

b) Draw up a list of the evidence that these improvements were limited.

c) After considering this evidence, how far would you agree with the view that the Cuban Missile Crisis was a hinge that produced the possibility of a changed direction in the arms race?

Unit summary

What have you learned in this unit?

The development of an arms race based on developments in nuclear technology was promoted by a combination of pressures including domestic factors, issues to do with national pride and reputation and the personalities of the individual leaders of the superpowers. What made these factors so potent was that they operated within a period of growing international tension. As each superpower tried to gain the upper hand in the Cold War, it is no surprise that they sought to apply developments in weapon technology to their own advantage.

Nuclear weapons, with their enormous destructive potential, posed the dilemma of whether they should ever actually be used. The Cuban Missile Crisis illustrated the predicament of the US policy of brinkmanship: it risked going to the edge of nuclear war. Yet the crisis was to provide a shock to the leaders of the two superpowers, resulting in them reaching agreements on controls and restrictions that would prevent MAD reaching its ultimate conclusion.

Nuclear weapons and their devastating effects not only exercised the minds of the political leaders, military leaders and scientists of each side. They were also to grip the popular imagination. Booklets such as 'Protect and Survive', from which the extracts at the beginning of this chapter are taken, were to help fire this imagination and keep the public in a state of alert. The purpose of these booklets was, of course, to reassure the public that there were measures that could be of use in the event of a nuclear attack. Experts have admitted that these measures would, in reality, be little more than useless.

What skills have you used in this unit?

You have been able to practise your skills in argument and making a judgement based on reasoning. The exercises in this unit have given you opportunities to reach your own substantiated judgements on the reasons for and impact of the nuclear arms race on superpower relations.

Exam style questions

This unit covers one of the issues that are assessed in Section A of the examination. The questions in this section will require you to analyse a historical issue or problem and come to a reasoned judgement. Questions are likely to ask 'how far/to what extent . . .' you agree with a statement or interpretation. For example:

- To what extent did the nuclear arms race make the world a more dangerous place in the years 1949–63?

Exam tips

This topic can pose a trap for students in that it can lead to you towards what might seem like the most obvious answer (yes, it did make the world more dangerous) rather than provide discussion and a reasoned argument.

When planning an answer to this specific question think through the arguments for both sides.

- *Yes, it did make the world more dangerous.* Here you could include the destructive potential of nuclear war, the development of more powerful weapons such as the hydrogen bomb and the improvements in delivery systems. The Cuban Missile Crisis should be used to illustrate the dangers of brinkmanship. (Here lies another danger – the temptation to describe the crisis in detail. You do not need to do so. Keep focused on the specific question.)
- *No.* Here there are several points to discuss. The nuclear arms race highlighted the dangers and therefore encouraged the superpowers to use other methods of conflict, e.g. the concept of limited war, the use of conventional weapons. Leading in the arms race provided the West with a useful deterrent that prevented the escalation of conflict. MAD could be argued to be the ultimate deterrent. The Cuban Missile Crisis woke up the superpowers to the need for mechanisms to restrict nuclear weapons. The result was the Test Ban Treaty.

RESEARCH TOPIC

Film as a source of information: *Dr Strangelove* and *Thirteen Days*

Feature films can be useful both as a source of information about historical events and in portraying the atmosphere at the time. They also provide a window into public attitudes during the period when the film was made. Two useful films on this topic are:

- *Dr Strangelove* (1963), directed by Stanley Kubrick, which takes a humorous slant on the dangers of nuclear war
- *Thirteen Days* (2001), directed by Roger Donaldson, which examines Kennedy's actions during the Cuban Missile Crisis.

Your task is to view at least one of these films. Consider the usefulness of the film in deepening your historical understanding of the period and the events it covers.

6 How did Sino–Soviet relations change in the period 1949–76?

What is this unit about?

This unit focuses on relations between the USSR and China during the period 1949 to 1976. The relationship between the two communist superpowers was to change from one of friendship and alliance to one of tension. This changing relationship was to have an impact on the dynamics of US foreign policy. This unit will give you an understanding of the ways in which Sino–Soviet relations changed, the factors that were responsible for these changes and the impact this had on the wider context of the Cold War. In this unit you will:

* examine the role of Communist China in advancing world communism between 1949 and 1953
* discover the reasons for the Sino–Soviet Split
* investigate examples of tension between the two communist superpowers
* examine the reasons why a rapprochement took place between China and the USA after 1969
* assess the achievements of China's rapprochement with the USA after 1969.

Key questions

* How, and why, did relations between the USSR and China change in the period 1949–76?
* What impact did the Sino–Soviet Split have on China's relationship with the USA between 1970 and 1976?

Timeline

1920s–1949	Tension over Stalin's support for the Chinese Nationalists and the USSR's interests in the Chinese province of Manchuria
1950	Treaty of Friendship, Alliance and Mutual Assistance signed. Some Chinese resentment at unequal terms of the Treaty
1954 October	Khrushchev's first visit to Beijing Khrushchev refused to lessen Soviet ties in Mongolia or allow China to expand its control in North Korea
1956	Khrushchev gives speech criticising Stalin at the Twentieth Congress of the Soviet Communist Party. The policy of De-Stalinisation begins. Mao criticises Khrushchev as a revisionist
1958	Khrushchev criticises Mao's policy of the Great Leap Forward as being impractical Mao accuses the USSR of being too cautious and detached during the crisis over Quemoy

1959	
June	USSR cancels Sino–Soviet Agreement on atomic cooperation
September	Khrushchev visits the USA. Mao condemns the Soviet Union's rapprochement with the USA
1960	The USSR pulls out all economic aid and advisers from China
1961	China gives economic support to Albania after it splits with the USSR
	China also encourages Romania to become more independent of Soviet interference
1963	A meeting between Party leaders of both China and the USSR fails to improve relations
	China claims that its border with the USSR is the result of 'unequal treaties'
1964	Khrushchev and Mao resort to bitter personal attacks
14 October	Khrushchev is dismissed as Soviet leader
16 October	China explodes its first nuclear bomb in a test at Lop Nor
	Zhou Enlai, the Chinese Prime Minister, visits a series of countries in the developing world to present China as the leader of world revolution
1965	The USSR develops its policy of trying to isolate China in international affairs by strengthening its ties with Mongolia, North Korea and North Vietnam
1968	Mao's attacks on the Soviet Union's leadership as revisionists increase during the Cultural Revolution, Mao's attack on revisionist elements within China
1969	Heavy fighting at Damansky Island on the Ussuri River in March when Chinese troops attack Soviet border guards
1970	Relations between China and the USSR improve slightly with the visit of Kosygin, the Soviet Prime Minister, to China
1971	Henry Kissinger, the US Secretary of State, visits China and paves the way for a visit by US President Richard Nixon. Chinese relations with the USSR deteriorate

Introduction

In November 1957 the Soviet Union called a conference of representatives from communist parties throughout the world. Many of the key players in the communist world were in Moscow for the conference. Among those players was Mao Zedong, the Chinese leader. Mao had always held the greatest respect for Stalin and considered him to be the guiding head of the world revolutionary movement. But Stalin was now dead. Would Mao view Khrushchev, the politician who had emerged as the Soviet leader, in the same way as he had Stalin? The early signs were very encouraging for the Soviet leadership. On the eve of the conference Mao stated: 'The socialist camp must have one head, and that head can only be the USSR.'

Yet by 1972 superpower relations had been profoundly altered. A deep and serious split had occurred between the two communist superpowers that threatened to escalate into nuclear warfare. At the same time as China's relations with the USSR deteriorated, those between China and the USA improved.

In 1971 an American table tennis team visited China at the invitation of its government. In 1972, in a move that surprised many observers, US President Richard Nixon visited Beijing for talks with China's communist leaders. As a mark of respect Nixon was presented with a gift of two giant pandas, Ling-Ling and Hsing-Hsing. Nixon responded by sending back a pair of musk oxen.

The talks between Nixon and Mao may have been more symbolic than substantive; nevertheless, there was rather more to the new relationship than ping-pong and pandas.

What role did Communist China take in advancing world communism between 1949 and 1958?

The communist takeover of China in 1949 was viewed by the US government as another victory for the forces of world communism. Mao was seen as an instrument of the Soviet Union's bid to spread worldwide revolution. In February 1950 Mao signed a Treaty with Stalin that seemed to confirm American perceptions that China was ready to do Stalin's bidding in the struggle against the forces of capitalism and imperialism. Reality was to show a more complex relationship between the two communist powers. The Sino–Soviet Treaty of 1950 was heavily favourable to the USSR, a reflection of the relationship between the two countries at the time. The USSR treated China very much as a junior partner in the communist alliance. One way the Chinese could improve their standing in this relationship was by proving their loyalty to the cause of world communism. In this context the new People's Republic of China was to take an active role in attempting to advance world communism.

The relationship between Stalin and Mao was not an easy one. Stalin had always been cautious in providing help to the Chinese Communist Party (CCP) during the civil war against the Guomindang (Nationalists). To Stalin the Guomindang seemed to offer a better bulwark against the Japanese expansion in China that occurred during the 1930s and the Second World War. As a result the Soviet Union gave the Guomindang aid. It was only after the CCP had taken over China in October 1949 that Stalin was prepared to place relations with Mao on a firmer footing.

Alliance with the USSR was to be the cornerstone of Mao's foreign policy in 1949. Mao believed that it was only through the assistance of the USSR that Communist China could receive the protection it needed against attack from the USA and anti-communist forces in China. He also wanted the help of Soviet experts to ensure a socialist society was developed within China.

Source A

Mao presents his vision of Chinese foreign policy under the CCP

We must unite in a common struggle with those nations of the world that treat us as equal and unite with the peoples of all countries – that is, ally ourselves with the Soviet Union, with the People's Democratic Countries, and with the proletariat and the broad masses of the people in all other countries, and form an international united front . . . We must lean to one side.

From 'On People's Democratic Dictatorship', a statement issued by Mao (30 June 1949)

The USSR agreed to help, and Liu Shaoqi, Mao's second in command, visited Moscow in the summer of 1949 to start negotiations. The Chinese position was outlined in a report Liu sent to Stalin.

Source B

The Soviet Communist Party is the main headquarters of the international Communist movement, while the Chinese Communist Party is just a battle-front headquarters. The interests of a part should be subordinated to international interests and, therefore, the CCP submits to decisions of the Soviet Communist Party. If on some questions differences should arise between the CCP and the Soviet Communist Party, the CCP, having outlined its point of view, will submit and will resolutely carry out the decisions of the Soviet Communist Party.

From the official report from the CCP presented to Stalin (4 July 1949)

This was enough to bring about a face-to-face meeting between Mao and Stalin in Moscow in December 1949, the only time the two communist leaders were to meet. The result of this meeting was to confirm the terms of the Sino–Soviet Treaty.

The Sino–Soviet Treaty of Friendship, Alliance and Mutual Assistance, 1950

Its terms were as follows:

- a formal alliance between the two countries
- economic aid in the form of credits worth $300 million: much of this was spent on machinery and equipment needed for defence industries; technical assistance included help for a large aluminium plant at Henan, a rare metals plant at Hunan and a cable factory at Jiantan
- Soviet military assistance in case of attack from either Japan or the USA; military aid to help China develop its air force
- a Soviet promise to restore Chinese sovereignty over the province of Manchuria; the USSR agreed to transfer control over the railways in Manchuria to China

- an agreement to ban all non-Soviet foreigners from Manchuria, as requested by the USSR.

Yet China failed to secure Soviet agreement on other aspects of policy:

- Mongolia remained a Soviet sphere of influence
- Stalin refused to give aid to conquer Taiwan, which remained in the hands of the Guomindang. Stalin feared provoking the USA into action
- No joint revolutionary strategy was devised for East Asia. Stalin forced Mao to drop plans to send support to the Vietminh in their struggle against the French in Indochina.

The Treaty in action: The Korean War, 1950–53

The outbreak of the Korean War in June 1950 gave Mao a chance to test the content of the Treaty and to put himself forward as a regional liberator in the name of communism.

Mao believed that the only way to unite Korea was through military action but he was not in favour of the North Koreans attempting to do this in 1950. He feared that a North Korean attack on the South would result in a much greater American presence in the Far East, which would jeopardise Mao's plans to invade Taiwan. The Korean War was not Mao's or Stalin's war but that of Kim Il Sung, the North Korean leader. Mao's decision to return nearly 70,000 Korean volunteers back to North Korea during the second half of 1949 can only have helped convince Kim that the chances of a successful invasion of the South were high. These Koreans had volunteered to fight for the CCP against the Nationalists during the Chinese Civil War. Now that the war in China was over, they could be returned for possible military action in Korea.

To Mao the Korean War presented an opportunity to show the commitment of China to the revolutionary cause, although he was more hesitant in deciding how much military support China should send. At the start of the war Mao sent military advisers to help North Korea but told Stalin on October 2 that he would not commit any Chinese troops to the war. Nonetheless there were several factors that pushed Mao towards military intervention in Korea: the threat of US action spilling into China, the debt owed to North Korean volunteers who had helped the CCP during the Chinese civil war and the opportunity the war provided for showing China's credential as a world revolutionary force. Yet the timing of Chinese intervention points to Stalin as having the decisive role in bringing China into the war. Stalin pushed for Chinese military involvement in preference to a direct Soviet presence in Korea. Stalin even presented the Chinese leadership with a communist version of the domino theory, warning them that to let North Korea succumb to the forces of American imperialism would lead to the fall of further dominoes in the Far East as communism rolled back.

After a series of meetings between the two sides Stalin was able to get the Chinese to change their mind. Chinese intervention began on 19 October.

The Chinese provided the troops and bore the brunt of the casualties – 900,000 dead or wounded by the end of the war. The USSR provided air support through a division of MiG-15 fighters and also military advisers.

During the war Stalin left matters of strategy to Mao but reserved the right to intervene and overrule where he felt it necessary. Differences between Soviet and Chinese military advisers were common, but it was the views of the Soviet officers that prevailed.

Stalin and Mao always consulted on the major decisions to be taken during the war: the decision whether to cross the 38th parallel in January 1951 and whether to start negotiations towards ending the fighting in May–June 1951. Yet it became clear to Mao that Stalin's actions and behaviour were driven by self-interest rather than proletarian internationalism. The Soviet demand that China should pay for the military support it received from the USSR particularly struck home. As the historian Chen Jian states, 'Stalin's stinginess made the Soviets seem more like arms merchants than genuine Communist internationalists.'

Despite the obvious inequality of the relationship Sino–Soviet affairs had been cemented by the Korean War. The Chinese had emerged from the war as a power of some note. The Chinese People's Liberation Army had played a key role in pushing back the forces of the UN from North Korea to below the 38th parallel. By working with the USSR during the war a feeling of comradely cooperation between the communist powers had been engendered. Yet the nature of this relationship gave Mao a sense of both inequality and moral superiority: if the USSR was not able to help out fellow comrades, then China would. Thus, the seeds of the future Sino–Soviet split were also sown during the Korean War.

The Treaty in action: The Taiwan Straits crises of 1954–55 and 1958

One of the most dangerous points of tension during the whole of the Cold War was the Taiwan Straits. After the Chinese Communists had seized the mainland, the remnants of the Guomindang had fled to the island of Taiwan. In addition to Taiwan the Guomindang held onto control of smaller islands such as Quemoy (Jinmen), Matsu and Yijiangshan in the Taiwan Straits (See Source E). To Mao the liberation of China under the Communists would not be complete without these islands.

In July 1953 the Korean War came to an end, and Mao could once again turn his attention to Taiwan. By 1954 Mao had decided to shell the Guomindang-held island of Quemoy. He wanted to highlight the issue of Taiwan, register the displeasure of Communist China at the establishment of **SEATO** in September and help galvanise the Chinese population in the cause of socialist reconstruction. It was also hoped that the tension would help cement the alliance with the USSR. Despite the CCP not informing the Soviet leadership of their plans, Khrushchev was willing to support China militarily.

SKILLS BUILDER

1 How did the Korean War reveal the inequality of the relationship between the USSR and China?

2 In what ways did the Korean War raise the reputation of China as a force for advancing communism?

3 'Chinese involvement in the Korean War was merely as an instrument of Stalin's foreign policy rather than as a force for spreading communist revolution.' How far do you accept this interpretation?

Definition

SEATO

The South East Asian Treaty Organisation formed in 1954: a defensive treaty designed to restrict the expansion of communism in the region. It was made up of Western states such as the USA, Britain, France, Australia and New Zealand and their close allies. The organisation never gained much respect from the independent nations of South East Asia.

The Guomindang did not back down in the face of the heavy bombardment of Quemoy in September 1954. Their defiance was helped greatly by US support and military backing. The crisis therefore had the potential to turn into a USA–Chinese war, possibly one involving nuclear weapons. In 1955 the Guomindang abandoned the Taschen Islands to the Communists but held onto Quemoy and Matsu. At the same time the CCP took a more moderate line and negotiations were started. The first Taiwan Straits crisis was over.

Tension came to the surface again in 1958. Mao announced that he would be taking a leading role in military decision-making, and this was the prelude to a new wave of shelling of Quemoy. There were several reasons for this:

- There was frustration at Taiwan's lack of concessions at negotiations started after 1954
- There was a desire on the part of Mao to test the American commitment to Taiwan
- It was part of Mao's attempt to stir up 'revolutionary enthusiasm' in the Chinese masses by highlighting the struggle against capitalist/imperialist forces. The historian Chen Jian sees the crisis as a product of Mao's domestic policies that were preparing for the Great Leap Forward
- It was an opportunity to tie the USSR to the defence of China by highlighting the threat of the USA.

Source C

Mao highlights the advantages of provoking tension

Besides its disadvantageous side, a tense international situation can mobilise the population, can particularly mobilise the backward people, can mobilise the people in the middle, and can therefore promote the Great Leap Forward in economic construction . . . Lenin said that a war could motivate people's spiritual condition, making it tense. Although there is no war right now, a tense situation caused by the current military confrontation can also bring about every positive factor.

Mao Zedong in a speech to the Supreme State Council of the CCP,
5 September 1958, as quoted in Chen Jian,
Mao's China and the Cold War (published in 2001)

Although divisions between China and the USSR had opened since the first Taiwan Straits Crisis, the tension generated in 1958 was to partly close this split. The USSR had serious misgivings over Chinese tactics but felt that the forces of communism needed to stand together against the USA.

Thus, Mao had secured the inclusion of China under the protection of Moscow's nuclear umbrella.

By October Mao and the Chinese Politburo had come to the conclusion that there were advantages in leaving Quemoy and Matsu in the hands of the

Guomindang. By doing so Mao had a valuable tool through which pressure could be applied to the USA and the Guomindang. In Mao's own words, 'Whenever we are in need of tension, we may tighten this noose, and whenever we want to relax the tension, we may loosen the noose'. The Chinese bombardments of Quemoy subsided.

SKILLS BUILDER

1 Explain how Mao used the Taiwan Straits crises to the advantage of the People's Republic of China by:

   a) applying pressure on the USSR

   b) applying pressure on the USA.

2 Explain how the Taiwan Straits crises were linked to Mao's policies within China.

Source E

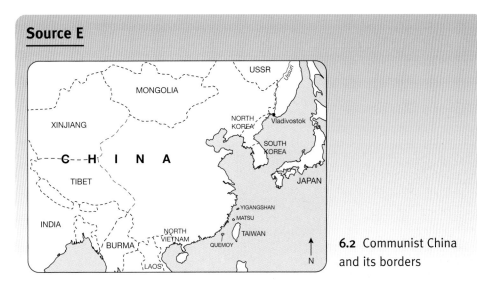

6.2 Communist China and its borders

Source D

Khrushchev's announcement in 1958

. . . attacking the People's Republic of China is attacking the USSR . . . It's necessary to put an end to interference into China's internal affairs. The American navy should be recalled from the Taiwan Straits, and American soldiers should leave Taiwan and go home. We are entirely on the side of the Chinese government, the Chinese people. It's their policy that we support and will support.

From a letter sent by Khrushchev to Eisenhower, the US President (7 September 1958)

Why did the Sino–Soviet Split occur after 1953?

Tensions between China and Russia had long existed. In fact, the period of close relations between 1949 and 1956 are better seen as an exceptional interlude in a much longer historical pattern of mutual hostility.

Long-shared borders, however, provided not just opportunities for disputes but also ties. These ties were to be in the ascendant after 1949 as the neighbouring governments of the Soviet Union and China were both based on communist ideologies. The new relationship between the two countries was cemented by the Treaty of Friendship, Alliance and Mutual Assistance of 1950. Yet by the early 1960s tensions between China and the Soviet Union had produced a split between the two communist superpowers. Verbal attacks and a failure to cooperate had progressed to more serious manifestations of the dispute: in 1967 Chinese Red Guards attacked the

Russian Embassy in Beijing; China encouraged fellow-communist Albania and Romania to assert greater independence from Moscow; the Chinese openly competed with the USSR in supporting communist groups in the developing world and by the early 1960s rival communist terrorist groups existed in some parts of the developing world. By 1969 border disputes had developed into an armed battle at the Ussuri River.

The causes of the Sino–Soviet Split are a mix of national and ideological factors that are often inextricably linked and difficult to disentangle. National interests were often dressed up in the language of ideological differences and separating the real reasons from the excuses is not an easy task.

1 *Ideological differences*

Arguments arose over the best way to pursue communist revolution. Since 1917 the Russian Communist Party was expected to give the definitive answer to this issue, but the Chinese Communist Party had adapted communism to a rural-based society and was accustomed to making its own decisions. The Soviet leadership had used Comintern, and later Cominform, to exercise control over other communist countries, but these organisations were not enough to prevent the Chinese criticising the Soviet Union.

In terms of the pecking order within the communist world Mao had considered himself junior to Stalin, but in 1953, with Stalin dead, Mao felt himself senior to Khrushchev and found much to dislike in the new Soviet leader's policies:

- Khrushchev had pursued a policy of reconciliation with Tito, the Yugoslav leader who had been unwilling to impose Stalin's policies in 1948. Mao regarded this as ideological revisionism

- Mao was heavily critical of Khrushchev's pursuit of improved relations with the USA. The policy of Peaceful Coexistence seemed to Mao to be showing weakness against the capitalist power. This criticism was heightened during Khrushchev's visit to the USA in 1959. Mao saw Peaceful Coexistence as abandoning those millions of comrades struggling to free themselves of capitalist and imperialist oppression

- Khrushchev's speech at the Twentieth Party Congress of February 1956 made disturbing criticisms of Stalin's domestic policies. The message was clear: Stalin's application of ideology contained errors, and communism must be applied in different ways. Many of Mao's domestic policies were based on Stalin's and he was greatly offended by 'De-Stalinisation'. In addition Mao had not been consulted on the speech before it was delivered

- Mao criticised Khrushchev for failing to see that a privileged elite had developed that would stop the progress from socialism towards communism in the Soviet Union. The use of strong tactics was needed against these revisionists or the revolution would be threatened

- Khrushchev had been highly critical of the **Great Leap Forward** in 1958, especially its plan for building 'back-yard steel furnaces' in rural areas, and this did nothing to dispel the Chinese feeling that Soviet economic and military aid would be very limited

- Khrushchev criticised Mao for splitting the communist movement and therefore helping the capitalists.

2 National interests

- Arguments arose over the USSR's refusal to reduce its ties to Mongolia, which China considered to be within its own sphere of influence.

- The USSR constantly blocked China's request to expand its control in North Korea.

- Border disputes between China and Russia had a long history that the communist regimes of both countries could not ignore. The Soviet Union had 15 army divisions stationed along the Chinese border in 1967. This figure had doubled by 1970.

- The Soviet invasion of Czechoslovakia in 1968 had a profound effect on Chinese perceptions of the USSR. Czechoslovakia had been invaded in order to bring a more independent communist government back into line with Moscow's direction. The Chinese understood the message: that the USSR could use the actions elsewhere.

The fact that the Chinese Communist Party itself traces the beginning of the dispute to Khrushchev's speech criticising Stalin at the Twentieth Party Congress of 1956 suggests that ideological differences were important. Khrushchev was labelled as a 'Rightist' and 'Revisionist'. Yet this was encouraged by the manoeuvrings within Chinese domestic politics. The Hundred Flowers Campaign of 1957 and the subsequent Great Leap Forward of 1958 consolidated the power of the Left in the CCP by attacking revisionism as the enemy. These issues came to the fore again in 1968 when Mao launched another attempt to strengthen his political power in China – the Cultural Revolution.

Border disputes, such as those over the Ussuri River, were usually manifestations of division rather than its cause. Long borders are shared between countries that remain on stable relations – the USA and Canada for example. Manchuria had previously been the main source of conflict between Russia and China, but the Russians had withdrawn from this area in 1954. Yet the multinational make-up of both the Soviet Union and China with the same ethnic groups (Kazakhs, Mongols) on both sides of the border provided tensions and concerns that could be exploited when needed. With a shared border 2,738 miles long there were plenty of opportunities for tension.

Both ideology and border disputes clearly had a role in the development of the Sino–Soviet Split. Ideology often provided the excuses and the language in which to present the divisions. Since the communist takeover of 1949 China was determined to play a leading role in the world communist

Definition

Great Leap Forward

The campaign launched by Mao in 1958 to increase production in industry and agriculture. The campaign involved building dams, reservoirs and roads, setting up small-scale steel and iron furnaces in country areas and establishing communes as the best way of organising agriculture. The campaign was an economic disaster and at least 17 million died directly as a result of these policies. Soviet impatience at Chinese methods led them to withdraw economic aid in 1960.

movement but found its ambitions thwarted by a Soviet Union that possessed atomic weapons, had developed a successful space programme with the launching of Sputnik in 1957 and had ICBM capability, yet refused to share these technologies. At its heart the Sino–Soviet Split was about China's struggle to become a world power and the Soviet Union's determination to prevent it.

Investigation: Mao, Khrushchev and the Sino–Soviet Split

Source F

The view of Khrushchev and the Soviet Politburo in 1958

We sensed that Mao had aspirations to be the leader of the world Communist movement.

From Nikita Khrushchev, *Khrushchev Remembers*, published by Sphere (1971)

Source G

I remember that when I came back from China in 1954 I told my comrades, 'Conflict with China is inevitable.' I came to this conclusion on the basis of various remarks Mao had made. During my visit to Beijing, the atmosphere was typically Oriental. Everyone was unbelievably courteous and ingratiating, but I saw through their hypocrisy . . . It was all too sickeningly sweet. The atmosphere was nauseating. In addition, some of the things Mao said put me on my guard. I was never exactly sure that I understood what he meant . . . Some of Mao's pronouncements struck me as being much too simplistic, and others struck me as being much too complex.

From Nikita Khrushchev, *Khrushchev Remembers*, published by Sphere (1971)

Source H

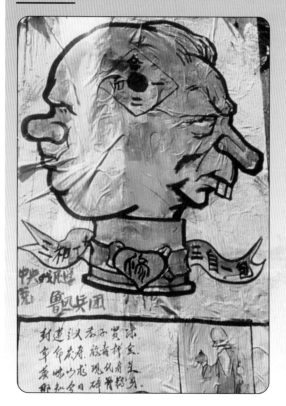

6.3 Propaganda poster issued by the CCP of Khrushchev and Liu Shaoqi as revisionists from the Cultural Revolution

Source I

To a considerable extent, the evolution of the quarrel in its early years between 1956 and 1964 had seemed impelled by the attitudes, prejudices, and egos of the leading actors, Mao and Khrushchev. The post-Khrushchev Soviet leadership, sensing this, attempted to find a basis for understanding with China in November 1964, immediately after Khrushchev's removal. Both sides were apparently disappointed to discover that this was impossible because the vested interests on each side were incompatible.

Subsequently, therefore, the Soviets resumed their long wait for the death of Mao, expecting no improvement in his lifetime but hoping for better things thereafter. When this event at last occurred in September 1976, Moscow immediately probed the attitude of his successors, but was at once again rebuffed.

From Harry Gelman, 'The Sino–Soviet Dispute in the 1970s', in Herbert Ellison (ed.), *The Sino–Soviet Conflict: a Global Perspective*, published by University of Washington Press (1982)

Source J

Let me also talk about Sino–Soviet relations. In my view, wrangling will continue . . . As far as I can see, circumstances are beyond what persons, even those occupying high positions, can control. Under the pressure of circumstance, those in the Soviet Union who still want to practice big-power chauvinism will invariably encounter difficulties. To persuade them remains our current policy and requires us to engage in direct dialogue with them. The last time our delegation visited the Soviet Union, we openly talked about some issues . . . as those people are blinded by lust for gain, the best way to deal with them is to give them a tongue-lashing. What is their asset? They have achieved nothing but digging a few things out of the earth, turning them into steel, thereby manufacturing some airplanes and automobiles. This is nothing to be proud of. They, however, turn these achievements into huge burdens on their back and hardly care about revolutionary principles.

Conflict will always exist. All we hope for at present is to avoid major clashes so as to seek common ground.

From *The Selected Works of Mao Zedong on Foreign Affairs* (published in 1994)

SKILLS BUILDER

1 What do Sources F–J suggest as the main causes of the Sino–Soviet Dispute?

2 Using the evidence from Sources F–J and your own knowledge, assess the validity of the view that the Sino–Soviet Dispute was a product of the personalities of Mao and Khrushchev.

Case study: the Ussuri River Dispute, 1969

Source K

An account of the border clash at Damansky Island on the Ussuri River, March 1969

Under cover of the wintry night of 1–2 March, approximately 300 Chinese soldiers, camouflaged in white uniforms, crossed the Ussuri River to Damansky Island and established a bivouac area for the night. Early the next morning, the Soviet guard on duty at Lieutenant Strelnikov's outpost noticed some 20 to 30 armed Chinese moving towards the Soviet side, shouting Mao slogans as they approached. Strelnikov and some of his men set off to meet the Chinese. Arriving on the island, they went forward to confront the approaching Chinese.

The Soviets strapped their automatic rifles to their chests and linked arms to prevent the Chinese from passing. The Chinese positioned themselves in rows and gave the appearance of being unarmed. When they had approached within about twenty feet of the Soviet soldiers, the first row stepped aside and a second row pulled out submachine guns from under their coats and opened fire on the Soviets. Strelnikov and six of his men were killed outright. At the same time, from an ambush on the Soviet flank, the Chinese let loose an enfilade which obviously caught the Soviet unit by surprise. Mortar and machine-gun fire joined in, and then the Chinese apparently charged with hand-to-hand fighting resulting. Under such an onslaught, the Soviet unit was overrun, and according to Soviet figures the Chinese killed nineteen men on the spot.

Lieutenant Bubenin had witnessed the battle from his outpost, and with his men he raced to the scene. He forced the Chinese to divide their fire, but in the process he was also wounded. A wild melee ensued, and when the confusion had died down the Soviets eventually forced the last group of 50 to 60 Chinese to retreat to their side of the river. The battle lasted some two hours, and both sides claimed victory.

From Colonel Donald M. Marks, 'The Ussuri River Incident as a Factor in Chinese Foreign Policy', published in *Air University Review* (July–August 1971)

On 2 March Soviet forces suffered 31 dead and 14 wounded. Further and more serious clashes occurred on 15 March when the Chinese once again attacked Damansky (Zhenbao) Island (see Source E for its location). The Soviet forces withdrew from the island, thus encouraging the Chinese to mass their troops opposite it. The Soviet forces then attacked the Chinese on a long front of several kilometres, exposing the Chinese weakness either side of the island. According to Soviet sources, the Chinese lost 800 soldiers compared with about 60 Soviet dead.

Both sides accused the other of provoking the incident, but the fact that on 2 March it was Soviet forces, consisting of border guards, that suffered heavy casualties suggests that it was the Chinese who initiated the clash.

Arguments over the exact position of the Sino–Soviet border had been long-standing and had often been sources of tension between Tsarist Russia and Imperial China. What made the issue of laying down borders along the

Ussuri River so difficult was the geographical condition of the area. The Ussuri River is one of the largest in China and as such it is subject to widespread flooding, which means its course can alter and islands in the middle of the river can appear and then be washed away.

In 1964 a preliminary agreement had been reached by which the USSR was prepared to hand over Damansky Island to China. But when Mao spoke openly about this being the first of many Chinese territorial gains from the USSR, Khrushchev was outraged and cancelled the agreement.

The Soviet invasion of Czechoslovakia in 1968 produced a real fear of invasion in China. In response the Chinese military developed a strategy of 'active defence' whereby they would make a pre-emptive strike against the USSR where Chinese forces were in the advantage in the hope of deterring the USSR from an invasion. It was a risky strategy. The dispute had the potential to escalate, especially as both sides now possessed nuclear weapons. Rumours spread that the USSR was prepared to use a nuclear strike against China; the appointment of Colonel General Tolubko, deputy commander of the USSR's Strategic Rocket Forces, to command Soviet forces in the Far East did little to ease these concerns.

The consequences of the Ussuri River Dispute, 1969

- Damansky Island remained in Soviet hands.

- The border dispute was left unresolved.

- Tensions increased along the border. In the west at Xinjiang on 13 August 1969 a serious clash occurred between Soviet and Chinese troops that resulted in the elimination of an entire Chinese brigade.

- When Kosygin, the Soviet Prime Minister, met **Zhou Enlai** (see page 131), his Chinese counterpart, in September 1969 relations remained frosty. Kosygin was returning from the funeral of Ho Chi Minh and made a stop at Beijing. The talks took place in the airport.

- The dispute of 1969 seems to have been of key significance in persuading Mao that China's foreign policy needed to be re-appraised. The result was a changed approach to the USA, which was to have a profound impact on the Cold War and shatter the bipolarity that had existed since 1945.

Why did a rapprochement take place between China and the USA after 1969?

One of the key consequences of the Sino–Soviet Split was the change it brought about in relations between China and the USA. After 20 years of directing insults at the USA as a dangerous capitalist power, the Chinese government decided that it was in its interest to seek a rapprochement with their enemy. Its main motive was the need to strengthen its position against the power that had emerged as the more important threat to Chinese security, its former communist ally, the USSR.

SKILLS BUILDER

1 Explain Mao's motives for provoking the Ussuri River Dispute of 1969.

2 What does the Dispute of 1969 tell us about the nature of Sino–Soviet relations at the time?

3 Explain how the Dispute brought about a change in the attitude of China to the USA.

Questions

1 By reference to the content and origin of Source L, how does the source reflect on the reasons for seeking a rapprochement with the USA?

2 Using your own knowledge, how far do you accept the validity of the interpretation that China's rapprochement with the USA was a product of geopolitical considerations?

The conventional interpretation offered to explain why China sought a rapprochement with the USA has stressed the role of geopolitical considerations. Writers such as Qian Jiang in *Behind the Ping-Pong Diplomacy* (1997) and Henry Kissinger in *Diplomacy* (1994) argue that Chinese security interests could not be adequately protected by sustaining its hostility to the USA at the same time as relations with the USSR had deteriorated to a dangerous level. The result was that some sort of accommodation with the USA was necessary.

The geopolitical interpretation highlights the threats to Chinese security in the late 1960s:

* an escalating war in Vietnam that threatened to increase US involvement in the region
* continued conflict with Taiwan
* hostile neighbours such as South Korea and Japan
* tension with India over their shared border: a short war had developed in 1962 over border disputes and further clashes occurred in September 1967 – tension remained high.

Thus China seemed to be surrounded by hostile states. The split with the USSR and the dispute over the Ussuri River in 1969 seemed to complete a dangerous encirclement of China by states who posed a threat to her national security.

This interpretation has much to commend it and offers a convincing explanation of why a rapprochement with the USA took place when it did. Historians such as Chen Jian in *Mao's China and the Cold War* (2001) argue that it was domestic political factors that underlie the reasons why China changed its policy to the USA.

The geopolitical interpretation sees ideology as unimportant and to be ignored when it is in conflict with national security needs. Yet Chen argues that this view is too simplistic. Ideology was central to the change in attitudes towards the USSR and the USA. Mao saw the USSR as developing into a reactionary and conservative society where a new privileged bureaucratic class had become entrenched in power. Mao's Cultural Revolution, which started in 1966, was an attempt to prevent this happening in China. Thus, the USSR was now labelled as the enemy in ideological terms as representing 'social imperialism'. Foreign policy and domestic policy were inextricably linked as Mao sought to strengthen his position as leader of China and of the movement for world revolution. Revisionism among the communist movement was now a much greater threat than the USA, now considered to be a declining power.

What did Sino–American relations achieve between 1970 and 1976?

Tentative feelers had been made on behalf of the Chinese and US leaderships since 1969. By 1971 both sides were willing to progress these contacts to a higher level but were unsure how to proceed. One key obstacle remained US support for Taiwan, but other differences existed: the military situation in Vietnam; the division between North and South Korea; and how to deal with the emergence of Japan as an economic world power. What was needed was an event that would provide an excuse for representatives from both countries to get together. In April 1971 one such event occurred; the World Table Tennis Championships in Nagoya, Japan. After several unplanned encounters between the Chinese and American players, the US team made it known that they would be happy to accept an invitation to visit China and play against their national team. Mao decided that such an invitation should be given. The result was the start of a series of contacts between the two superpowers that helped establish a rapprochement between them.

Source M

6.5 Nixon and Mao during the Beijing visit of 1972

- In 1971 an American table tennis team was invited to China. The Chinese let the American players win most of the matches and they treated their guests with courtesy and friendship. Allowing their guests to win was seen by the Chinese as an indication of their superiority. The tour received enormous publicity within China. This **ping-pong diplomacy** led to further contacts.
- Trade and travel restrictions were relaxed.
- In July 1971 Kissinger, the US Secretary of State, visited China. He had six meetings with Zhou Enlai lasting for a total of 17 hours. The two men respected each other and established a good working relationship.
- In February 1972 Nixon, the US President, visited China. At the end of the summit a communiqué was produced that allowed both sides to stress their differences as well as their common ground. This meant that both Mao and Nixon could present the visit as a diplomatic success that did not involve an abandonment of their principles. As the historian Chen (2001) states in *Mao's China and the Cold War*, for Mao the great

Definition

Ping-pong diplomacy

The term given to the tentative contacts between the Chinese and US governments in 1971 whereby sporting links between the two countries were used as opportunities to start diplomacy.

Biography

Zhou Enlai (1898–1976)

A key member of the Chinese Communist Party who became Prime Minister in 1949 and remained in this position until his death in 1976. He was a well-educated man, seen as a moderating force on Mao. He survived China's upheavals of the Great Leap Forward and the Cultural Revolution. He had been foreign minister between 1949 and 1958 and it remained a policy area he was interested in. He was in favour of the rapprochement with the USA.

victory was 'the simple fact that Nixon and Kissinger came to *his* study to listen to *his* teachings'.

- In 1975 Ford, who had replaced Nixon as US President, visited China.

- The Chinese government put pressure on the USSR in Europe by visiting countries in Eastern Europe in order to strengthen their ties with China at the expense of the USSR. Visits to Yugoslavia and Romania were particularly successful.

- Trade between China and the USA grew considerably from $5 million to $500 million a year in the space of just a few years. The USA refused to trade in goods that might have military applications but did not stop its allies from doing so. In 1975 Britain secured an order to supply Rolls-Royce jet engines to China.

- America's allies in the Far East, especially Taiwan, South Vietnam and South Korea, were shocked by her closer links to China.

- The USA toned down its foreign policy in the Far East. The US government became more critical of the repressive regime of Park in South Korea. US support for Taiwan diminished as the US government issued its 'two Chinas' policy. In 1971 Taiwan was expelled from the Security Council of the United Nations, an action taken with US backing. By 1978 the USA had given diplomatic recognition to the communist regime in China and withdrawn it from Taiwan.

- The improved links with America caused tension between China and its allies. North Vietnam was annoyed by China establishing friendly relations with Nixon when they appeared to have the USA very much on the defensive in the war in Vietnam. Albania, which had been China's staunchest communist ally, now accused China of betraying the world proletarian revolution.

- For Mao the links with the USA did much to restore his damaged standing within China after the chaos of the Cultural Revolution. They also helped enhance the power of Zhou Enlai, who was a strong advocate of opening up China's relations with the rest of the world. The closer relationship with the USA may also have played a part in the downfall of Lin Biao, who had opposed closer links. Lin was killed when his plane crashed in mysterious circumstances during an attempt to flee from China. Official Chinese propaganda accused Lin of having planned to turn China into a colony of the Soviet Union – a ridiculous but telling accusation.

- The links provided a series of opportunities for both China and the USA to embarrass and undermine the USSR. A communiqué issued after Nixon's visit to China announced that neither China nor the USA 'should seek hegemony in the Asia–Pacific region and each is opposed to efforts by any other country or group of countries to establish such hegemony'. This implied a joint stand against the actions of the USSR.

- For the USA, closer links with China were a valuable way of exerting pressure on the USSR in order to extract concessions from them. This was to become a key feature of the negotiations that took place during the period of Détente.

SKILLS BUILDER

1 What did closer relations between China and the USA achieve for:

a) China

b) the USA?

2 Source M shows cordial relations between the Chinese and Americans. Was this merely a publicity stunt or did the rapprochement between China and the USA achieve anything of substance?

What were the implications of the Sino-US rapprochement for US–Soviet relations?

One of the key results of the developing rapprochement between the US and China was to be its impact on US-Soviet relations. The US governments of the 1970s took pleasure in the discomfort that closer relations with China caused the Soviet leadership. The idea of a communist bloc acting as one had been severely dented by the new direction taken by the Chinese leadership.

The Soviet Union had not foreseen a Sino-American rapprochement and it forced them to change their thinking in international relations. The world now had to be seen in multi-polar terms. The USSR now had to engage in triangular diplomacy, involving both the US and China. This was to be a much more complex affair as each power tried to play off one against the other. Chinese support for the Soviet position in international affairs could no longer be guaranteed. If the USSR did not offer concessions to the US it could be pushed further towards a closer friendship with China.

This weakening of the Soviet position was in part responsible for bringing the Soviet Union to the negotiating table and once there to make concessions. Nixon's visit to China in 1972 had the effect of making the USSR more amenable to US wishes. This all fed into the pressures that promoted Détente: the more permanent relaxation in superpower relations of the 1970s that produced agreements on trade, arms limitations and human rights.

SKILLS BUILDER

Using Sources N and O and your own knowledge, explain how the Sino-American rapprochement caused 'the most profound shift in the international balance of power'.

Source N

The Nixon administration had initiated contacts with the People's Republic of China (PRC) shortly after taking office, but divisions within the Chinese leadership on the possibility and the value of improved relations with the United States had prevented progress. The May 1970 US invasion of Cambodia caused further delays.

Nixon's visit to China in February 1972 put further pressure on the Soviets to head off a Sino-American strategic partnership. A public relations and a geopolitical success, the visit ended with a final communiqué that proclaimed Chinese and US opposition to Soviet 'hegemony' in Asia. Although the communiqué noted their differing views on the future of Taiwan, it also pledged the United States to work toward a full normalisation of relations with the PRC by 1976.

From David Painter, *The Cold War, An International History*, published by Routledge (1999)

Source O

The Sino–American rapprochement, along with the deterioration of relations between Beijing and Moscow, caused the most profound shift in the international balance of power between the two contending superpowers. Whereas the great Sino–Soviet rivalry further diminished Moscow's capacity to wage a global battle with the United States, the Sino–American rapprochement enormously enhanced Washington's strategic position in its global competition with the Soviet Union. More importantly, the great Sino–Soviet split buried the shared consciousness among Communists and Communist sympathisers all over the world that communism was a solution to the problems created by the world-wide process of modernisation. Nothing could be more effective in destroying the moral foundation of communism . . . Although the Cold War did not end until the late 1980s . . . one of the most crucial roots of that collapse certainly can be traced to the reconciliation between Beijing and Washington in 1969–72.

From Chen Jian, *Mao's China and the Cold War*, published by Chapel Hill (2001)

Unit summary

What have you learned in this unit?

You have learned from this unit that the foreign policy of the People's Republic of China had produced a profound shift in the dynamics of the Cold War. From a position of greatly strengthening the power and position of the Communist Bloc in the period from 1949 to 1956, China had, by 1972, split irrevocably with the USSR and brought about a rapprochement with its former enemy the USA. Although this change seemed on the face of it to be a dramatic about-turn, it was largely the result of continuity in Chinese foreign policy – the desire to protect Chinese national security against foreign powers.

The change in Chinese policy was to shatter the perception of a bipolar world that had existed since the beginning of the Cold War. Superpower relations were now best described as a triangular process involving China, the USSR and the USA.

What skills have you used in this unit?

You have been able to practise your skills in argument and making a judgement based on reasoning. The exercises in this unit have given you opportunities to discuss the changes in Sino–Soviet relations and their impact on US foreign policy. As a result of this you should now feel confident to present your own substantiated judgements on this topic.

Exam style questions

This unit covers another of the four issues that are assessed in Section A of the examination. Don't forget that the questions in this section will require you to analyse a historical issue or problem and come to a reasoned judgement. Questions are likely to ask 'how far/to what extent . . .' you agree with a statement or interpretation. One example on this topic would be:

- How far was the Sino–Soviet Split of the late 1960s the result of ideological differences between the two communist powers?

Exam tips

This question is asking you to develop an argument on a judgement given about the reasons for the Sino–Soviet Split.

- Was it the result of ideological differences? What were these differences? What role did they play in the split? Were they real reasons/excuses/opportunities for the split?
- What other factors played a role? This will allow you to assess 'How far'. Other factors to examine would include:
  - the role of personality: Mao and Khrushchev
  - national interests.

Did these factors work in combination? What were the links between them?

Introductions

The introduction is a very important part of any essay answer and requires thought before launching into your response. A good introduction can get your answer off to a good start that shows the examiner that you understand the demands of the question, have an argument to offer and know the range of material that needs to be addressed in order to answer the question in an effective manner. Thus a good introduction will have the following features:

- show a clear awareness of the issue under discussion
- outline your argument
- give an indication of the areas you will be looking at to develop your argument.

Common weaknesses include:

- starting the essay as if telling a story and using the introduction to set the scene
- focusing on the topic of the question rather than addressing the specific angle of the question
- giving no indication of an argument. Think about how you argue orally. If you are asked 'What do you think of Manchester United?', your answer will almost inevitably start with an assertion of your viewpoint, which you will then go on to develop and support. It would seem odd if you were to say 'Well, there are some good things and bad things about Manchester United and I will try to weigh them up.' Written answers are no different. Be assertive and state your argument at the beginning. Obviously you are likely to become more assertive if you are confident with the material and topic. This is where practice helps. Remember that the highest levels on the A Level mark scheme are for answers that have a sustained argument. 'Sustained' requires you to argue from the beginning to the end.

RESEARCH TOPIC

Mao Zedong

One of the key figures of the twentieth century is Mao Zedong, the leader of Communist China from 1949 until his death in 1976. Mao's domestic policies have been a source of much debate. They seem to be instruments of Mao's struggle for supremacy in China, but they also had a major impact on China's relations with the two superpowers.

Your task is to research the following campaigns initiated by Mao:

- The Great Leap Forward, 1958

- The Cultural Revolution, 1966.

For each campaign find out how it affected China's relationship with:

a) the USSR

b) the USA.

- Do you think these campaigns were a reflection of Mao's strengths as leader of China or a reflection of his weaknesses?

- Did these campaigns strengthen or weaken China's position in world politics?

7 What were the causes and achievements of Détente?

What is this unit about?

This unit focuses on the period of improved relations between the USA and the USSR during the 1970s, known as Détente. This period saw significant agreements between the superpowers that seemed to provide stability in their relations. Yet the development of Détente faced critics on both sides and its fragility became evident when it collapsed in 1979. In this unit you will:

- examine the factors that pushed both superpowers towards Détente
- assess the key features of the main agreements of Détente: the Strategic Arms Limitation Talks of 1972, the Anti-Ballistic Missile Treaty of 1972 and the Helsinki Accords of 1975
- examine the ways in which Détente was criticised by opponents on both sides
- understand and analyse the role of the factors that brought about the end to Détente.

Key questions

- What factors promoted Détente and to what extent was it a successful method of conducting Cold War conflict?
- Why did Détente come to an end in 1979?

Timeline

1969	
January	Nixon becomes President of the USA, appoints Henry Kissinger as his National Security Adviser
	Willy Brandt becomes Chancellor of West Germany
1972	
May	SALT I agreed, including the ABM Treaty
December	West and East Germany sign the Basic Treaty, accepting the existence of each other as separate states
1973	
January	USA signs Paris Peace Settlement and agrees to withdraw troops from Vietnam.
July	NATO and Warsaw Pact countries begin talks that lead to the Helsinki Accords in 1975
September	Kissinger becomes US Secretary of State
1975	
17 July	Apollo–Soyuz link-up
August	Helsinki Accords signed

1976	
November	Jimmy Carter elected US President.
1977	
January	Carter appoints the neo-conservative Zbigniew Brzezinski as his National Security Adviser.
1979	
May	Margaret Thatcher becomes British Prime Minister
June	Vienna Summit between Carter and Brezhnev leads to signing of SALT II Treaty
December	Soviet forces invade Afghanistan
1980	
January	USA suspends ratification of SALT II in protest at Soviet invasion of Afghanistan
November	Right-winger Ronald Reagan elected President of the USA

Introduction

Source A

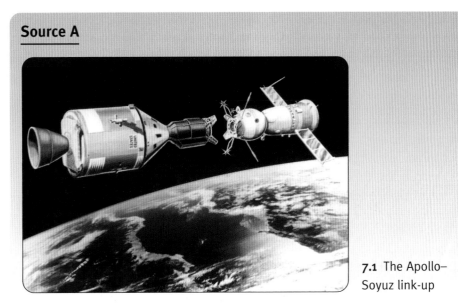

7.1 The Apollo–Soyuz link-up

The illustration Source A shows what was considered by both US and Soviet governments to be one of the highlights of Détente. Instead of the confrontations that had marked superpower dealings up to 1962, Cold War relations were to change to a period of 'more permanent relaxation' known as Détente.

Negotiations for a link-up of Soviet and US spacecraft had begun in 1970 and were to bear fruit on 17 July 1975. In an event broadcast live on global television two Soviet cosmonauts entered the American Apollo spacecraft through a docking module and shook hands with waiting astronauts. The two crews conducted experiments together, shared accommodation and meals and received messages from the American President Ford and the

Soviet leader Brezhnev. After two days the two spacecraft returned to earth.

The Apollo–Soyuz link-up had been a symbol of what greater cooperation between the two superpowers could achieve. Yet it was a mission that was not without its difficulties. On re-entry to the earth's atmosphere the thrusters on the Apollo spacecraft released a highly toxic gas into the cabin. Catastrophe was averted, but it caused the astronauts to choke. As Détente progressed, this was an experience that the leaders of both sides came to identify with, as Détente involved making compromises that were often unpalatable and seemed to achieve little more than show.

What were the causes of Détente?

The Cuban Missile Crisis of 1962 had highlighted the underlying tensions between the USA and the USSR, but it also helped to accelerate the moves towards reducing these tensions that had started during the so-called 'Thaw' of the late 1950s. Détente, a more permanent relaxation of relations, was to develop after 1962. It was a trend that was encouraged by both international tension and the domestic considerations of the two superpowers. Détente was also stimulated by initiatives taken by European leaders keen to reduce tension in Europe. As these factors came together Détente was to gather enough momentum to produce agreements that offered some tangible evidence of greater cooperation.

The fear of war

The Cuban Missile Crisis of 1962 had highlighted the danger of a superpower confrontation resulting in nuclear war. President Kennedy's threat to use American nuclear missiles if Soviet missile bases were not withdrawn from Cuba had caused anxiety across the world. With the nuclear arms race leading to the development of ever more efficient missiles the fear of future war continued to increase. By 1969 the USSR had matched the capability of the USA for mutually assured destruction: each superpower now had enough nuclear missiles to destroy the other in the event of a first strike by the opponent. This situation not only posed a threat to the economic well-being of both superpowers but also provided a balance of power that would, it was hoped, act as a deterrent. The pressure to forge ahead in the arms race did, however, threaten constantly to disrupt this delicate balance. The necessity of reducing the risk of future nuclear war pushed both East and West towards Détente.

The needs of the USSR

After 1964 the new Soviet leadership, led by Leonid Brezhnev, made little change to Khrushchev's foreign policy. Peaceful Coexistence continued to be pursued because it was seen to further the interests of the USSR. Although ideological considerations pointed towards the inevitability of conflict between the powers of communism and capitalism, national security interests were to be the overriding factor determining Soviet foreign policy, and this pushed the USSR towards Détente. This was nothing new. The Nazi–Soviet Pact of 1939 had been a prime example of security being placed above ideological differences.

The advantage of coming to an accommodation with the USA in the late 1960s was the perceived weakness of the USA during the latter stages of the Vietnam War. The USSR had also achieved a greater degree of parity in nuclear weapons at this time, which allowed it to contemplate arms limitation agreements from a position of strength. It would also stop the USA trying to forge ahead in the arms race by developing new technology that the USSR feared it would not be able to keep pace with.

Accommodation with the USA would help stabilise the Soviet hold over Eastern Europe. The USSR hoped to gain recognition from the West for its influence and control over the Eastern Bloc, giving it a legitimacy that it had failed to gain by imposing communism on the region after 1945. Romania's development of a more independent foreign policy, the Czechoslovakian Crisis of 1968 and strikes in the Polish city of Gdansk in 1970 were signs that the Soviet hold on Eastern Europe needed strengthening.

The Sino–Soviet Split was another factor that pushed the Soviet Union towards an accommodation with the West. If conflict was to occur with China, then the USSR wanted to ensure that the USA would not get involved and that Western Europe was stable. Détente could help achieve this.

In addition, there were important domestic forces that were pushing the Soviet leadership towards Détente. The Soviet Politburo faced mounting economic problems and needed to divert resources away from the military sector of the economy to deal with these. The Soviet population had failed to gain the improvement in living standards they had been led to expect by Khrushchev and Brezhnev. With the continuation of the arms race, the Soviet government found it difficult to transfer production capacity in industry to consumer goods. Détente would provide the international background necessary to make this possible.

Improved relations would allow the USSR access to much-needed Western technology and grain supplies. Great strides had been made towards competing with the US economy, but Soviet successes had been in areas that were becoming outdated. Soviet production of steel, cement, oil and pig iron exceeded that of the USA by the end of the 1970s, but these were vital elements of an industrial age that was giving way to a post-industrial society based on microchips and computers. The Soviet leadership was aware that it needed access to the new technologies developing in the West. The Eighth Five Year Plan (1966–70) tried to address technological weakness in the car industry by making deals with Fiat and Renault to import technology into the USSR. More of this would be possible if friendly relations could be established with the USA.

Thus, for Brezhnev there were strong reasons for developing links with the USA and the West. It would further the interests of the Soviet Union and engage the USA in a manner that suggested the USSR was a partner of equal status. Yet Détente did not involve the USSR giving up Cold War conflict. By stabilising relations with the West in Europe, the Soviet Union could focus on helping liberation movements in the developing world with a freer hand.

The needs of the USA

For the USA Détente was a way of coming to terms with the realisation that there were limits to its power on the world stage. It was the American experience in the Vietnam War that was to change US public opinion. The failure of the USA to secure victory in Vietnam led to a re-evaluation of America's power in the world and recognition of the painful reality of the Vietnam War: there were limits to the power of the USA. In 1969 President Nixon and his National Security Adviser, Henry Kissinger, had to grapple with the impact of the Vietnam War on America. Both were right wing in terms of domestic policy, but they were practical politicians. The Vietnam War had caused high inflation, a large budget deficit and had led to a decline in support for foreign intervention in the wider world. Western Europe was also showing greater independence from the USA. De Gaulle, the French President, had gone as far as withdrawing France from NATO in 1966. Détente would offer the USA an opportunity to uphold its interests without the need for military intervention that might not succeed. More could be gained by negotiation than confrontation.

It is significant that it was Nixon and Kissinger who pursued the policy of Détente. Both had established credentials as anti-communists and this allowed them to carry a large degree of American right-wing support with them. Trade and arms agreements were presented as methods of restraining the USSR. The rapprochement with China that occurred during Détente allowed the policy to be seen as one that weakened the Communist Bloc rather than as one that gave in to communism. Thus, Nixon was able, due to a temporary demoralisation of the powerful right in America caused by Vietnam, to pursue Détente at this time.

Détente would, in addition, allow the influence of the powerful industrial-military complex to be reduced. Plans for social reform in America had been undermined by a lack of resources due to continued military spending. Kennedy had a vision of a New Frontier, Johnson a New Society: both were sacrificed for increased armaments. The urban riots that broke out across the USA in 1968 provided the evidence that social issues within America needed to be tackled as a matter of urgency. Moves to Détente would allow resources to be released from the military budget to improve the lives of the American people. From a purely economic standpoint Détente would allow America to invest more resources in its own commerce and financial services, areas in which Western Europe was becoming a serious rival.

For the USA, Détente was a method of adapting to a world where its power seemed to be weaker. US interests could be pursued by negotiation without reducing its influence internationally and at the same time addressing serious domestic issues.

European needs and Ostpolitik

The pressure for Détente did not derive solely from the superpowers. Developments in Europe during the late 1960s also encouraged links across the Iron Curtain. In 1968 events showed substantial instability on both sides of the Iron Curtain in Europe. The Soviet invasion of Czechoslovakia revealed the continuing tension in Eastern Europe. In France large-scale student demonstrations had resulted in a general strike that threatened both President de Gaulle and the French system of government. Political disorder posed a danger to East and West in Europe. The West German politician Willy Brandt was to take the lead in promoting links across the divide. Brandt served as West German Foreign Minister (1966–69) before taking over as Chancellor (1969–74). He saw a stabilisation of European relations as essential to the interests of the continent as a whole. By reducing tension and establishing links between East and West, the divisions that had scarred Europe since the early Cold War would be gradually eroded. Brandt's response to this situation was to develop his 'Eastern Policy', better known as 'Ostpolitik'. By opening up channels between East and West in Europe Ostpolitik aided greatly the impetus towards Détente. Brandt's policy encouraged other European countries to establish links across the East–West divide, such as the French government's policy of establishing friendly relations with Romania.

By 1969 there was in existence a range of factors that provided considerable pressure for a Détente to be reached in international relations. Yet Détente did not mark an end, however temporary, to Cold War conflict; it developed out of a recognition that there was more to gain in the struggle between East and West by a degree of cooperation rather than confrontation. Thus, Détente represented a change in the tactics of superpower conflict rather than an end to the Cold War.

Key individual: Henry Kissinger

Henry Kissinger was one of the key players in Détente. He was Nixon's National Security Adviser after 1969 before becoming Secretary of State in 1973. When Nixon resigned as President in 1974 Kissinger continued as Secretary of State for the new President Gerald Ford until 1977.

Kissinger was born in Germany in 1923, of Jewish background. He fled with his family to the USA in 1938 to escape Nazi persecution. He studied foreign policy at Harvard University and quickly developed a reputation as an expert on foreign affairs. He had studied European diplomacy in the nineteenth century and was an admirer of statesmen such as the Austrian chancellor Metternich who was very successful by adopting a practical approach to international relations that has been termed 'realpolitik'.

SKILLS BUILDER

1 Assess the role of Nixon and Kissinger in the development of Détente.

2 To what extent was Détente a product of the domestic considerations of the superpowers rather than a response to the fear of nuclear conflict?

3 How significant were economic realities in pushing both sides towards Détente?

Source B

7.2 Henry Kissinger during the early 1970s

Kissinger, with the support of Nixon, is said to have supported the views of the 'realist' school of diplomacy, pursuing realpolitik in his own foreign policy. This involved down-playing ideological differences and seizing opportunities available to secure national interests.

His main achievements were:

- developing Détente with the USSR
- establishing a rapprochement with China
- securing an end to the US war in Vietnam.

His approach was at odds with traditional American views of the USSR, and critics accused him of being soft on communism and abandoning those people living under communism.

Source C

The war in Indochina was the culmination of the disappointment of a decade that had opened with the clarion call of a resurgent idealism and ended with assassinations, racial and social discord, and radicalised politics. The collapse of these high aspirations shattered American self-confidence.

From Henry Kissinger, *The White House Years*
(published in 1979)

Source D

If we were perceived to block détente, we would lose the support of our West European allies, who would then speed up their own contacts with the East, with no co-ordinated strategy; they would be too weak to resist simultaneous domestic and Soviet pressures. We found ourselves in the paradoxical position that we would have to take a leadership role in East–West relations if we wanted to hold the Alliance together and establish some ground rules for East–West contacts.

From Henry Kissinger, *The White House Years*
(published in 1979)

SKILLS BUILDER

1 Explain what is meant by the term 'realpolitik'.

2 Using Sources C and D, discuss the ways in which Kissinger can be considered to have pursued realpolitik in his foreign policy.

What role did economic realities play in superpower relations during the 1970s?

1 The impact of the oil crisis of 1973

The potential of oil to be used as a weapon in international affairs was to be illustrated starkly by the oil crisis of 1973. Its impact was to change the dynamics of superpower relations by initially weakening both the USA and the USSR. The challenges posed by the crisis led to different reactions that ended up widening the gap between them.

Both superpowers had an insatiable demand for oil that increasingly could not be met by their own domestic production. As a result they were to be drawn into the affairs of the Middle East, a region that might otherwise have played little role in the Cold War. In 1973 Egypt and Syria, supported by other Arab nations, invaded Israel in what became known as the Yom Kippur War. In October the delegates at a meeting of OPEC (The Organisation of Petroleum Exporting Countries) decided to raise the price of their oil by seventy per cent as a way of putting pressure on those countries like the US and Britain who supported Israel. As the historian David Stone has commented, this action transformed oil 'from a strategic commodity into a strategic weapon'. OPEC also decided to cut supplies to those countries that supported Israel in the War, leading to a full oil embargo on supplies to the United States later in October. These moves sent shock waves through the Western world. There was a widespread mood of panic and uncertainty which manifested itself in panic buying of many goods, leading to a further rise in prices. In Britain the government struggled with an economic situation made worse by a wave of industrial strikes which merely exacerbated shortages. The historian Daniel Yergin has described it as follows:

'The prospect, at best, was gloomy: lost economic growth, recession and inflation. The international monetary system could be subject to extreme dislocation. Moreover, the United States, the world's fore-most superpower and the underwriter of the international order had now been thrown on the defensive, humiliated, by a handful of small nations.'

The American government became worried that these strains would lead to social unrest within her allies in Western Europe, fracturing the alliance that had become part of the Cold War system. These worries resulted in a series of actions aimed at resolving the situation. In February 1974 the US government called the Washington Energy Conference which produced agreement on harmonising Western energy policies. This had the effect of reducing the worse of the crisis. The US then abolished capital controls which allowed US banks and financial institutions to take advantage of surplus dollars now available. Thus, the impact of the oil crisis was to strengthen the large institutions of US capitalism in the long term.

There were also benefits to oil companies in the West who were able to profit from the general rise in the price of oil and the related processes of refining and marketing of oil. Much of the increased amount of money flowing into the Middle East tended to find its way back into the West through investments, contracts for arms, airports and schools as well as an increased demand for fine wines and casinos. Thus, Arab wealth became a stimulus for the global economy.

In the immediate term the economic strains and uncertainties caused by the oil crisis were to increase the pressure towards achieving Détente with the USSR. The enormous costs of US military spending, aimed at achieving supremacy over the USSR, seemed unsustainable given the economic situation produced by the oil crisis. Negotiation and compromise seemed an attractive solution. Yet, although many western leaders felt more vulnerable due to the weaknesses highlighted by the oil crisis, ultimately the western world showed itself to be resilient and even strengthened by it. For the Soviet Union the impact was to be different.

2 Soviet economic problems in the 1970s

Despite its enormous potential in terms of resources the Soviet Union failed to fully exploit its economic wealth and by the 1970s was to face serious problems with its economy. The opening up of vast oil reserves in Siberia was to cushion the USSR from some of the negative impact of the oil crisis. It also gained from the increase in the world price for oil through the extra hard currency to be gained by exporting some of its own oil. But these benefits could not disguise the long term economic problems facing the USSR.

- Much of the resources of the USSR were diverted into propping up the military-industrial sector to ensure that it did not fall too far behind in the arms race. 30 million people out of a working population of 100 million were engaged in this sector.

- Vast sums of money were used to support its communist allies: Vietnam received over $1 billion a year; Cuba $4 billion each year. $4 billion worth of arms was sent to African satellite states such as Ethiopia and Angola. Nearly three quarters of the hard currency earned by the Soviet Union went on aid and arms to its allies.

- The rigid planning required of the communist system used in the USSR made its economy inflexible and easily disrupted by unforeseen events. The oil crisis of 1973 was one such event.

- Soviet technology was falling behind that of the West, despite attempts to spread new techniques under the Ninth Five-Year Plan of 1971–75.

- The over-emphasis on heavy industry meant that consumer goods were constantly in short supply. This had a negative impact of attempts to raise living standards.

- Agriculture was very inefficient compared to the rest of Europe and the USSR struggled to produce enough grain to feed its own population. In the 1970s the USSR relied on nearly $15 billion worth of imported grain, some of which came from the US.

Overall, the Soviet economy was inefficient, plagued by shortages, poor quality and inflexibility. In the 1950s the annual growth rate for the Soviet economy averaged 7%, in the 1960s it was 5%, and by the 1970s it had fallen to 3%. The economy of the USSR gave the impression of a vast beast gradually grinding to a halt. This made Détente an attractive option to the Soviet leadership. Agreements could be reached on reducing the strains caused by the arms race so that resources could be released for sectors that were more likely to improve the lives of those living under communism.

SKILLS BUILDER

Explain how economic realities of the 1970s promoted Détente.

What was achieved by the SALT treaties?

The SALT treaties mark the highpoint of Détente as well as illustrating the difficulties of reaching a meaningful agreement. The talks that led to SALT were long drawn out affairs, starting in 1968 and not bearing fruit until SALT I was agreed in 1972. Further negotiations produced a SALT II treaty in 1979 but by this time relations between the USA and the USSR had deteriorated and the agreement was never ratified.

SALT (Strategic Arms Limitation Talks) I

Early attempts to negotiate treaties on nuclear weapons, such as the Rapacki Plan of 1957, had failed. The Cuban Missile Crisis had shocked the superpowers into reaching some agreements to limit the use of nuclear arms. The Nuclear Test Ban Treaty (1963) and the Non-Proliferation Treaty of 1968 provided the first moves in this direction and this continued under Détente. In 1968 the Soviet Union had been ready to talk about limiting strategic nuclear weapons, but the Soviet intervention in Czechoslovakia to replace a liberalising government with one more in line with Soviet expectations had caused outrage in America, and the talks were delayed. When they resumed later in the year the talks were to prove slow and protracted. It was not until 1972 that both sides were ready to sign a final agreement.

The key issues over which the two superpowers found agreement difficult were how arms should be limited and which types of weapon should be included in the arrangements. The differing weapons systems of each side made comparison difficult. There was also a tendency to focus on setting limits for existing weapons, as the USA in particular recognised that the arms race would only be won through the development of newer technologies.

Nixon's visit to China in February 1972 caused concern in the USSR. The Soviet government was anxious to avoid an agreement between its two superpower rivals, and this worked to exert pressure on the USSR to sign the SALT I treaty in May. Agreement was reached in three areas: first, on the use of anti-ballistic missile (ABM) systems; second, on offensive nuclear weapons; and third, on a code of conduct.

- *The ABM Treaty* reduced the tension caused by the destabilising impact of defensive systems. With ABM systems in place the ability to retaliate if hit by a nuclear missile was uncertain and therefore encouraged each side to strike first. By limiting ABM systems to two sites, the deterrence provided by the knowledge that the other side could strike back was maintained. Thus the USA and the USSR agreed to a limit of two ABM systems each, one for their capital city and one to protect their nuclear missiles.

- *The Interim Treaty* on offensive nuclear missiles was much barer. Both sides could only agree to an interim agreement, which would expire in 1977. Limits were placed on the number of ICBMs (intercontinental ballistic missiles) and SLBMs (submarine-launched ballistic missiles) of 1,618 and 740 respectively for the USSR and 1,054 and 740 for the USA. The Soviet Union was allowed more of these missiles because in other areas, such as strategic bombers, the USA had a large lead. This was an important step towards limiting nuclear arms, but it omitted new technological developments such as the MIRVs (multiple independent re-entry vehicles), which carried multiple warheads on a single missile. Each side could replace old, obsolete missiles with new ones within these limits, and the technological advantage lay with the USA.

- *The Basic Principles Agreement* laid down some important rules for the conduct of nuclear warfare. The Seabed Pact of 1971 had banned the placing of warheads on the seabed. The Basic Principles Agreement extended the guidelines to be used by both sides to minimise the development of nuclear war. The USA and the USSR pledged 'to do their utmost to avoid military confrontations' and to 'exercise restraint' in international relations. Trade was to be encouraged between the two superpowers. This agreement marked a shift from the atmosphere of confrontation even if the principles were little more than a statement of intent.

A lot remained unsettled in the SALT treaties. The treaty on offensive weapons was, in particular, thin on substance. Each superpower retained enough nuclear weapons to destroy the other several times over. Nonetheless, they indicated a desire to move away from dangerous confrontation. US–Soviet trade increased as a result of the agreements, but it tended to be limited to grain supplies for the USSR. In the 1970s the Soviet Union came to rely on American grain to make up shortfalls in domestic production. The American government recognised that trade could be used as a lever to extract further concessions from the Soviets.

Despite its limitations SALT marked the high point in the spirit of cooperation engendered by Détente. Nixon visited Moscow in 1972 and 1974; Brezhnev visited Washington in 1973. These visits were symbolic of the new accord between the superpowers.

SALT II

SALT I had been an interim agreement and there had been an intention to negotiate further, but SALT II ran into difficulties. An agreement for SALT II was outlined at the Vladivostok Summit in 1974 between Brezhnev and the new US President, Gerald Ford. It set equal limits for missile launchers and strategic bombers but, importantly, left out cruise missiles where the USA had a significant lead. The proposed treaty was too much for right-wing American senators, who saw all arms control as a mechanism for allowing the USSR to catch up with superior American weaponry. Led by Senator Henry Jackson, the right was too powerful for Ford to ignore. When Jimmy Carter became President in 1977, he attempted to renegotiate the SALT II treaty in order to reduce the number of Soviet missiles. It was not until 1979 that precise figures could be agreed, and the SALT II treaty was signed by Carter and Brezhnev at a summit in Vienna in June. The treaty was highly technical and detailed, and according to the historian Ralph Levering it was not understood by 'the average senator'. One wonders whether Brezhnev, the now aged and increasingly senile Soviet leader, understood the treaty. In America public opinion as well as the opinion of senators was turning against arms control agreements with a Soviet government considered to be untrustworthy. Increasing conflict in the Third World, especially in Iran, Angola and Afghanistan, led to the Senate's rejection of SALT II in 1980.

SKILLS BUILDER

1 Make a list of the successes and a list of the limitations of the SALT treaties.

2 Who gained the most out of these treaties: the USA or the USSR?

3 Make an overall judgement: did SALT achieve anything other than to highlight the difficulty of bringing about arms limitation?

Did the Helsinki Accords of 1975 achieve anything meaningful?

The other key agreement of Détente was the Helsinki Accords of 1975. Thirty-three states from both NATO and the Warsaw Pact attended the Conference on Security and Cooperation in Europe in Helsinki, which began in 1973 and produced an agreement in 1975.

At the conference the Warsaw Pact countries wished to secure US recognition of the European borders established after the Second World War. The USA saw this as an opportunity to gain concessions from the Soviet government in return. The result was an agreement covering three 'baskets'.

Basket one declared the borders of European countries to be 'inviolable'. This meant they could not be altered by force. By signing this agreement, all countries accepted the existence of the Soviet Bloc in Eastern Europe, including East Germany. This received a lot of criticism from the right wing in the USA, but it merely acknowledged the reality of the situation that had existed since the late 1940s.

Basket two covered trade and technology exchanges to promote links across the Iron Curtain.

Basket three contained the concessions the West had tried to gain from the USSR. It included an agreement to respect human rights, such as freedom of speech and freedom of movement across Europe. For the communist states of Eastern Europe to accept this was seen by the West as a significant step forward. The West hoped this would undermine the hold of the repressive Soviet regimes in Eastern Europe. Organisations were established to monitor governments and their actions against these principles.

7.3 *Time* magazine, June 1979, showing Carter and Brezhnev at the Vienna Summit

Investigation: attitudes to the Helsinki Accords

Source E

The effects, to put it mildly were unpredictable. It is unlikely, for example, that the aging leaders in Moscow followed the fortunes of a scruffy, anti-establishment Czechoslovak rock band, the 'Plastic People of the Universe', formed in the aftermath of the invasion of that country in 1968. Given to performing in secret while dodging the police, the band ran out of luck in 1976, when its members were arrested. Their trial provoked several hundred intellectuals into signing, on January 1 1977, a manifesto called Charter 77, which politely but pointedly called upon the Czech government to respect the free expression provisions of the Helsinki Final Act, which with Brezhnev's approval it had signed.

From John Lewis Gaddis, *The Cold War* (published in 2005)

Source F

Ronald Reagan gives his view of the Helsinki Accords. Reagan was a right wing Republican who was standing against President Ford for the Republican nomination in the presidential election of 1976

At Kissinger's insistence, President Ford flew halfway round the world to sign an agreement at Helsinki which placed the American seal of approval on the Soviet Empire in Eastern Europe.

As quoted in Martin Walker, *The Cold War* (published in 1994)

SKILLS BUILDER

1 What interpreta-
tions do Sources
E and F offer of
the impact of the
Helsinki Accords
on dissident
groups?

2 How far would
you agree with
Reagan's
assessment of the
Helsinki Accords
given in Source F?

To what extent was Détente a successful method of conducting Cold War conflict?

In order to assess fully the achievements of Détente it is necessary to look at the developments that occurred at the level of inter-European cooperation. There was more to Détente than SALT and the Helsinki Accords.

European Détente

Brandt's policy of Ostpolitik abandoned the Hallstein Doctrine, which had been designed to snub East Germany by refusing to recognise its existence as a separate state. Brandt preferred to establish links between East and West in Europe as a method of reducing barriers. The results of this policy included several treaties that involved a recognition of reality rather than an abandonment of the principle of reunification. Treaties with Poland and the Soviet Union accepted the Oder–Neisse Line as the border between Germany and Poland as well as recognising the border between East and West Germany. An agreement by the USA, the USSR, France and Britain in 1971 gave a legal basis to access routes from West Germany to West Berlin and provided some security for the Western half of the city. The most significant agreement was, however, the Basic Treaty of 1972, in which West Germany accepted the existence of East Germany as a separate state and agreed to increase trade links between the two countries. Ostpolitik played a major role in reducing tension in Europe and contributing to Détente, but it was at a cost. West Germany had to accept Soviet control over Eastern Europe and in doing so gave it a legal recognition and a reinforcement of the division of Cold War Europe.

An assessment of Détente

After the dangers of potential war and nuclear destruction that had been evident in the confrontations of the late 1950s and early 1960s, Détente was a welcome trend to those who wished to reduce the sources of tension. The achievement of Détente was that superpower relations had been stabilised and risks minimised. Yet on substantial matters little was achieved: armaments had increased during this period, and many of the signed agreements were ignored, as in the case of the Helsinki Agreement, or withdrawn later, as in the case of SALT II. In addition, Détente did not reduce tension in all areas of international relations. Europe was more stable, but tension between the USSR and China remained high. Conflict continued and even intensified in the Third World. Events in Iran, Angola and Afghanistan showed that the USSR had extended its influence during the period of Détente. This situation was to produce a lot of the renewed suspicion and mistrust that led to the breakdown in Détente in 1979. The collapse of Détente showed its fragility.

Interpretations of Détente

Not surprisingly, historians have been divided in their assessment of Détente. To many historians on the American left and in the centre of the political spectrum Détente has been viewed as a positive step in the reduction of tension, and its stabilising effect on international relations has been highlighted. This was the standard view during the early and mid-1970s when there was optimism that Détente would limit the arms race and reduce the threat of nuclear war. Not surprisingly, the autobiographies of Nixon and Kissinger, the main architects of Détente on the American side, give a positive view of their own attempts to bring about Détente.

The view that Détente was a beneficial policy for both sides has gained support from some post-revisionist historians, such as Gordon Craig and Alexander George in *Force and Statecraft* (1983). They present a more detached analysis that emphasises Détente as a method pursued by both superpowers in order to create a less dangerous and more useful international relationship.

Yet by the end of the 1970s disillusionment with Détente on the American right resulted in a more critical approach that has tended to dominate historical thinking. Détente was seen as a sign of weakness and of being 'soft' on communism by allowing the Soviet Union to continue the Cold War. This view was developed by many American writers in the 1980s who supported Ronald Reagan's massive rearmament programme.

The collapse of the Soviet Union in the late 1980s was viewed as a result of the pressure of matching the USA in the arms race, and therefore Détente can be seen as prolonging the Cold War rather than a realistic step towards bringing about its end. An evaluation of Détente from the perspective of the right has been presented forcefully by Richard Pipes in *US-Soviet Relations in the Era of Détente* (1981). This view does, however, tend to neglect the advantages Détente held for the USA during a time when American self-confidence was under serious threat.

Source G

The rise of détente can be understood as a process of adaptation in the international system and on the part of its leading members. The cold war system based upon a stark bipolarity . . . began to give way to a more complex order, with other power centres developing to challenge the superpowers, at least on some issues. Furthermore, the development and deployment of large numbers of nuclear weapons by both sides made it imperative that the superpowers managed their competition in a way which prevented them from degenerating into hostilities. Détente represented a new stage in the process of adapting to these changes in the distribution of power and instruments of influence.

From M. Bowker and P. Williams, *Superpower Détente:*
A Reappraisal (published in 1988)

Source H

(Détente) did not free the world from crises, but the new spirit of cooperation did seem to limit their frequency and severity: Soviet-American relations in the late 1960s and the early 1970s were much less volatile than during the first two decades of the Cold War . . . This was a major accomplishment, because with the superpowers now commanding roughly the same capacity to destroy one another, the risks of escalation were even greater than they had once been. Détente was turning a dangerous situation into a predictable system, with a view to ensuring survivability for the post-1945 geopolitical settlement, as well as for humanity at large.

Humanity, however, was not particularly grateful . . . Détente sought to freeze the Cold War in place. Its purpose was not to end that conflict – the differences dividing its antagonists were still too deep for that – but rather to establish rules by which it would be conducted . . . What that meant was that certain nations would continue to live under authoritarian rule while others could elect and remove governments by constitutional means.

It became harder to defend the idea that a few powerful leaders at the top, however praiseworthy their intentions, still had the right to determine how everyone else lived. Despite its elite origins, détente required support from below, and this proved difficult to obtain. It was like a building constructed on quicksand: the foundations were beginning to crack, even as the builders were finishing off the façade.

From John Lewis Gaddis, *The Cold War* (published in 2005)

Source I

An outline of Soviet actions in the developing world after 1975

Evil or improving, the USSR remained an empire on the march. The fall of the Portuguese Empire in Africa saw an unprecedented expansion of Soviet influence there, where revolutionary governments in Angola and Mozambique were armed and supported by the Soviet Union . . . In the Horn of Africa the Soviets switched their backing from Somalia to the revolutionaries who had toppled Haile Selassie in Ethiopia . . . The fall of Saigon offered the Soviet navy a new port in the Pacific.

From Martin Walker, *The Cold War* (published in 1994)

SKILLS BUILDER

1 Why have historians differed in their views of Détente?

2 What do Sources G and H suggest were the positive achievements of Détente?

3 Using Source I, and your own knowledge, explain why Détente can be seen as a fragile system.

4 How does Source I suggest Détente was a weakness for American policy?

5 As a foreign policy adviser to the US government in 1978:
EITHER
a) write a report outlining the arguments for continuing the policy of Détente with the USSR.
Mention:
- the achievements in arms control
- The Helsinki Accords
- the use of rapprochement with China to weaken the USSR
- developments in Europe that aid Détente
OR
b) write a report outlining the arguments for abandoning Détente in favour of adopting a more aggressive stance against the USSR.
Mention:
- the limited success of SALT
- the failure of the USSR to apply the Helsinki Accords
- continued Soviet support for liberation movements in the developing world
- the use of an arms race to weaken the USSR and its economy.

Investigation: the rise of the neo-conservatives in the USA and their impact on decision-making

The Democrat Jimmy Carter was elected US President in 1976. He hoped to use respect for human rights as the basis of his foreign policy with the USSR in order to reduce tension. Unfortunately, Carter lacked experience in foreign affairs and failed to realise that a constant emphasis on human rights as they were defined in the West was likely to increase rather than reduce tension.

It was during Carter's presidency that critics of Détente became more vocal. The view that Détente had been too soft on communism gained strength as America regained its confidence after the debacle of the Vietnam War. More strident anti-communist views were associated with the rise of neo-conservatives who recommended a more forceful approach to the Soviet Union. This approach would involve resuming the arms race in order to make the superior technological and economic resources of the USA count against the USSR.

Although the rise of the neo-conservatives has been associated with the presidency of Ronald Reagan, which succeeded that of Carter, their growing influence was evident before 1980 and was to have an impact on foreign policy decision-making under Carter.

Carter has often been portrayed as a 'dove', soft on communism, but this view is misleading. It is more accurate to see Carter's foreign policy as a struggle between two opposing positions: on the one hand, the approach of using negotiation to lessen tension, as advocated by Cyrus Vance the Secretary of State; and on the other, a more hard-line approach advocated by **Zbigniew Brzezinski**, Carter's National Security Adviser. Because of his inexperience Carter was heavily reliant on the advice of these two men, and perhaps the central weakness of his foreign policy was the inconsistency in choosing which advice to follow.

Source J

Brzezinski outlines his concerns on Soviet actions in Ethiopia, 1978

Soviet leaders may be acting merely in response to an apparent opportunity, or the Soviet action may be part of a wide strategic design. In either case, the Soviets probably calculate, as previously in Angola, they can later adopt a more conciliatory attitude and that the USA will simply again adjust to the consolidation of Soviet presence in yet another African country.

From Z. Brzezinski, *Power and Principle* (published in 1983)

Biography

Zbigniew Brzezinski (b.1928)

A Pole by birth who became an American citizen. His background led him to be highly suspicious of Soviet policy. He gained a reputation as an academic who specialised in foreign affairs, was appointed as National Security Adviser in 1977 and became influential in the formulation of Carter's foreign policy. He clashed with Cyrus Vance, the Secretary of State, who favoured a continuation of negotiation under Détente. Brzezinski articulated the views of the neo-conservatives, which called for a show of American strength that would make the Soviet leadership change its policy.

Source K

Particularly troubling for Moscow was the emergence of Brzezinski to a dominant position . . .

In March 1979 Brzezinski initiated a review of Soviet military activities in Cuba. Almost inevitably, this increased attention resulted in increased indicators of Soviet activity. New information was combined with existing files in ways which suggested that the Soviet Union had introduced a 'combat brigade' into Cuba. In fact, all that was new was the designation: the Soviet troop presence in Cuba went back to 1962, and in 1963 'the Kennedy administration had agreed to a Soviet brigade remaining in the location where the combat brigade was discovered in 1979 . . . Both Vance and President Carter announced that they were not satisfied with the status quo in Cuba.

From M. Bowker and P. Williams, *Superpower Détente: A Reappraisal* (published in 1988)

Source L

Brezhnev addresses the Soviet Politburo in June 1978

A serious deterioration and exacerbation of the situation has occurred. And the primary source of this deterioration is the growing aggression of the foreign policy of the Carter government, the continually more sharply anti-Soviet character of the statements of the President himself and of his closest colleagues – in the first instance those of Brzezinski.

Carter is intent upon struggling for his election to a new term as President of the United States under the banner of anti-Soviet policy and a return to the 'cold war'.

As quoted in Jussi Hanhimaki and Odd Arne Westad, *The Cold War*, published by OUP (2003)

Source M

Maintaining good relations with the Soviet Union was more difficult, partly because while Secretary of State Cyrus Vance supported Détente, Carter's national security adviser, Zbigniew Brzezinski, was strongly anti-Russian. Carter fluctuated between the two approaches yet seemed blissfully unaware of his ambivalence. He could complain about Soviet human rights violations one day, and praise the idea of a new arms limitation agreement the next.

From John Garraty, *The American Nation*, published by HarperCollins (1991)

SKILLS BUILDER

1   What does Source J reveal about the views of Brzezinski?

2   How far do Sources K–M support the view that Brzezinski was able to influence the direction of foreign policy during Carter's presidency?

3   What were the likely consequences of the growing influence of the neo-conservatives for Détente?

Why did Détente come to an end in 1979?

An explanation of the reasons for the development of the Second Cold War usually takes the Soviet invasion of Afghanistan in 1979 as its starting point. The invasion led to widespread condemnation of the USSR and was perceived in the West as evidence of the continuation of the expansionist tendencies of the USSR. Yet the relaxation in superpower relations that had taken place under Détente in the 1970s had already broken down before Brezhnev ordered Soviet tanks into Afghanistan. The development of renewed superpower hostility can be seen as early as 1976 during the US presidency of Jimmy Carter.

- Increasing Soviet influence in the Third World, especially in Angola, Mozambique and Ethiopia, was used by the neo-conservatives as evidence of continuing Soviet ambitions to spread communism. Carter increased supplies of arms to anti-communist groups and governments in the developing world, such as in El Salvador and Nicaragua, to prevent the spread of Soviet influence.

- Soviet violations of the human rights agreements reached in Helsinki troubled the conscience of many in the American government.

- Carter reached agreement with Brezhnev on the SALT II Treaty in June 1979, but he was under growing pressure from critics at home. Opposition to SALT II was mounting in the US Senate and it was looking increasingly unlikely that the agreement would be ratified even before the invasion of Afghanistan.

- By the late 1970s negotiation with the Soviet Union had become increasingly difficult because of Brezhnev's failing health. He had suffered a series of heart attacks since the mid-1970s, and by 1979 he could only function with the aid of drugs. Without firm guidance at the top, Soviet decision-making became very slow and painstaking. It was easier for the Americans to adopt the hard-line approach recommended by Brzezinski.

- In November 1979 Islamic militants occupied the US Embassy in Teheran and held the US diplomats and their families hostage. Carter refused to negotiate with the militants. The hostages were not released until January 1981, and the whole incident seemed to symbolise America's growing impotence in world affairs. The American right called for a firmer stance against aggressors.

Thus, Détente was already breaking down. Opposition to continued Détente also existed within the USSR. Discussions within the Politburo revealed growing unease with the criticism directed at the USSR over the Helsinki Accords. Pressure was also being exerted by the Soviet military to resume increases in arms in order to support Soviet policy in the developing world and to strengthen its position against the USA.

The Soviet invasion of Afghanistan of December 1979 was the last straw for Carter, who condemned the action and withdrew the SALT II Treaty from the Senate. There seemed little chance that Détente would now serve the needs of the USA.

Case study: the impact of the Soviet invasion of Afghanistan, 1979

The events in Afghanistan marked the end of any further negotiation between the superpowers. Détente was dead. Lying south of the USSR, Afghanistan was viewed by Moscow as an important buffer state. The situation in this region had been complicated by events in nearby Iran. In January 1979 the US-supported Shah of Iran had been removed by a popular uprising led by the Muslim Fundamentalist Ayatollah Khomeini. The new government of Iran was violently anti-American, and US oil assets were under threat. But the Iranian Revolution also posed a threat to Soviet interests. The spread of Muslim Fundamentalism through the region was a danger to the stability of the Soviet Union. The Central Asian republics of the USSR, which bordered Afghanistan, contained Muslim populations whose integration into the Soviet Union had always been superficial. Thus, the importance of maintaining a pro-Soviet government in Afghanistan was given added significance.

The chaotic situation in Afghanistan was in danger of escalating when, in the summer of 1979, the CIA threatened to support an anti-Soviet faction. The prospect of US involvement in Afghanistan was too much for Brezhnev who decided to send in Soviet troops to install a pro-Soviet government. The new Afghan regime remained unpopular, and the Soviet Union had to send over 100,000 troops to ensure its survival. Afghanistan was to become a Soviet Vietnam: a war that they could not win against an enemy located in the countryside and using guerrilla tactics.

The consequences of the invasion for US–Soviet relations:

- President Carter was unwilling to let the USSR get away with another intervention in the affairs of a foreign country so easily. His language in condemning the Soviet action was more strident than had been expected.

- As well as withdrawing the SALT II Treaty from the Senate, he cut off trade contacts between the USA and the USSR and encouraged a Western boycott of the Moscow Olympics in 1980.

- Carter decided to increase arms spending. Presidential Directive 59 authorised an increase in the American nuclear arsenal: the era of arms limitation was at an end.

- The more strident approach of the USA was encouraged and supported by Margaret Thatcher, the new staunchly anti-communist Prime Minister of Britain.

- The Soviet invasion of Afghanistan had been one of the key issues of the US presidential election of 1980. Carter's perceived weakness at dealing with yet another example of Soviet aggression was one of the deciding factors that resulted in defeat for Carter and victory for Ronald Reagan. A staunch right winger, Reagan's hatred of communism was well known. He saw the USSR and communism in unsophisticated moral terms as the embodiment of evil. Reagan, a former B-movie actor, had difficulty handling complex political ideas, but he was highly skilled at articulating a vision of world affairs that was shared by a large section of the American population. Reagan's forthright hostility towards the USSR symbolised the change in American public opinion caused by the growing disillusionment with Détente.

Source N

With the Soviet intervention in Afghanistan the US response was swift. Combined with the turmoil in Iran and the expansion of Soviet influence in the Horn of Africa (Ethiopia), the USA was gravely concerned that Soviet designs were not confined to Afghanistan but the wider region and the Persian Gulf in particular . . . The USA returned to a much more militarised and confrontational approach to dealing with the USSR and laid the foundations for the intensification of militarised containment (and rollback) under the instinctive critic of détente, Ronald Reagan, who assumed the presidency the following year.

From Richard Saull, *The Cold War and After* (published in 2007)

7.4 Soviet forces fighting in Afghanistan

Source P

The mood in Washington in the mid-1970s was extraordinary . . . Both Republicans and Democrats began to campaign with increasing stridency for an end to détente and a new robustness. The coalition was the more effective in that it crossed party lines.

American trade unions had been a loyal member of the Cold War coalition because of their support for the principle of free trade unions for Eastern Europe . . . Jewish groups . . . because of their anti-Communism developed a powerful campaign around the cause of Soviet Jews and their right to emigrate. Human rights was a cause everyone in the Democratic Party could agree upon.

There was no single Soviet action which turned the scale, more than an accumulation of worries which widened the suspicion of détente to many other than the predictable hawks.

From Martin Walker, *The Cold War* (published in 1994)

Source O

There were many reasons why US–Soviet détente collapsed as a political project. Some historians argue that the failure was inherent in the project itself: because Americans and Soviets had different notions of what détente consisted of, conflict would replace co-operation sooner or later. Others claim that super-power détente was less a policy of co-operation than an attempt, partially through covert means, to outmanoeuvre the other side and gain advantages in an ongoing Cold War.

From Jussi Hanhimaki and Odd Arne Westad, *The Cold War* (published in 2003)

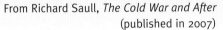

SKILLS BUILDER

1 What does Source N tell us about the role the Soviet invasion of Afghanistan played in the collapse of Détente?

2 What do Sources O and P suggest were the causes of the collapse of Détente?

3 Using the sources, and your own knowledge, discuss the view that the Soviet invasion of Afghanistan was more a symbol than a cause of the collapse of Détente.

Unit summary

What have you learned in this unit?

It had suited the USA and the USSR to use Détente as a method of conducting the Cold War in the 1970s because both thought it would work to their own interests in the ongoing battle for superpower influence. Thus, Détente was not the beginning to an end of the Cold War but rather its continuation through other means. Brezhnev described Détente as 'the way to create more favourable conditions for peaceful socialist and communist construction'. Détente worked to the advantage of the USSR in allowing it to continue to compete in the arms race. It also proved useful to the USA when it was feeling the strains of the Vietnam War. When it no longer served its purpose, Détente fell apart.

It is perhaps too easy to condemn the policy of Détente as achieving very little, even prolonging the Cold War by stabilising relations and providing legitimacy for the Soviet Union to continue to impose its authoritarianism on large parts of the world. Yet within the context in which it developed Détente had much to commend it to the leaders of both sides.

What skills have you used in this unit?

You have been able to practise your skills in argument and making a judgement based on reasoning. The exercises in this unit have given you opportunities to reach your own substantiated judgements on causes and achievements of Détente as well as considering the role of the factors that brought about its collapse.

Exam style questions

This unit covers one of the issues that are assessed in Section A of the examination. The questions in this section will require you to analyse a historical issue or problem and come to a reasoned judgement. Questions could ask you to consider a statement or interpretation. For example:

- How advantageous was the policy of Détente to the management of the USA's Cold War diplomacy with the USSR in the 1970s?

RESEARCH TOPIC

The role of economic realities in superpower relations during the 1970s: the impact of the oil crisis of 1973

While working through this unit you will have been made aware of the role that economic realities had in promoting Détente.

Your task is to research the following aspects of the oil crisis of 1973:

- What were the causes of the crisis?
- What was the impact of the crisis on the West?
- What impact did it have on the Communist Bloc?
- How might the oil crisis have strengthened Détente?
- How might it have weakened the process towards Détente?
- What do the actions of OPEC in 1973 tell us about their attitude towards the superpowers?

8 How did the Cold War come to an end in the 1980s?

What is this unit about?

This unit focuses on the events of the 1980s which produced an end to the Cold War that had developed between the superpowers. It will give you an understanding of the ways in which both US and Soviet foreign policy changed in the 1980s. Ronald Reagan and Mikhail Gorbachev were to change the landscape of the Cold War, and their policies were to have consequences that produced an end to the USSR and to the Cold War itself. In this unit you will:

- examine the philosophy that lay behind the Reagan Doctrine
- find out what factors weakened the hold of the USSR over Eastern Europe
- discover the ways in which Mikhail Gorbachev changed Soviet Foreign policy in the 1980s
- investigate the significance of the fall of the Berlin Wall
- understand the sequence of events that was involved in the ending of the Cold War.

Key questions

- How and why did US and Soviet foreign policy change in the 1980s?
- How did the Cold War come to an end?

Timeline

1981
January   Ronald Reagan becomes US President
                Wave of strikes in Poland organised by the illegal trade union, Solidarity

1982
November   Brezhnev dies, Andropov becomes new Soviet leader

1983
March   Strategic Defense Initiative announced by USA

September   South Korean airliner KAL 007 shot down by Soviet air force

October   US troops invade Grenada to depose left-wing government

1984
February   Andropov dies; Chernenko becomes new Soviet leader

1985
March   Chernenko dies; Mikhail Gorbachev becomes new Soviet leader

November   Geneva Summit between Reagan and Gorbachev

1986	
October	Reykjavik Summit between Gorbachev and Reagan
1987	
December	Washington Summit. The INF (Intermediate Nuclear Forces) agreement is signed
1988	
May–June	Moscow Summit between Reagan and Gorbachev
December	Gorbachev announces major reductions in Soviet forces in Europe
1989	
September	First free elections in Poland; Solidarity wins and forms government
	Hungary opens border with Austria
November	Fall of the Berlin Wall, dismantled by crowds
	Collapse of communist regimes in Czechoslovakia and Bulgaria
December	Malta Summit between Gorbachev and Bush
	Collapse of communist regime in Romania
1990	
October	Reunification of Germany
1991	
August–December	Baltic States and Ukraine vote for independence from USSR
December	USSR formally dissolved

Introduction

In November 1982 the tensions of the Cold War seemed permanent.
If anything, those tensions had increased. The USA had been under the
presidency of Ronald Reagan since January 1981. His more strident
attitude towards the USSR had done little to improve international
relations. Leonid Brezhnev, the aged Soviet leader, had died and had been
replaced by Yuri Andropov. To dissidents living within the USSR, the hope
for change diminished as Andropov clamped down on any action that
might undermine the power of the Communist Party. It was a period when
fear predominated over hope. Yet despite this seemingly permanent
situation international relations were soon to be transformed, resulting in
the end of the Cold War and the collapse of communist regimes throughout
Eastern Europe, including the USSR. In the words of one Soviet dissident,
'History is like a mole. It burrows away unnoticed.' By 1989 a lot of the
'burrowing' was to finally produce results in a sequence of events that saw
hope triumph over fear.

How did Ronald Reagan view the USSR and in what ways was the Reagan Doctrine designed to bring about an end to the Cold War?

One of the factors identified as having a vital role in helping to undermine the Soviet Union has been the role of Ronald Reagan and his policy of militarised counter-revolution.

The start of Reagan's presidency in January 1981 is often heralded by the American right as marking a fundamental shift in US foreign policy towards a more aggressive, strident anti-communist approach. This shift had, however, been one of the trends during the presidency of Jimmy Carter (1977–80), as witnessed by the growing influence of Brzezinski as National Security Adviser. Nonetheless, under Reagan this approach was to be clearly in the ascendant. Reagan's anti-communist rhetoric indicated that he was ready to pursue the so-called Second Cold War with vigour on all fronts.

*The key features of Reagan's **militarised counter-revolution***

1 Increasing nuclear arms

Reagan was able to convince the US Congress to increase military spending on a scale that was unprecedented in American history. The actions of the Soviet Union in Afghanistan and the decision of the USSR to deploy the more accurate SS-20 nuclear missiles in Eastern Europe were used to bolster Reagan's argument. Defence spending was increased by 13 per cent in 1982 and over 8 per cent in each of the following two years. New methods of deploying nuclear missiles were developed, including the Stealth bomber and Trident submarines. Central to this arms build-up was the Strategic Defense Initiative, announced in 1983. SDI, or 'Star Wars' as it was better known, was the development of anti-ballistic missile systems in space. It was a system that would require vast sums of money and resources to develop, and in order for the USSR to keep pace with this they would face bankruptcy. The aim of this arms programme was to regain American military supremacy against the Soviet Union to the extent that they would not be able to continue the Cold War. Thus, supremacy in arms would allow the USA to gain more meaningful concessions from the Soviet leadership through a position of strength.

> **Definition**
>
> **Militarised counter-revolution**
>
> Those policies implemented by Ronald Reagan as US President to undermine the forces of communism. It was a much more aggressive strategy than Carter's policy towards the USSR and included extensive re-arming and providing covert help to those fighting against communist forces or governments.

2 The Reagan Doctrine

Reagan took decisive measures to try to halt the growth of Soviet influence in the Third World by developing what became known as the Reagan Doctrine. This term was given to the policy of sending assistance to anti-communist insurgents as well as anti-communist governments. In Nicaragua, the doctrine was used to supply military aid to the Contras, a right wing guerrilla group fighting against the communist government of the Sandinistas. In El Salvador the USA supported an unpopular right-wing government facing a growing popular revolt by the left.

8.1 Ronald Reagan

The Reagan Doctrine was designed to weaken the Soviet Union 'at the edges' and to supply counter-revolutionaries with enough support to ensure that Soviet support for revolutionary regimes would entail a much greater military, political and economic cost. The advantage for the USA was that, in reality, it led to very few instances of direct use of American troops. One example was the invasion of the Caribbean island of Grenada in 1983 when US forces deposed its left-wing government. More often, however, covert methods were used. The strategy entailed a massive rise in CIA operations in support of counter-revolutionary groups. In Afghanistan Stinger anti-aircraft missiles were supplied to the mujahedeen who were fighting the Soviet forces. In Europe radio broadcasts such as 'Voice of America' and 'Radio Free Europe' were used to encourage those living in Eastern Europe to protest against their communist governments. When the Polish government banned the independent trade union Solidarity, US loans and bank credits to the country were cut off and tariffs placed on Polish exports to the USA.

The actions undertaken under the Reagan Doctrine were not always popular in the wider world and were often counter-productive. US actions in Grenada, Nicaragua and El Salvador showed the apparent willingness of the USA to interfere in the internal politics of other countries. These actions were often criticised by liberals and socialists in the West as a threat to the freedom of people to choose their own destiny. This sentiment was also supported by governments in the developing world who were left-wing. Some of the regimes supported by the USA, such as the Marcos government in the Philippines, may have been anti-communist but they had a very poor record on human rights. Nonetheless, the Reagan Doctrine showed the Soviet Union that the USA was prepared to take forceful action against communism and its expansion.

What made Reagan's approach more effective was the support he received from Margaret Thatcher, the British Prime Minister. The two leaders shared a view of the USSR as the 'evil empire'. Thatcher's harsh attacks on communism led the Soviet press to dub her the 'Iron Lady'. She established a highly effective working relationship with Reagan, and her agreement to have US nuclear missiles based in Britain was of vital importance in putting pressure on the Soviet Union. Without European bases the threat to use nuclear missiles against Soviet territory would have been much diminished.

Source A

Reagan's view of the Soviet Union

During the late seventies, I felt our country had begun to abdicate its historical role as the spiritual leader of the Free World and its foremost defender of democracy. Some of our resolve was gone, along with a part of our commitment to uphold the values we cherished. Predictably, the Soviets had interpreted our hesitation and reluctance to act and had tried to exploit it to the fullest, moving ahead with their agenda to achieve a Communist-dominated world . . . The Soviets were more dedicated than ever to achieving Lenin's goal of a communist world . . . I deliberately set out to say some frank things about the Russians, to let them know there were some new fellows in Washington.

From Ronald Reagan, *Ronald Reagan: An American Life* (published in 1990)

Source B

Reagan makes a private joke at a radio station but forgets the microphone is on

My fellow Americans, I am pleased to tell you I just signed legislation which outlaws Russia forever. The bombing begins in five minutes.

Ronald Reagan, spoken during a radio microphone test (1984)

Source C

How do you tell a communist? Well, it's someone who reads Marx and Lenin. And how do you tell an anti-Communist? It's someone who understands Marx and Lenin.

Ronald Reagan, speech on communism delivered to US business people (September 1987)

Source D

In Britain's Margaret Thatcher, Reagan found a triple ally. First, she shared his ideological belief in free markets and an unleashed capitalism as the path to prosperity, and as the buttress against socialism at home and abroad . . .

Second, Mrs Thatcher's strategic loyalty was rooted in the Atlantic Alliance, and in the old 1940s' perception of the world which held that the ambitions of the Soviet Union would only be kept in check by a full revival of the old special relationship between London and Washington.

Third, Mrs Thatcher shared one key aspect of the Reagan temperament, a belief in the importance of morale in public life. He spoke of the American spirit, she of the national soul. She too talked in terms of spiritual revival, of the bracing effects of freedom on both the economic and above all the moral fibre of the nation.

From Martin Walker, *The Cold War* (published in 1994)

Source E

From the minutes of a meeting of the Soviet Politburo, 31 May 1983. The meeting is chaired by the Soviet leader, Yuri Andropov. Also speaking is Mikhail Gorbachev from the reforming wing of the Communist Party

Andropov: The actions of President Reagan, the bearer and creator of all anti-Soviet ideas, creator of all untrue insinuations regarding our country and the other countries of the Socialist community, deserve very critical and harsh reactions from our side . . . The imperialist countries of the West want to put together a bloc against the USSR.

It is true that we shouldn't scare people with war. But in our propaganda we should show more clearly and fully the military actions of the Reagan administration and its supporters in Western Europe, which in other words means disclosing the full scale aggressive character of the enemy. We need that, so we could use facts to mobilise the Soviet people for the fulfilment of social and economic plans for development of the country. We can't, comrades, in this situation forget the defence needs of our country.

Gorbachev: You said it right, Yuri Vladimirovich [Andropov], that the time now is calling us to increase our actions, taking the necessary steps to develop a broad programme of counter-measures against the aggressive plans of the Western countries.

As quoted in Jussi Hanhimaki and Odd Arne Westad, *The Cold War* (published in 2003)

SKILLS BUILDER

1 How do Sources A–C illustrate Ronald Reagan's views of the USSR?

2 Use your own knowledge to explain how Reagan's foreign policy was designed to bring the Cold War to an end?

3 Using Source D, and your own knowledge, assess the importance of Margaret Thatcher in reinforcing Reagan's foreign policy.

4 To what extent does Source E show Reagan's foreign policy towards the USSR to be successful?

Investigation: Star Wars

Source F

SDI was a technologically ambitious and extremely expensive plan to develop a nationwide ballistic-missile defense system that would deploy weapons in outer space to destroy enemy missiles in flight. Popularly known as Star Wars, SDI threatened to violate several US–Soviet agreements, including the Limited Test Ban Treaty of 1963, the Outer Space Treaty of 1967, and the ABM Treaty of 1972 . . .

Many analysts regarded SDI as a dangerous and destabilising attack on mutual deterrence, which was based on each side's ability to retaliate against a nuclear attack . . . [they] also warned that SDI would accelerate the arms race.

In addition to re-establishing US military superiority, which they believed had been lost during Détente, and regaining the initiative in the Cold War, Reagan and some of his supporters later claimed that they planned to use an arms race, especially in fields where the United States was technologically superior, to place great strain on the Soviet economy. Although the US build-up, and especially SDI, alarmed the Soviets, there is no evidence that Soviet defense spending, which had begun to level off in the mid-1970s, increased significantly in response to Reagan's initiatives.

From David Painter, *The Cold War: An International History* (published in 1999)

Source G

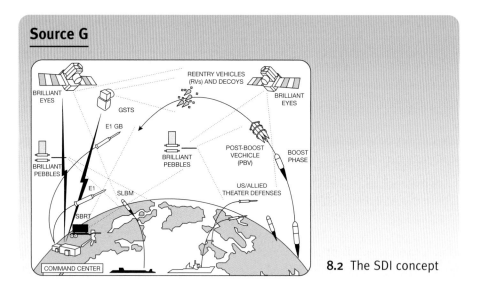

8.2 The SDI concept

Source H

Reagan was deeply committed to SDI: it was not a bargaining chip to give up in future negotiations. That did not preclude, though, using it as a bluff: the United States was years, even decades, away from developing a missile defense capability, but Reagan's speech [of 8 March 1983] persuaded the increasingly frightened Soviet leaders that this was about to happen. Having exhausted their country by catching up in offensive missiles, they suddenly faced a new round of competition demanding skills they had no hope of mastering. And the Americans seemed not even to have broken into a sweat.

The reaction, in the Kremlin, approached panic.

From John Lewis Gaddis, *The Cold War* (published in 2005)

SKILLS BUILDER

1 Using Sources F and G, outline the key features of the SDI.

2 Using Source F and your own knowledge, explain how the US government hoped to use SDI against the Soviet Union.

3 To what extent do Sources F and H support the view that SDI weakened the USSR?

What factors weakened the hold of the Soviet Union over Eastern Europe in the early 1980s?

By the early 1980s considerable pressure was building within many of the states of Eastern Europe that threatened the hold of the Soviet Union over the region. Internal weaknesses became more pronounced, and public opinion in Eastern Europe was more critical of their regimes.

There were many reasons for popular discontent against the governments of Eastern Europe.

Economic issues

By the 1980s there were clear signs that the socialist economies of Eastern Europe were unable to deliver the degree of prosperity evident in the West. The state-controlled industries of Eastern Europe were inefficient both in terms of quality and quantity of goods produced. Since the 1950s most of the countries of Eastern Europe had concentrated their resources on heavy industry rather than consumer goods, and as a result food, clothing and housing were in short supply and often inadequate. Industrial pollution was bad enough to have a serious impact on the health of the people of the region. Management had become a privileged group with little concern for innovation as long as their position in society was maintained. The increase in oil prices in the mid-1970s had made it difficult for governments to get credit for foreign exchange and investment. By the 1980s the technology used in the region was becoming rapidly out of date. The USSR was slow to develop new technologies, such as personal computers, robotics and video equipment. Eastern Europe had become reliant on Soviet technology and as a consequence also fell behind the West.

Living standards in Eastern Europe had long fallen behind those of the West, but by the 1980s the expectations of its population were different. On the borders of East Germany and Czechoslovakia West German television stations could be received, with images of life under capitalism. Western music, cinema and fashion also had some influence on the people of Eastern Europe. The mass consumer society of the West provided a sharp contrast to living standards in the East. Not only did Western-style capitalism seem more attractive but the failure of socialism to provide the living standards expected was evident to more and more of the citizens of Eastern Europe. A sense of impending economic crisis was helped by the slowdown in the rate of growth in industrial production. By 1985 all of the socialist economies of the Eastern Bloc had growth rates that were virtually negligible, including the more developed economies of East Germany and Czechoslovakia. The impression was given of a vast bureaucratic economic system grinding to an inevitable halt.

Calls for political reform

Criticisms of the regimes of Eastern Europe were not restricted to economic issues; there was often a conflict between those leaders who wished to maintain a hard line communist approach and others, including Communist Party members, who pressed for reform. The leaders of the Communist Parties of the Eastern Bloc were often portrayed in the West as uninspiring, mediocre men more interested in their personal power than the needs of their country. Although there is some truth in this view, it underestimates the conviction of some communist leaders who had suffered for their beliefs before 1945 and had, like Zhivkov, the Bulgarian leader, played an important role in resisting the German occupation during the Second World War. But by the 1980s the regimes of Eastern Europe were led by men who were increasingly out of touch with the needs of their country and had been in position long enough to enjoy the trappings of power. They were leaders who were reluctant to change a system that worked for them. Janos Kadar had been leader of Hungary since 1956, Gustav Husak had dominated Czechoslovak politics since 1968, Todor Zhivkov had led Bulgaria since 1956. With Communist Parties dominant and the use of a repressive police network, opposition in these countries was severely limited.

East Germany (the DDR or GDR) had a particularly effective system of surveillance. The **Stasi**, East Germany's secret police, kept files on 5.5 million East Germans through an elaborate system of informers. Over 600,000 people were employed directly by the Stasi with an additional 100,000 informers. When government files were opened after the country collapsed it was clear that husbands were informing on their wives who in turn were informing on their husbands. The leadership of **Erich Honecker** had little respect from his own people. The position of the DDR was unique in that the country was itself an artificial creation of the Cold War. Attempts to forge a sense of national unity through sporting achievements had produced lots of medals but also popular resentment at the privileges and pampering given to athletes by the government. Most East Germans adopted an attitude of resignation, making the most of life under a regime they had little choice but to accept. It was not exactly a ringing endorsement of the 'people's' republic but it was enough to keep the regime of Honecker relatively secure.

In Romania the leadership of **Nicolae Ceausescu** was firmly entrenched by the early 1980s despite his growing paranoia and megalomania.

Definition

Stasi

The East German secret police.

Biography

Erich Honecker (1912–94)

East German leader from 1971 to 1989. Honecker had been responsible for implementing the building of the Berlin Wall in 1961. He was a hard-line communist and against reform. Popular protests forced him to resign as leader in 1989. Despite attempts to arrest him and put him on trial for abusing his power, Honecker was allowed to go into exile in the USSR.

Ceausescu's regime was one of the most repressive in Eastern Europe. His secret police, the **Securitate**, ruthlessly crushed any opposition. There was a very tight system of censorship, which involved the registration of all typewriters by their owners every year. Government propaganda was the only source of information for the vast majority of Romanians. As Ceausescu's hold on power grew, so did his ability to push through more extreme policies. In the mid-1980s he introduced a policy of 'systematisation', which involved the demolition of whole villages to be replaced by agro-industrial complexes. Ceausescu seems to have chosen villages for this policy on a whim, and the policy was very unpopular.

Although Ceausescu had been courted by the West because of his independent stance in foreign affairs, by 1985 he had alienated virtually the entire Romanian population, with the exception of the Securitate.

Thus the nature of the governments of Eastern Europe and their policies produced discontent and latent opposition. The events in Hungary in 1956 and Czechoslovakia in 1968 showed that the USSR would not permit the governments of Eastern Europe to go too far in placating the wishes of those who wished to reform. This pattern was again followed in 1981 when discontent in Poland threatened to get out of hand.

Attempts by the Polish government to increase prices as a response to economic problems were met with unrest. This unrest was strengthened by the emergence of Solidarity, an illegal, independent trade union in 1980–81. Those seeking to challenge communist rule received encouragement from the visit to Poland of Pope John Paul II, a Pole himself by birth, in June 1979. His message of 'Do not be afraid' gave consternation to the Polish government and courage to Solidarity. **Lech Walesa** (see page 166), the leader of Solidarity and a devout Catholic, was popular enough to wield considerable influence over the industrial workers of the shipyards in Gdansk. Edward Gierek, the Polish Communist Party leader, decided to negotiate with Solidarity, leading to an agreement that gave Solidarity legal status as an independent trade union. The USSR was concerned that this concession would encourage groups elsewhere within the Soviet Bloc and threaten the hold of communism over Eastern Europe. As the USSR undertook army manoeuvres along its border with Poland, the message was clear. **General Jaruzelski** (see page 166), the new Polish leader, declared martial law on 12 December 1981 and used the army to quell the unrest. Although greatly despised by many Poles for his action, Jaruzelski realised that the alternative was a Soviet invasion to restore order. This option would have probably led to greater bloodshed. As it was, the actions of the Polish army restored order. Solidarity was abolished, but millions of trade unionists continued to work together underground. They hoped that circumstances would become more conducive to change in the future.

The prospects of change were limited at the beginning of the 1980s, but it was not long before external factors were transformed to give encouragement to those forces seeking reform.

Biography

Nicolae Ceausescu (1918–89)

Communist leader of Romania from 1965 to 1989. He pursued policies of forced industrial development and heavy repression. He developed a cult of personality to extreme proportions and by the mid-1980s most of his support was manufactured rather than real. His rule was not merely ruthless but also vindictive. In 1989 popular unrest led to the overthrow of Ceausescu. He and his wife were executed on Christmas Day 1989.

Definition

Securitate

The Romanian secret police under Ceausescu.

Biography

General Wojtech Jaruzelski (b.1923)

A general in the Polish army who served as Minister of Defence before becoming Prime Minister in 1981. His appointment was made in order to use the army to suppress unrest organised by the trade union Solidarity. He remained Prime Minister until 1989 when the Communist Party lost power after free elections. He served as President from 1989 until 1990 when he was succeeded by Lech Walesa, the leader of Solidarity.

Biography

Lech Walesa (b.1943)

An electrician at the Lenin shipyard in the Polish port of Gdansk. Walesa was active in the trade union movement and in 1980 founded the independent trade union Solidarity. It soon had a membership of 10 million, and in 1980 the communist government in Poland gave in to pressure and gave it legal status. When General Jaruzelski became Polish leader in 1981 Solidarity was banned. Walesa and his supporters continued to operate underground until the government reopened negotiations in 1986 and agreed to legalise Solidarity again. When free elections were held in 1990 Walesa was elected President of Poland, a post he retained until 1995.

Source I

8.3 Pope John Paul II meeting crowds in Poland in 1979

SKILLS BUILDER

1 What were the main causes of popular discontent in Eastern Europe at the beginning of the 1980s?

2 Why would the Soviet Union find the scene shown in Source I embarrassing?

3 What do the events in Poland in 1981 tell us about the strength of the Soviet hold over Eastern Europe at this time?

4 In what circumstances might the Soviet hold over Eastern Europe be threatened?

Why was the Soviet leadership so ineffective in responding to international relations between 1980 and 1985?

The election of Ronald Reagan as American President in 1980 resulted in foreign policy changes. Soviet policy in the early 1980s, however, was grinding to a halt. No new initiative was possible from the Soviet leadership because of the nature of its leaders during this period. A succession of old and infirm leaders, sometimes referred to as a **gerontocracy**, resulted in inertia in decision-making. The increasingly aged and confused Brezhnev finally died in 1982. His physical incapacity had prevented any change in the direction of Soviet foreign policy. Brezhnev's successor was Yuri Andropov who, at 69 years old, was only seven years younger than Brezhnev. It seems likely that Andropov would have introduced policy initiatives – he attempted to start domestic reform – but he was an ill man. Being wired to a dialysis machine for most of his time as leader led to the joke that he was 'the most switched-on man in the Kremlin'. He succumbed to kidney failure in February 1984. His replacement was Konstantin Chernenko, a conservative who represented the desire of the majority of the Politburo to avoid reform. Chernenko was unable to have an impact on policy. He was dying of emphysema when he became leader and lived little more than a year in office. As Ronald Reagan commented, 'How am I supposed to get any place with the Russians, if they keep dying on me?'

An example of the impact inertia had on relations between the superpowers is shown by the response to the shooting down of the Korean airliner KAL 007 by Soviet fighters in 1983. The incident, which cost the lives of all 269 passengers, caused outrage in the West. The aircraft had been en route from Alaska to Seoul when it strayed into Soviet airspace. The Soviet authorities assumed it was a spy plane and shot it down. The Politburo showed its inflexibility during the furore that followed. Gromyko, the Soviet Foreign Minister, ignored questions from the West, and the Soviet military merely reiterated the standard line that any unidentified aircraft flying over Soviet airspace would be treated in exactly the same way. Old age and illness had rendered the Soviet leadership incapable of action. It was unable to respond to the incident in any meaningful manner. The 1970s had shown that the best method of improving relations was by face to face meetings between the US and Soviet leaders. The condition of Andropov had made this impossible during the KAL 007 affair. The incident marked a low point in the Second Cold War.

When Chernenko died in March 1985, after only 13 months as leader, the Soviet Politburo chose **Mikhail Gorbachev** as his successor. At 54, Gorbachev represented a younger generation. Change was now possible.

What was the impact of Mikhail Gorbachev's New Political Thinking?

As a committed communist Mikhail Gorbachev's aim on gaining the Soviet leadership in 1985 was to make the Soviet system more productive and

---

Definition

Gerontocracy

Rule by the elderly (geriatrics). The term is used to describe the Soviet leadership in the years 1980–85, i.e. the last years of Brezhnev, Andropov and Chernenko. At a time when the Soviet Union was in desperate need of reform it was led by a series of men whose physical condition prevented strong, decisive leadership.

Biography

Mikhail Gorbachev (b.1931)

Leader of the USSR from 1985 to 1991. Gorbachev represented a younger generation of Soviet politicians who believed socialism needed to be reformed. His policies aimed to make the Communist Party more responsive and to liberalise the economy. He encouraged those in Eastern Europe who wished to make similar reforms. In international relations Gorbachev recognised the inability of the USSR to compete with the USA in the arms race and called for limitations on nuclear weapons and an end to the Cold War. Gorbachev's political career came to an end with the collapse of the USSR in 1991.

responsive. 'We can't go on living like this,' he had told his wife in 1985. Gorbachev recognised that in order to achieve change within the USSR, military spending had to be reduced. This could only be done if arms limitation talks were reopened with the USA. Arms agreements would allow Gorbachev to reduce military spending without leaving the USSR exposed to attack, thereby avoiding opposition at home from the Soviet armed forces.

Gorbachev's new approach was strengthened by the emergence and promotion of like-minded individuals of ability. One such individual was Eduard Shevardnadze, who replaced the veteran Gromyko as Foreign Minister in 1985. Together Gorbachev and Shevardnadze launched a charm offensive on the West with their New Political Thinking. Margaret Thatcher had met Gorbachev in 1984 and declared, 'This is a man with whom I can do business.' To the new Soviet leadership confrontation between the superpowers was viewed as unproductive because it led to an escalation in arms and retaliatory measures that increased insecurity.

The Soviet experience in Afghanistan led to a re-evaluation of Soviet intervention in the affairs of other countries. The Afghan War had dragged on without a decisive result and highlighted the cost of making a commitment to supporting communist regimes. Over 15,000 Red Army soldiers were killed in the war, which cost $8 billion per annum. Supporting communist regimes in Cuba, Vietnam and Afghanistan, and even in Eastern Europe, had become a drain on Soviet resources. The USSR spent approximately $40 billion annually on propping up communist governments throughout the world. This money could be used to promote domestic reform. Instead of seeing foreign policy as an implement of class struggle against the forces of capitalism, Gorbachev focused on universal values of human rights to promote the interests of all peoples. Thus, Soviet foreign policy was 'normalised': it would no longer be an instrument for furthering the interests of world communism.

The impact of the New Political Thinking was felt quickly.

1 *November 1985: Geneva Summit.* Reagan and Gorbachev met. Little was decided at the summit, but it was important in establishing a personal rapport between the two leaders. Reagan hated everything the Soviets stood for but liked Gorbachev and the other Soviet representatives he met. Gorbachev soon realised Reagan found detail hard to grasp and ensured discussions focused on general principles. The Geneva Summit was important in laying the foundations for future negotiation in an atmosphere of cordiality.

2 *October 1986: Reykjavik Summit.* Gorbachev proposed phasing out nuclear weapons and offered a series of ever-increasing concessions that took the US leadership by surprise. The price of these concessions was to be the withdrawal of the American SDI (Strategic Defense Initiative) programme. At Reykjavik Reagan was not prepared to put SDI on the negotiating table and no agreement was reached.

3 *December 1987: Washington Summit*. At this summit the deadlock was broken. The INF (Intermediate Nuclear Forces) agreement was signed, leading to the scrapping of all intermediate-range ballistic missiles. It was the first time the superpowers had agreed to arms reduction rather than arms control.

4 *May–June 1988: Moscow Summit*. At this meeting Reagan and Gorbachev signed agreements on the more complex detail of the INF Treaty. In December Gorbachev met Reagan in New York and announced further cuts in Soviet arms. Gorbachev also met George Bush, who was due to become US President in January of the following year.

5 *December 1989: Malta Summit*. At this first full summit between Gorbachev and Bush the two leaders established a good working relationship. No new agreements were made but both leaders declared that the Cold War was over. Shevardnadze was able to announce that the superpowers had 'buried the Cold War at the bottom of the Mediterranean'.

Gorbachev's New Political Thinking was also to have a considerable impact on domestic reform within the USSR. He recognised that the whole Soviet system, which had become so entrenched, was performing badly. As a committed communist, Gorbachev made a genuine attempt to rejuvenate the Soviet Union. His policies included:

- *Perestroika*: a restructuring of the economy that involved a measure of private enterprise to promote production, efficiency and higher quality goods

- *Glasnost*: a policy of openness that encouraged the population to put forward new ideas and show initiative

- *Democratisation*: an attempt to get more people involved in the Communist Party and political debate.

The result of these policies was to lead to a more critical approach towards communism, and this encouraged reformers to push for further liberalisation. Within four years popular opinion in the Soviet Union had shifted towards an adoption of some aspects of the political and economic ideas of the West: others called for a wholesale rejection of communism. Gorbachev's policies encouraged reformers in the Communist Parties of Eastern Europe to press for similar measures. By 1988 'Gorby-mania' was sweeping much of Eastern Europe as those pushing for change called for Gorbachev's ideas to be implemented in their own country. In September 1989 a non-communist government was elected in Poland, and the floodgates were opened. What made these changes different to previous attempts to liberalise was the changed attitude of the USSR towards Eastern Europe. In 1985 Gorbachev had made it clear that he would not uphold the Brezhnev Doctrine.

The end of the Brezhnev Doctrine

The so-called Brezhnev Doctrine had been formulated after the Soviet intervention in Czechoslovakia in 1968. Brezhnev had made it clear that, 'Whenever internal and external forces hostile to Socialism try to reverse the development of a Socialist country towards the restoration of capitalism . . . this becomes the concern of all Socialist countries.' Gorbachev, however, decided that he would not uphold the right of the USSR to intervene in the affairs of other Socialist countries. Why?

1 There was growing disillusionment with the Soviet intervention in Afghanistan.

2 Supporting unpopular and inefficient regimes in the Soviet sphere was costly. Even before Gorbachev the Soviet leadership had decided not to use the Brezhnev Doctrine in 1981 when Poland was destabilised by unrest and the growth of Solidarity. Andropov informed the Politburo that using armed force 'will be very burdensome for us'. Yet the USSR did not make this known for fear of the consequences. It was able to convince the Poles that they would apply it so that its own government would clamp down on the unrest and restore order.

3 Gorbachev had a genuine belief that the way to rejuvenate socialism was by introducing a degree of liberalisation.

4 He believed the use of armed intervention was, in most cases, morally wrong. He refused to use force to keep the population under control.

5 Without the tensions generated by the Cold War, there was no longer a need for the USSR to exert control over Eastern Europe.

The end of the Brezhnev Doctrine meant the peoples of Eastern Europe could now choose their own governments. The consequences of this change were to be spectacular.

Source J

8.4 Mikhail Gorbachev meeting Margaret Thatcher

What were the consequences of the ending of the Brezhnev Doctrine?

Gorbachev's reforms in the USSR led to attempts by some governments in Eastern Europe to reform in response to the new Soviet lead and to an increase in the pressure for change from the public. This trend gathered momentum and the pace of events took many by surprise. Those governments that resisted these trends were to become quickly isolated.

The ending of the Brezhnev Doctrine posed a particular problem for those Eastern European leaders who wanted to resist reform. They could not rely on Soviet military intervention to buttress their regimes. Evidence that Gorbachev meant what he said came in 1989 when Hungary adopted a multi-party system and Polish elections returned a non-communist government. The USSR took no action; Gorbachev even offered his encouragement. The result was to be the collapse of communist regimes in Eastern Europe.

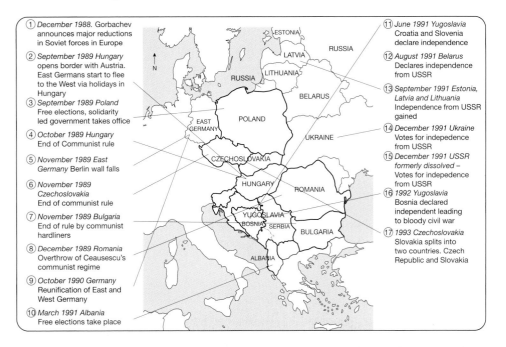

① *December 1988. Gorbachev announces major reductions in Soviet forces in Europe*

② *September 1989 Hungary opens border with Austria. East Germans start to flee to the West via holidays in Hungary*

③ *September 1989 Poland Free elections, solidarity led government takes office*

④ *October 1989 Hungary End of Communist rule*

⑤ *November 1989 East Germany Berlin wall falls*

⑥ *November 1989 Czechoslovakia End of communist rule*

⑦ *November 1989 Bulgaria End of rule by communist hardliners*

⑧ *December 1989 Romania Overthrow of Ceausescu's communist regime*

⑨ *October 1990 Germany Reunification of East and West Germany*

⑩ *March 1991 Albania Free elections take place*

⑪ *June 1991 Yugoslavia Croatia and Slovenia declare independence*

⑫ *August 1991 Belarus Declares independence from USSR*

⑬ *September 1991 Estonia, Latvia and Lithuania Independence from USSR gained*

⑭ *December 1991 Ukraine Votes for indepedence from USSR*

⑮ *December 1991 USSR formerly dissolved – Votes for indepedence from USSR*

⑯ *1992 Yugoslavia Bosnia declared independent leading to bloody civil war*

⑰ *1993 Czechoslovakia Slovakia splits into two countries. Czech Republic and Slovakia*

8.5 The collapse of communism in Eastern Europe

1 Poland

In Poland General Jaruzelski had suppressed the independent workers' organisation Solidarity in 1981 and declared a state of martial law. Despite the fact that Solidarity had to operate illegally, its support remained high due to a failure of the government to solve economic difficulties. This support included the endorsement of the Catholic Church, reinforced by further Papal visits in 1983 and 1987. By 1988 the government had lifted martial law and was prepared to introduce some reforms in response to Gorbachev's policies in the USSR. Solidarity was legalised, and, in an important step, the government decided to allow it and any other political groups to stand in elections. In the general elections of 1989 Solidarity was able to defeat the Communist Party by a landslide. In the face of this lack of support, the Communist Party collapsed as an organisation and by 1990 it held no position in the coalition government formed after the election of 1989. The USSR had done nothing to stop these events happening; indeed, Gorbachev seemed to approve of the Poles deciding their own future. The message was clear to all those pressing for change in other East European states: the USSR no longer had any wish to impose itself on the internal affairs of Eastern Europe.

2 The communist collapse spreads

a) Hungary

In Hungary the pressure for reform came from within the Communist Party, and in 1988 Kadar, the hard-line leader who had been in office since 1956, was sacked. The government, now dominated by reformers, decided to allow other political parties to contest elections. The decision of the Hungarian government to open its borders to the West in September 1989 was to seriously undermine East Germany. Thousands of East Germans on holiday in Hungary were now free to travel to the West. On one day alone, 11 September, 125,000 East Germans crossed into Austria and the freedom of the West. The exodus was highly embarrassing to the hard-line East German regime of Erich Honecker.

b) East Germany

The end of the Brezhnev Doctrine was of particular concern to the East German regime. The creation of East Germany had been a result of superpower tension and hostility after the Second World War. As an artificial country, East Germany was more reliant on Soviet support than the other regimes of the region. When Gorbachev visited East Berlin in October 1989 he became the focus of those East Germans who wanted to reform the country. Erich Honecker, the East German leader, refused to contemplate reform of any kind, and his intransigence led to his removal by other members of the East German Politburo. With mass demonstrations on the streets of East German cities, the pressure for reform became unstoppable. Earlier in the year the Chinese government had responded to demonstrations calling for reform by using force. The massacre of students in Tiananmen Square, Beijing, in June had illustrated one method of dealing with the situation. Egon Krenz, the new East German leader, refused to sanction widespread repression and amidst the growing chaos decided to open access across the Berlin Wall. On 9 November the Berlin Wall, the symbol of Cold War Europe, was dismantled by 'people power'.

c) Czechoslovakia

Also in November 1989 the communist regime in Czechoslovakia was forced to make concessions in response to public demonstrations calling for reforms. An organisation called Civic Forum emerged to coordinate the campaign to get rid of the communist government. Under severe public pressure the communists caved in, reforms were introduced and in 1989 Vaclav Havel, a leading playwright and opponent of communism, was elected President. Despite the scale of the demonstrations in Czechoslovakia, there was little violence. Thus, the events in Czechoslovakia were described as **the Velvet Revolution**. Another consequence of the collapse of communism was the separation of the country into the Czech and Slovak republics.

d) Romania

Throughout the turbulent events in Eastern Europe that took place in 1989, Romania seemed the most immune to calls for change. Ceausescu was confident enough to leave for a visit to Iran in early December after receiving 67 standing ovations at the Communist Party Congress. The crisis that brought about the collapse of Ceausescu started with the seemingly unimportant actions of Laszlo Tokes, a priest from Timisoara in northern Romania. Tokes had broken the law by allowing poetry to be recited in public during his services. The police ordered him to be transferred out of the area. When he refused, crowds demonstrated in support. Being close to the border with Hungary, the people of Timisoara had some awareness of events in the rest of Europe via Hungarian television and radio stations. Ceausescu sent the army in and opened fire on the demonstrators. Despite attempts to keep knowledge of the massacre of 71 people from the Romanian people, rumours spread quickly. When Ceausescu appeared at a rally in Bucharest, a week later, the crowds booed. The noise of the crowd could be clearly heard above the tape-recorded cheers that were usually played at rallies. This time the army was unwilling to take action against the demonstrators. Ceausescu and his wife were forced to flee Bucharest by helicopter but were later arrested by the army. The Securitate remained loyal to Ceausescu and continued to engage in fierce street fighting until the execution of Ceausescu and his wife, on Christmas Day. Communism, and the man who had completely discredited the system, had been overthrown in Romania.

The situation by the end of 1989

People power had played a large part in the dismantling of communism in Poland, Czechoslovakia, East Germany and Romania. In Hungary the hard-line leaders were dislodged by reformers within the ranks of the Communist Party. A similar pattern occurred in Bulgaria where Zhivkov was deposed by his own ministers. Across Eastern Europe the forces of communism had collapsed. It had been a swift and largely peaceful process, with the exceptions of Romania and Yugoslavia. In Yugoslavia the collapse of communism was accompanied by the disintegration of the country and a bloody civil war as Slovenia, Croatia and Bosnia attempted to break away from Serbian dominance.

The role of Gorbachev was vital in changing the context in which the communist regimes of Eastern Europe operated. The USSR was no longer willing to support unpopular communist governments, which were no longer crucial to its security and were in danger of becoming a political embarrassment and a financial drain.

Definition

The Velvet Revolution

A term used to describe the collapse of communism in Czechoslovakia in 1989. The communist regime was brought down by widespread demonstrations and protests that involved little violence. The revolution was therefore relatively smooth compared to the violence that marked the overthrow of communism in some of the other Eastern European states such as Romania.

SKILLS BUILDER

1 How far would you accept the view that the collapse of communist regimes in Eastern Europe was the result of 'people power'?

2 Explain why the collapse of communism in Eastern Europe was a key stage in the ending of the Cold War.

By the end of 1989 every pro-Soviet communist government in Eastern Europe had disintegrated.

To what extent was the fall of the Berlin Wall a result rather than a cause of the end of the Cold War?

One of the most symbolic acts of the Cold War was the dismantling of the Berlin Wall in November 1989. It was a symbol of the changes that had swept through Europe in 1989 and of the end of the divisions that had marked the essential character of the Cold War: the ideological split between capitalism and communism.

In 1989 the DDR was 40 years old and the East German leadership prepared to celebrate its anniversary. At what should have been an event to consolidate the country, the tide was turning against the regime.

Gorbachev's reforms had important consequences for the very existence of East Germany as a separate country. The DDR was a product of Cold War tensions, which had prevented the unification of Germany after the Second World War. Without these tensions there seemed little reason for Germany to remain divided. Honecker recognised that the DDR could still have a reason to exist if it remained socialist and therefore different from West Germany. Honecker was not in favour of any reform, but the East German population could not be isolated from events in the rest of Europe.

Large numbers of East Germans had fled from the country via Hungary during the summer of 1989, but even more serious for the government were those who were staying put. Gorbachev's reforms of communism in the USSR had encouraged many East Germans to push for change. Political groups such as New Forum were formed. When huge crowds of demonstrators gathered in the city of Leipzig they were shouting 'We are staying.' Honecker seemed paralysed by events. He was seriously ill for much of 1989, and in his absence government decision-making ground to a halt. It was in these circumstances that, in October, Gorbachev visited Berlin to attend a parade to mark the 40th anniversary of the DDR.

Source K

Guests – including Gorbachev himself – were arriving in East Berlin for the official commemorations on October 7–8, 1989. To the horrors of his hosts, the Soviet leader turned out to be even more popular than he had been in Beijing. During the parade down Unter den Linden the marchers abandoned the approved slogans and began shouting, 'Gorby, help us! Gorby stay here!' Watching from the reviewing platform next to an ashen Honecker, Gorbachev could see that 'these were specially chosen young people, strong and good-looking . . . The regime was doomed'.

Gorbachev tried to warn the East Germans of the need for drastic changes: 'One cannot be late, otherwise one will be punished by life.' But trying to get through to him [Honecker] was 'like throwing peas against a wall'.

From John Lewis Gaddis, *The Cold War* (published in 2005)

Honecker decided to meet further protest with police action. He was in favour of using the tactics followed by the Chinese government in June 1989, when students protesting in Tiananmen Square in Beijing had been massacred by the armed forces. Fortunately, the East German Politburo overruled Honecker and he was sacked as leader, to be replaced by Egon Krenz. Krenz was aware of the need for reform but as a former head of the Stasi his reputation did not endear him to the public. With popular pressure forcing events to run out of his control, on 9 November 1989 Krenz decided that the Berlin Wall should be opened.

Source L

As the newly appointed Central Committee Secretary for the Media, Schabowski was entrusted with announcing the new travel regulations. It soon became apparent under questioning that he was not familiar with the details. He had only received them from Krenz (the General Secretary) shortly before the conference and he had not been present when the document had come before the Politburo earlier in the day. What Schabowski did confirm was that applications for private visits . . . could take place via Checkpoints in Berlin with 'immediate effect'. He had, however, overlooked the reference in paragraph three of the document that the new dispensations should not be introduced until the following day.

Did this mean that the Berlin Wall was about to be lifted? Immediately after the end of the conference, a flustered Schabowski acknowledged that 'it is possible to go through the border' . . .

Thousands flocked through into West Berlin and joyous celebrations began on the Kurfurstendamm and the city's other streets. At the Brandenburg Gate young people climbed and danced on top of the Wall. Even if Krenz had not wished to open the Wall . . . the popular pressure was so intense that the final lifting of the Iron Curtain could not have been long delayed.

From Mike Dennis, *The Rise and Fall of the German Democratic Republic* (published in 2000)

Source M

8.6 Crowds dismantling the Berlin Wall, 1989

SKILLS BUILDER

1 What does Source K tell us about the influence of Gorbachev on the people and government of East Germany?

2 Using Sources L–N, explain the role of popular pressure in the fall of the Berlin Wall.

3 How far would you agree with the view that the fall of the Berlin Wall occurred by accident?

4 Was the fall of the Berlin Wall more a result than a cause of the ending of Cold War tensions?

Source N

A misunderstanding was born and it caused an avalanche. The false information spread like wild fire and the rumour became the truth. This was not how the SED* leadership had envisioned the new DDR travel law: masses of people storming the Berlin border-crossings in the middle of the cold night, cheering, celebrating, disrespectfully dancing on the Wall and turning the Anti-Fascist Protective Wall into a farce.

In November 1989, the DDR leadership no longer held the reins of History. Back on August 13 1961, the communist state leadership had taken its residents by surprise. Twenty eight years later, on the night on November 9, the population caught its rulers and their henchmen off guard . . . The citizens of the DDR had run out of patience. They were running the show now: on the streets, at demonstrations, in their demands for democracy and the right to travel.

From Christian Bahr, *Divided City* (published in 2008)

*the Socialist Unity Party, the name given to the Communist Party in East Germany

Events followed quickly from the fall of the Berlin Wall. The government of the DDR was shocked by the pace of events, and revelations of corruption weakened the Communist Party.

The future position of Germany, however, still remained in Gorbachev's hands. If Germany was to reunite, Gorbachev wanted it to be neutral. Helmut Kohl, the West German Chancellor, called for German membership of NATO, and bolstered by the election results in East Germany in March 1990, which saw a victory for parties favouring unification, Kohl was able to persuade Gorbachev to accept a reunified Germany with NATO membership. The Soviet Union also gave up any claim to occupy German soil. Gorbachev appears to have seen these developments as inevitable, but the close relationship between himself and Kohl certainly helped speed up the process.

On 3 October 1990 the process of German reunification was formally completed.

How did the Soviet Union come to an end?

By the summer of 1991 the superpowers had signed the START (Strategic Arms Reduction Talks) Treaty. Nuclear arsenals were to be rapidly reduced. The hostility between East and West was gone. Cold War conflict was a thing of the past, but for those who saw the Cold War as a conflict between the competing ideologies of the superpowers the fall of the USSR in 1991 was the final conclusion to a conflict that had threatened the world since 1945.

Feted as a hero abroad, Gorbachev had become increasingly unpopular at home. His policies for economic restructuring had failed to improve the living standards of the Soviet population. Food queues, strikes by workers in key industries who had not been paid wages for months, inflation and rising crime were all features of Soviet life by 1988. Most Soviet citizens felt that life had become more difficult since Gorbachev had attempted to breathe new life into the communist system. This situation was coupled with a growing freedom of the Soviet people to express their own opinion and the call for greater democracy. Glasnost had encouraged wider discussion of political issues in the USSR and was also responsible for the Soviet media presenting the public with information that the government would previously have withheld. Discoveries of mass graves in Belarussia and the Ukraine in 1988–89 were revealed as evidence of Stalin's terror. These revelations damaged the Communist Party, as did repeated cases of corruption by party officials. In 1985 Gorbachev had asked the Soviet people for new ideas on how to improve the communist system. By 1989 the answer was that a large section of the population wanted the entire system dismantled.

The forces for change unleashed by Gorbachev's policies ran out of his control. By the summer of 1991 the monopoly of the Communist Party was legally ended and reformers within the party were now free to establish the Democratic Reform Movement.

Gorbachev was caught between those liberals who wanted greater reform and conservatives who wished to uphold the communist system. As a result he gained the resentment of both sides. Conservative elements, supported by many from the upper echelons in the Soviet armed forces, feared a reduction in power that a break-up of the Soviet Union would bring. In August they staged a coup against Gorbachev, who was held under house arrest. The coup collapsed after three days in the face of huge popular protests led by the Russian president Boris Yeltsin.

When the coup collapsed Gorbachev was back in power but no longer in control of events. The rise of nationalist sentiment in the Soviet republics had led the Baltic States of Lithuania, Latvia and Estonia to declare their independence from Moscow by the end of 1990. In December 1991 the remaining republics dissolved the Soviet Union as a sovereign state. The Cold War was over.

Source O

Gorbachev and his allies did not anticipate the rapidity with which party rule in eastern Europe would collapse . . . The most critical decisions of 1987–89 were arguably those of Western leaders to withhold large-scale aid to perestroika, and those of hard-line east European leaders not to launch perestroikas of their own.

From Robert English, 'Ideas and the End of the Cold War', in S. Pons & F. Romero (ed.), *Reinterpreting the End of the Cold War*, published by Cass (2005)

Source P

The role of the nation's leader is crucial in explaining Soviet behaviour during the Cold War, both at the beginning of the conflict . . . and at its end, when Gorbachev's no less momentous choices made this confrontation irrelevant. Whilst it is impossible to imagine the end of the Cold War without the agency of such Western leaders as Ronald Reagan and George Bush, their contribution was secondary in importance. The contribution of Gorbachev, whatever his motives, was primary and absolutely crucial to events.

From Vladislav Zubok, 'Unwrapping an Enigma: Soviet Elites, Gorbachev and the End of the Cold War', in S. Pons & F. Romero (ed.), *Reinterpreting the End of the Cold War*, published by Cass (2005)

SKILLS BUILDER

Sources O, P and Q give different interpretations on the importance of Gorbachev in the end of the Cold War.

1 Summarize the view of each source in no more than 5 words.

2 What phrases or words would you quote from each source to illustrate their view?

3 State one way in which Source O agrees with Source P.

4 State one way in which Source P agrees with Source Q.

Source Q

... moments between 1970 and 1986 symbolised profound changes that, in the end, contributed to the end of the Cold War ...

Some scholars believe that moving the beginning of the end of the Cold War back by a decade would deny Mikhail Gorbachev and his Soviet leadership their place as the prime movers of change. This of course is not the case. Gorbachev's greatness consisted in recognizing many of these trends shortly after coming into office and having the courage to act in accordance.

From Odd Arne Westad, 'Beginnings of the End', in S. Pons & F. Romero (ed.), *Reinterpreting the End of the Cold War*, published by Cass (2005)

Unit summary

What have you learned in this unit?

In 1980 the division of Europe that had developed with the Cold War after 1945 looked to be entrenched. Yet despite this image of stability there were many forces that were to produce a dynamic situation. The election of more strident anti-communist leaders in the West, such as Ronald Reagan and Margaret Thatcher, was to result in the adoption of policies that aimed to undermine the Soviet Union by economic pressures. The response of the Soviet leadership was one of inertia until Mikhail Gorbachev became General Secretary in 1985. Gorbachev's New Political Thinking brought about change within the USSR and encouraged other communist regimes that had previously been tightly controlled from Moscow to reform and liberalise. This, coupled with the Soviet Union's renouncing of the Brezhnev Doctrine, made the hold of communism over Eastern Europe much more precarious. As popular pressure on communist regimes to reform increased, the governments of Eastern Europe found themselves isolated and bowed to the seemingly inevitable tide of events during 1989. The collapse of communism weakened the position of the Soviet Union and furthered calls by its own population for reform. Amidst this weakening position the USSR drew closer to meeting the demands for controlling arms that were presented by the USA. By 1989 the two superpowers had reached agreement on arms reduction and their relationship was cordial enough for their leaders to declare that the Cold War was now buried. The formal dissolution of the USSR in 1991 marked what many saw at the time as the final victory of the West in the Cold War.

What skills have you used in this unit?

You have been introduced to the key events that led to the ending of the Cold War between the superpowers during the 1980s. You will have understood the changes brought about by Ronald Reagan and Mikhail Gorbachev, the sequence of events that followed and how they played a part in the process of ending international tension between East and West. This understanding will be crucial for the work in the next unit where you will be studying the differing interpretations that have been put forward to explain why the Cold War came to an end.

Exam style questions

This unit has been concerned with setting the context for one of the key controversies of this topic, namely how and why historians' interpretations of the ending of the Cold War differ. It is, therefore, useful for you to reinforce your understanding of the content in readiness for the evaluation of interpretations regarding this controversy that you will consider in the next unit.

The questions centred on this controversy will appear in Section B of the exam. They will ask you to use two or three sources and your own knowledge to make a judgement on an interpretation. For example:

- How far do you agree with the view that the Cold War came to an end because popular protest in the Communist Bloc during the 1980s weakened the Soviet hold over Eastern Europe?

Exam tips

To answer this question you will need to examine the role played by popular protests in Eastern Europe in bringing an end to the Cold War and assess how it links to other factors such as Reagan's foreign policy, Gorbachev's New Political Thinking, the actions of Pope John Paul II and the pressure of economic weaknesses. Interpretations, such as the one given in this question, require you to use the sources you are presented with in the exam and your own knowledge. You will be examining examples of sources by historians in the next unit. To help you assess these by using your own knowledge, use the material you have covered in this unit to identify evidence that could be used to support the following:

- evidence that popular protests in Eastern Europe brought an end to the Cold War
- explain how this factor can be linked to:
  - Reagan's foreign policy
  - Gorbachev's New Political Thinking
  - the actions of Pope John Paul II
  - the pressure of economic weaknesses.

RESEARCH TOPIC

The end of communism?

A key factor in the ending of the Cold War was the collapse of communist regimes, often misleadingly termed 'the collapse of communism'.

Your task is to use your research skills to find out how many countries are still ruled by regimes who claim to be communist. Aim to find out:

- the key features of these regimes and their leaders
- why they have survived the collapse of the USSR
- why their survival has not produced a continuation of the Cold War
- what relevance, if any, communism has to addressing the problems of the modern world.

9 Why did the Cold War come to an end in the 1980s?

What is this unit about?

This unit focuses on the key historical controversy of why the Cold War came to an end in the 1980s. In the last unit you looked at the events that saw the ending of the Cold War; this unit builds upon that knowledge by examining the ways in which historians have debated the significance of the factors that produced these events. The relative importance of the causes that led to the end of the Cold War has been a highly contentious issue, and this unit seeks to help you explore the differing interpretations offered by historians. Ultimately, this will enable you to assess and evaluate these interpretations and present convincing arguments of your own. In this unit you will:

- consider the different interpretations of the role played by individuals in the process of ending the Cold War
- assess and evaluate historical interpretations of the causes of the ending of the Cold War
- come to your own reasoned judgement as to why the Cold War came to an end.

Key questions

- What roles were played by Reagan, Gorbachev, Thatcher and Pope John Paul II in the ending of the Cold War?
- How and why do interpretations of the end of the Cold War differ?

Introduction

Source A

9.1 A cartoon from 1989 showing Ronald Reagan on a horse riding into the sunset

Source B

9.2 Crowds gather outside the Communist Party Central Committee building in the centre of Bucharest, 22 December 1989

Discussion point

How do Sources A and B suggest different interpretations of the ending of the Cold War?

It is no surprise that events as momentous as the ending of the Cold War have produced a debate amongst historians over the relative importance of the factors involved. The Cold War is said to have ended with the fall of the Soviet Union, after which the unique ideological conflict between the two superpowers came to an end. Two key approaches have been adopted: one stresses the importance of external pressures on the USSR that helped undermine its control over Eastern Europe and its satellite states; the other focuses on the importance of internal factors that weakened the Soviet system from within.

Each approach, in itself, highlights a range of individual factors, events and key individuals. The purpose of this chapter is to examine these in detail in order to help a full evaluation to take place.

Problems facing historians examining the ending of the Cold War

For the historian a study of the ending of the Cold War poses particular challenges. The origin and development of the Cold War has attracted a lot of attention and a wide range of serious scholarly research. In contrast, the end of the Cold War, while attracting attention, has yet to be covered by a wide range of detailed analytical works. This has been largely the result of the problems the topic poses. These are as follows:

- Many records are unavailable due to matters of national security or because it is still in the interests of the various governments that exist today to restrict access to material that is considered sensitive.

- The events of this topic are relatively recent. The historian is still heavily influenced by the values and attitudes of societies that were moulded by the Cold War and affected intimately by its ending.

- History is often said to be written by the victors. In the case of the Cold War this has meant the Americans. In the case of the former Soviet Bloc it has been written by supporters of democracy and greater freedom and therefore by critics of the old communist system that collapsed with the ending of the Cold War.

- The ending of the Cold War coincided with the collapse of the Soviet Union, and this has left a lot of bitterness in Russia. It has made serious and detached reflection on the events very difficult.

- The impact of the process that brought about the end of the Cold War is difficult to assess due to the fact that only a limited amount of time has passed since the events themselves.

- Historians, political scientists and journalists have often been tempted to move on to examine the events that have followed the Cold War. The so-called war on terrorism, involving the wars in Iraq and Afghanistan of the 1990s and beyond, have drawn attention away from the ending of the Cold War itself. In fact, historians such as Denise Artaud have argued that the Cold War was merely one stage in a longer struggle between totalitarianism and democracy. Thus, the struggle continues and therefore the ending of the Cold War is of limited importance and interest.

All judgements by historians are provisional, and this is especially true of events that are recent, where the historian will struggle to detach him or herself from the issues and dilemmas they pose for the present day. This is not to invalidate the research conducted by historians on this topic but it should always be borne in mind.

The role of individuals in the end of the Cold War

In tracing the developments that led to an end to the Cold War, key individuals are identified as having an important role in determining the course of events. However, in order to assess fully their role it is necessary to consider the context within which these individuals operated. The following table highlights key information on these individuals.

SKILLS BUILDER

1 Using the information in the table, present a case for each of the key individuals, highlighting their role in the events that ended the Cold War.

2 After considering the role of each individual, rank them in order of their importance in bringing about the end of the Cold War.

3 Check your ranking against that of other students in your group. Do you agree? If not, why?

4 What factors could be highlighted as limiting the influence of all of these individuals?

Pope John Paul II

Basic details
Born 1920.
Real name Karol Wojtyla.
Son of a Polish army
lieutenant.
Entered the underground
seminary at Krakow in 1942.
Became bishop of Ombi in
1958, archbishop of Krakow in
1963.
Became Pope in 1978.
Died in 2005.
Character Inspiring and
courageous, willing to stand
up for beliefs. Sometimes
referred to as having 'heroic
faith'.
Ideas A conservative within
the Catholic Church on
theological matters. A believer
in the importance of human
rights and therefore critical of
communist regimes.
Policies Spoke out against
human rights abuses by the
governments of Eastern
Europe.
Influence His speeches
inspired those resisting
communism: 'Do not be
afraid! Open wide the doors
for Christ. To his saving power
open the boundaries of states,
economic and political
systems, the vast fields of
culture, civilisation and
development. Do not be
afraid!'
Visited Poland in 1979, 1983
and 1987. Each visit reinforced
support for Solidarity and
helped it gain concessions
from the government.
Lech Walesa, the leader of
Solidarity, was a devout
Catholic.
BUT
The Catholic Church was only
strong in Poland and the Baltic
States, and its impact was
limited in the other countries
of Eastern Europe.

Ronald Reagan

Basic details
Born 1911.
Son of a shoe store owner.
Developed a career as an
actor in Hollywood.
Joined the Republican Party
and then served as Governor
of California 1967–75.
President of the USA 1981–89.
Died 2004.
Character Astute rather than
intelligent. Could be very
strident when convinced he
was right. Generally
personable and able to
establish good relations with
other leaders.
Ideas Saw communism as
'evil', a view shaped by
traditional American values.
A staunch believer in free
market capitalism.
Policies Increasing nuclear
arms and developing SDI (Star
Wars) in an attempt to put
economic strain on the USSR.
Reagan Doctrine supplied aid
to groups against
communism.
Influence Caused difficulties
for the USSR in Afghanistan.
Put pressure on its
government to grant
concessions to Solidarity by
reducing financial aid to
Poland. SDI alarmed the
Soviet leadership.
BUT
May have delayed the end of
the Cold War by showing the
USSR that the USA was so
hostile.
Soviet leadership did not try
to engage in Reagan's arms
race.
SDI viewed by many as
unrealistic.
Sometimes supported regimes
that were not a good advert
for capitalism and freedom,
e.g. the Philippines.

Margaret Thatcher

Basic details
Born 1925.
Daughter of a grocer.
Secretary of State for
Education and Science
1970–74.
Leader of the Conservative
Party from 1975.
Prime Minister 1979–90.
Character Strident, forceful
approach to politics. Strong-
willed; dubbed the 'Iron Lady'
by the Soviet press.
Ideas Opposed to all forms
of communism. A strong
supporter of free market
economics.
Policies Allowed Ronald
Reagan to deploy Cruise
nuclear missiles to Britain in
the early 1980s.
Launched strong verbal attack
on Soviet invasion of
Afghanistan.
Influence Strong supporter of
Reagan and able to present
Reagan's perspective in
Europe.
Her decision to deploy US
missiles in Britain was crucial
to the success of Reagan's
policy.
Her strong personality gave
her considerable influence in
face-to-face meetings.
Established good relations
with Gorbachev in 1984.
BUT
Essentially a support player to
Reagan.

Mikhail Gorbachev

Basic details
Born 1931.
Son of an agricultural
mechanic.
Studied law at Moscow
University.
Became member of
Communist Party Central
Committee in 1971.
Youngest member of the
Politburo in 1980.
Elected General Secretary of
the Communist Party in 1985.
Soviet leader 1985–91.
Character Established good
relations with foreign leaders.
Affable and honest but prone
to hesitation and vacillation.
Ideas A communist, but he
believed that the Soviet
system needed to be reformed
to make it more responsive to
the needs of the Soviet
people.
Believed that the arms race
diverted too many resources
away from more productive
sectors of the economy.
Policies Glasnost: greater
freedom and openness.
Perestroika: restructuring of
the economy.
Democratisation: need to
make politics more
democratic.
Introduced moves to reduce
nuclear arms.
Ended the Brezhnev Doctrine.
Influence An inspiration to
those who wanted to reform
communism.
Ending of the Brezhnev
Doctrine weakened the hard-
line communist regimes in
Eastern Europe.
Prepared to make concessions
to reduce arms, which led to
progress towards the INF
Agreement, 1987.
His policies brought about the
collapse of the USSR.

How and why do interpretations of the end of the Cold War differ?

Discussion point

Who might Source C be referring to when it mentions 'other stories of . . . people, in different places and in different ways'?

Source C

The collapse of the Soviet Union ended the Cold War. But the story of why the Soviet Union collapsed is itself intimately linked to many of the other stories of how people, in different places and in different ways, broke out of the stranglehold that they felt the ideas and the practices of the Cold War represented.

From Jussi Hanhimaki and Odd Arne Westad, *The Cold War* (published in 2003)

Historians and political commentators have argued over the relative importance of the factors involved in bringing about an end to the Soviet Union. The Cold War came to an end primarily because of changes in the Soviet Union that affected its thinking. The Soviet leadership came to the conclusion that the Cold War was no longer worth fighting.

The causes of the end of the Cold War can be categorised as either external factors that bore down upon the USSR or as internal factors that undermined the Soviet system from within.

1 External factors

The role of changes in international relations are emphasised by the *Realist School* of historians.

a) The Triumphalists

The factor that has received a lot of attention from this school has been the role of Ronald Reagan and his policies towards the USSR. Politicians and historians from the American right credit the hard-line approach of the USA in the early 1980s as providing the pressure that caused the Soviet Empire to collapse. SDI was the final straw for a Soviet economy on the brink of bankruptcy. Unable to match the increased defence spending of the USA, the USSR had no choice but to call an end to the arms race and the Cold War. This view is presented by historians such as J. L. Gaddis, in *We Now Know* (1997), and by many writers who played a role in the formulation and implementation of Reagan's foreign policy, such as William Clark and Richard Allen.

Reagan's approach was strengthened by the support he received from Margaret Thatcher in Britain, which enabled him to deploy nuclear missiles in Europe as tangible evidence of his new anti-communist approach.

The importance of Reagan and Thatcher's hard-line stance against communism has been highlighted by historians of the Right who see firm action as the only effective way of standing up to aggression.

This approach has been reinforced by events of the late twentieth and early twenty-first century, such as the war in Iraq against the dictator Saddam Hussein. This perspective often comes from those who supported Reagan's stance against the Soviet Union and see it as the main factor that produced the US 'victory' in the Cold War. This school of historians has therefore tended to view the Cold War in a triumphalist manner, using the end of the Cold War as a justification for the foreign policies of Reagan.

The triumphalists include writers who served in the Reagan administration, such as Caspar Weinberger, Robert McFarlane, Richard Pipes and Richard Pearle. The historian Peter Schweitzer based a lot of his research on interviews with these individuals. It is perhaps of no surprise that in his book *Victory* (1994) Schweitzer argues that the end of the Cold War was due to Reagan turning away from the foreign policy of Détente towards a more aggressive stance against the USSR. In this respect Schweitzer has much in common with the views of other triumphalists who see Reagan's foreign policy as marking a change from that of previous US administrations.

b) Critics of the triumphalists

Critics of the triumphalists, such as George Shultz, argue that US pressure did little to help win the Cold War. A hard-line stance against communism had proved ineffective when applied in Vietnam in the 1960s. Thus there was no guarantee that a more aggressive approach to the USSR would bring about the desired change in Soviet policy. Nonetheless, they do see aspects of US foreign policy as effective. The fact that both Reagan and Bush made serious attempts to engage with Gorbachev in a dialogue that aimed to reduce international tension produced results that led to an ending of the Cold War.

c) Interpretations of Gorbachev's role

One of the key divisions between the views of the triumphalists and their critics has been on the role of Gorbachev. The triumphalists emphasise that it was difficult to trust Gorbachev because of his aims. They argue that Gorbachev's reforms were designed to strengthen the USSR by revitalising its economy and providing clear political leadership. This would allow the USSR to retain its place as a superpower with global interests and influence in ways that were wider and more effective than the old method of imposition through military means.

The critics of the triumphalists argue that Gorbachev's change in intentions and attitude to working with the West was the key factor that reduced mistrust and fear, and therefore international tension, between the superpowers. To some historians and commentators Gorbachev is the hero who brought about the end of the Cold War. These writers sympathised with Gorbachev's New Political Thinking. Raymond Garthoff, in his book *The Great Transition: American-Soviet Relations and the End of the Cold War* (1994), argues that the end of the Cold War was due to Gorbachev's New

Political Thinking and the concessions he was prepared to offer to the USA. As Archie Brown has argued in *The Gorbachev Factor* (1996), if Reagan had listened to the more conservative elements in his administration, he would not have taken the opportunities offered by Gorbachev but continued a policy based on mistrust and fear.

Russian historians and commentators are divided along lines that parallel those in the West when assessing the role of Gorbachev. Many veterans of the Gorbachev administration and former members of the Soviet secret police, the KGB, claim that the USA won because of pressure exerted on the USSR through subversive activities, often organised by the CIA. Due to this pressure Gorbachev gave in and 'surrendered' to the West. These views are still deeply held in Russia by nationalists who claim that the goal of the USA was not to end the Cold War but to destroy the Soviet Union and then weaken Russia. Sergei Akhromeyev and Georgi Kornienko have presented these views in *With the Eyes of a Marshall and a Diplomat: A Critical View of Foreign Policy of the USSR Before and After 1985* (1992).

The foreign policies of Gorbachev have been defended by Gorbachev himself and key members of his administration, such as Anatoly Chernyaev. They see the end of the Cold War as a separate event to the collapse of the Soviet Union. They highlight the importance of New Political Thinking as an alternative to the conduct of superpower relations based on fear and confrontation. Although these studies have come from individuals who played a part in the events themselves, they are often based on impressive use of evidence.

d) The role of Pope John Paul II

Another individual who is highlighted as having a significant impact on the Soviet system is Pope John Paul II. His speeches gave encouragement to those living under communist rule to stand up for human rights. The fact that John Paul II was Polish gave him considerable influence over the predominantly Catholic population of his home country. This influence has been highlighted by biographers of the Pope, such as Jonathan Kwitny in *Man of the Century: the Life and Times of Pope John Paul II*. Yet the role of the Catholic Church in leading opposition to the communist regimes of Eastern Europe can be overstated. Catholicism was strong in Poland, but elsewhere in Eastern Europe Protestantism or the Orthodox Church had more followers. Much of the opposition had no affiliation to any religion.

2 Internal factors

Domestic changes within the Soviet system have been highlighted by the *Ideational School*. The views of those on the right who see Reagan's role as key have been challenged by historians who point to the fact that Soviet leaders had already come to the conclusion that superpower rivalry was counterproductive before the arms programme of Reagan. Soviet scientists did not consider SDI to be a realistic policy – rather, something in the realm of science fiction. In the debates and discussions that went on among Soviet policy-makers – reflected in records of Politburo and Central Committee meetings that have become public – there is hardly mention of – let alone emphasis on – a race to catch up with Reagan's new weapons. A top general who proposed such an effort was fired for it in 1984.

The Soviets had a long-standing problem of over-committing resources to the military, a problem that burdened the United States as well. The Afghan commitment had been an enormous drain even in the days before Reagan. Thus Reagan's arms programme created little additional pressure. According to M. Bowker, in *Russian Foreign Policy and the End of the Cold War* (1997), Reagan's policies may have delayed the end of the Cold War by giving conservative elements within the Soviet leadership a better case for continuing the conflict by highlighting the hostility of the enemy.

Thus another school of historians has developed that focuses on internal factors that undermined the Soviet system. To those writers heavily critical of communism, the key factor has been the weaknesses inherent in the ideology of communism. Thus the collapse of the USSR and the end of the Cold War was inevitable. The inefficiencies in a state-controlled economy and the inability of a communist system to meet the needs of its people would eventually lead to crisis. By the 1980s this crisis had come to a head.

The development of popular protest movements – 'people power' – across Eastern Europe in 1989 was certainly a consequence of the failure of communist regimes, if not communism as an ideology. By the 1980s the regimes of Eastern Europe had become so entrenched that they had lost touch with much of their own population and even with members of their own party. The photographs of large crowds physically dismantling the Berlin Wall with hammers in November 1989 remains one of the abiding images of people power in action. Yet the popular movements that brought about the collapse of communist regimes were only possible because of the changes brought about by the Soviet leadership. In fact, people power played a small role in the collapse of the USSR itself. Yet change from above was to be the catalyst for change from below. Gorbachev's encouragement of new ideas for reforming communism coupled with a refusal to use force to support unpopular communist regimes was to transform the context within which change was to become not only possible but develop a life of its own. Thus Gorbachev's policies produced a chain of events that took almost everyone by surprise and resulted in an end to the Cold War.

3 The influence of attitudes and ideology

New evidence available from Soviet archives has allowed a revision of some of the previous views on the ending of the Cold War. This has resulted in a re-evaluation of the impact of national experiences and ideology on policy-making. One of the key factors highlighted has been the change in attitudes held by the Soviet people and leadership. The Russian historian Vladislav Zubok has drawn attention to this factor, arguing that the fading of the traumatic memories caused by the Second World War was to have a marked impact on how the USSR saw the West. Images of burning buildings, devastated land and millions of dead had produced a hostile view of the outside world after 1945. By the 1980s the survivors of the wartime generation were dying out. This generational shift in society was to be reflected by the generational change amongst the leadership. The attitudes and principles of the Soviet elite started to change. Out went the rigid adherence to communist ideology as decided by the Party. There was no longer seen to be a need to spread the ideology of communism or build up an empire based on it. Gorbachev's New Political Thinking rejected the idea that Soviet control over Eastern Europe could be justified by ideology or the need to defend itself against Nazism. Thus what made Gorbachev's impact so important was the change occurring in Soviet society during the 1980s.

No historian would see only one cause for an event as complex as the ending of the Cold War, but there is still plenty of debate to be had as to the relative importance of a range of individuals interacting with their wider context.

Source exercise: interpretations of the end of the Cold War

Source D

It was Gorbachev's acceptance of a non-communist government in Poland that, more than anything, opened the floodgates for political change in Eastern Europe . . .

While the events in Eastern Europe were unfolding, Gorbachev insisted on absolute Soviet non-intervention. As he explained to his Politburo, the Soviet Union could not afford to intervene, financially or in terms of the cost in its relationship with the West. But most importantly, Gorbachev believed that it would not be *right* to intervene . . .

From Jussi Hanhimaki and Odd Arne Westad,
The Cold War (published in 2003)

Source E

Mikhail Gorbachev did not suddenly emerge from nowhere. He, or some similar Soviet reformer, may even have been inevitable. He was the most prominent of that extraordinary generation of democratically minded reformers who suddenly broke through to the top of the Communist Party.

From Martin Walker, *The Cold War* (published in 1994)

Source F

Because of the pressing domestic, political and economic demands that confronted Gorbachev, he went further than any other Soviet leader in reducing Soviet commitments. But this was not abandonment but retrenchment. What ultimately mattered for the forces of international revolution was the domestic strength of individual revolutionary states with or without Soviet support.

From Richard Saull, *The Cold War and After* (published in 2007)

Source G

For Gorbachev any attempt to maintain control over unwilling peoples through the use of force would degrade the Soviet system by overstretching its resources, discrediting its ideology, and resisting the irresistible forces of democratisation that, for both moral and practical reasons, were sweeping the world ... 'It is obvious,' he argued, 'that force and the threat of force cannot be and should not be an instrument of foreign policy ... Freedom of choice is a universal principle, and it should know no exceptions.'

It suddenly became apparent, just as Reagan was leaving office, that the Reagan Doctrine had been pushing against an open door. But Gorbachev had also made it clear, to the peoples and the governments of Eastern Europe, that the door was now open.

From John Lewis Gaddis, *The Cold War* (published in 2005)

Source H

The upheavals of 1989 caught everyone by surprise ...

What no one understood, at the beginning of 1989, was that the Soviet Union, its empire, its ideology – and therefore the Cold War itself – was a sandpile ready to slide. All it took to make that happen were a few more grains of sand. The people who dropped them were not in charge of superpowers or movements or religions: they were ordinary people with simple priorities who saw, seized, and sometimes stumbled into opportunities. In doing so, they caused a collapse no one could stop. Their 'leaders' had little choice but to follow.

From John Lewis Gaddis, *The Cold War* (published in 2005)

Source I

What caused the collapse of communism?

... the communist economic crisis of the 1980s was about how the entire economy, domestic and military, was to be run. Poland and the other occupied states of Eastern Europe were in a similar economic bind, and they weren't trying to build a competitive 'Star Wars' system.

... One could also say that communism was doomed by technology. The arrival of the information age meant the end of mass industrial labour – Marx's proletarian class – in modern economies ...

... if Solidarity had not come along to take advantage of these sweeping technological changes, something else would have. But Solidarity did come along – not anything else.

Father Avery Dulles, the theologian and son of the US secretary of state who helped father the Cold War, says John Paul's role was 'crucial. It wasn't the whole thing, but it was decisive. Poland was the key to the end. It influenced the other countries in Eastern Europe. Walesa was on TV saying he never would have had the courage to act without the pope.

From Jonathan Kwitny, *Man of the Century: The Life and Times of Pope John Paul II* (published in 1997)

SKILLS BUILDER

1 How do Sources D and E differ in their view of the importance of the role of Gorbachev in ending the Cold War?

2 Using your own knowledge, assess the validity of these two views.

3 How might Sources F and G be used to challenge or modify the view that Gorbachev's role in the ending of the Cold War was important?

4 Using Source H, and your own knowledge, explain how far you agree with the view that popular protest was a significant factor in bringing an end to the communist regimes in Eastern Europe.

5 Using Source I, and your own knowledge, assess the role of Pope John Paul II in the collapse of communist regimes in Eastern Europe.

Linking the factors involved in ending the Cold War

Ronald Reagan's foreign policy	This reinforced Reagan's stand against the USSR by allowing US nuclear missiles in Europe
Mikhail Gorbachev's New Political Thinking	This greatly weakened the ability of the communist regimes to oppress their own population
The ending of the Brezhnev Doctrine	It threatened to economically bankrupt the USSR
The role of Margaret Thatcher	It turned many people away from communism as an answer to their needs
Popular protests in Eastern Europe	These gave encouragement to the people of Eastern Europe to demand change
The role of Pope John Paul II	It helped strengthen the resolve of those protesting against communism
The moral bankruptcy of communism	This showed the lack of support for the regimes of Eastern Europe that refused to reform

SKILLS BUILDER

1 Using the table above, find the box in the middle column that provides the link between a factor in the left-hand column and one in the right hand column.

2 What other links can you explain between the factors?

3 Which factors are highlighted by the realist school of historians?

4 Which factors are highlighted by the ideational school?

5 Does the exercise using the table suggest that these two historical approaches are incompatible?

6 You have now considered a range of differing interpretations for the ending of the Cold War. Which of these do you consider to be the most valid?

• Use your own knowledge to support your argument.

• Do not just accept the view of one interpretation without reasoning. For example, do you think that a combination of interpretations provides the most convincing explanation? Explain how you would link them.

• Explain why you reject the other interpretations.

Unit summary

What have you learned in this unit?

The Cold War came to an end when the USSR lost its will for empire. A range of factors combined to weaken the Soviet hold over Eastern Europe and ultimately over its own people. It is the relative importance of these factors and the ways in which they link together that have been the focus of debate by historians.

The role of the changes to US foreign policy brought about by Ronald Reagan has received a lot of attention from American historians, particularly those on the political right. Reagan's foreign policy was a strident attempt to get the Soviet leadership to change its ways. The USSR could not sustain the resources needed to pursue an empire it no longer felt it needed in order to secure itself against its enemies. Cold War conflict had involved the superpowers building empires abroad to secure spheres of influence. As the USA found in Vietnam and the USSR found in Afghanistan, empire building was a painful and costly policy.

Yet change in history is never driven by one cause only. Reagan's policies did not operate in a vacuum. The failings of the communist system had already persuaded reformers within the Soviet leadership that change was needed. The difference was that after 1985 Gorbachev was in a position to bring these changes about. The chain of events unleashed by Gorbachev's ideas and actions produced results he had not intended: the collapse of communism rather than its revitalisation.

Much of the historiography of the ending of the Cold War has been concerned with the role of individuals, but, perhaps ironically given the rejection of Marxism that the events entailed, the masses of Eastern Europe played their role in the collapse of the Soviet Bloc. It is tempting to see this process of 'people power' that swept Eastern Europe in 1989 as one force, but despite some common features the experience, attitudes and values of the people in each country also relate to their own stories.

The many dimensions of the ending of the Cold War give this topic a richness that is likely to provoke continued debate in the future.

What skills have you used in this unit?

You have examined the ways in which historians have debated the issue of what factors led to the ending of the Cold War between the superpowers during the 1980s. You will also have understood why historians have offered differing interpretations. This understanding has enabled you to assess the validity of these interpretations and to offer clear, reasoned judgements on them. As a result you can present your own interpretations with conviction and confidence.

Exam style questions

The questions centred on this controversy will appear in Section B of the exam. They will ask you to use two or three sources and your own knowledge to make a judgement on an interpretation. An example is given below.

Source J

Reagan and his foreign policy advisers came into office on a wave of hyperbole* about the Soviet threat designed to rally the American public to support a major military build-up. A number of Reagan's advisers belonged to an ideological faction whose views had not been substantively represented in Washington since the 1950s. Like their counterparts in the domestic arena who proudly proclaimed that they had come to create a 'revolution' in government, they were radicals, in a sense of going back to the roots, and their ambitions were high. Like their forebears in the Eisenhower years, they wanted to roll back the Soviet empire and win the Cold War.

From Frances Fitzgerald, *Way Out There in the Blue: Reagan, Star Wars and the End of the Cold War* (published in 2000)

*exaggerated statements

Source K

It was Gorbachev and the East Europeans themselves, not the Americans, who rolled back the iron curtain and ended the cold war. It is an exaggeration to claim that America's military spending in the 1980s prompted the Soviet counter-measures and economic dislocations that forced the evil empire to surrender. Not only does such an argument downplay Lech Walesa's Solidarity movement in Poland and Vaclav Havel's 'velvet revolution' in Czechoslovakia, it ignores the degree to which the cold war had become institutionalized on both sides by the 1980s . . . Worst-case analysis wherein generals and admirals overstated the strength of the adversary to justify larger weapons systems and budgets became standard operating procedure on both sides. If anything, the Reagan military build-up may have delayed an earlier Soviet move toward detente.

From J. Garry Clifford, 'History and the End of the Cold War: A Whole New Ball Game?', in *Organization of American Historians* (vol. 7, Fall 1992)

Source L

The pressure from the West in the early 1980s revived Cold War tensions, but it is hard to see it as a decisive factor in the end of the Cold War world order. The ending was, in a way, a 'victory' of the West, but attempts of some US leaders to take credit for this victory cannot be corroborated by the new evidence from the Soviet side. The role of longer-term processes within the Soviet Union (the erosion of ideology, the pent-up desire for relaxation) played a much greater role than the short-term measures of the Reagan or Bush administrations.

On the other hand, the personal roles of Gorbachev and other 'new thinkers', decisive as they were in the turn from the Cold War, should not be idealized. They let the war in Afghanistan continue, needlessly, for three more years under their leadership. In concrete terms, their new foreign policy gave them only limited achievements . . . What finally ended the Cold War was the process of liberalization inside the Soviet Union that they unleashed and over which they later lost control. As a domestic reformer, Gorbachev failed terribly . . . The end of the Cold War was, in many ways a byproduct of this failure. The new evidence demonstrates dramatically that it was not only Gorbachev's 'good will', but also the progressive paralysis of his 'revolution from above', the lack of guidelines and orientations, that made possible the collapse of communism in Eastern Europe.

From an article by Vladislav Zubok, 'Why did the Cold War End in 1989? Explanations of "the Turn"', in O. A. Westad (ed.), *Reviewing the Cold War* (published in 2000)

- Use Sources J, K and L and your own knowledge. How far do you agree with the view that Reagan's actions to roll back the Soviet empire led to the ending of the Cold War?

Exam tips

Note the instruction 'use Sources J, K and L *and* your own knowledge'. This is not a choice.

Weaker answers will tend to discuss the sources first and deal with own knowledge separately. It is much more effective to integrate your own knowledge with the sources. For example:

- Use your own knowledge to explain phrases in the source, to place the source into its context by clarifying what it is saying and the circumstances that it is about, and to test the validity of the interpretation in the source.

For example, in Source J:

- The rise of the neo-conservatives could be discussed in order to provide context for 'Reagan's advisers'.
- Your own knowledge should be used to explain how these attitudes led to policies such as the Reagan Doctrine.
- The debate over whether the Soviet leadership took seriously Reagan's SDI programme could be discussed.
- Why might a historian writing at this time be positive towards Reagan's policies?

For Source K:

- Discuss the assertion that 'It was Gorbachev and the East Europeans themselves . . . who ended the cold war'. This would require you to examine the validity of the supporting assertion 'It is an exaggeration to claim that America's military spending in the 1980s prompted the Soviet counter-measures and economic dislocations that forced the evil empire to surrender.'
- Explain the role of Lech Walesa's Solidarity movement in Poland and Vaclav Havel's 'velvet revolution' in Czechoslovakia.
- Is the date of publication of this source significant?

For Source L:

- This source challenges the interpretation given in the question. You need to explain how. This is an opportunity to cross-reference this source with Source J.
- Source L finds some agreement with Source K, another opportunity for cross-referencing.
- But Source L offers another interpretation that needs to be assessed for its validity. Own knowledge should be used to explain how Gorbachev's domestic failures led to the collapse of the Soviet Union.

Note that you will be asked to refer to at least two sources in your answer. These sources will be deliberately chosen to remind you that there is more than one interpretation on the issue and that you are dealing with a historical debate. Your answer should therefore engage in this debate and give a reasoned judgement on the interpretation of the issue highlighted in the question.

RESEARCH TOPIC

Biographies

The events that produced the ending of the Cold War appear to have been dominated by several key players. Biographies are often used as a source of information for the historian but can pose particular dangers if not used with care.

Compile a list of biographies available on the key individuals involved in the end of the Cold War.

- Why might these biographies be both useful and misleading to a historian of the Cold War in the 1980s?

To help you think about this question consider the purpose of a biography and how this differs from a piece of historical analysis.

Which school of historians is a biography most likely to support? Why?

Afterthoughts

In February 2008 I took a group of students to Berlin for a study visit. Part of the trip involved a visit to the Stasi prison at Hohenschönhausen. Our guide Marita was a former inmate of the prison. Now in her fifties, she described how her life had been shattered by the secret police of the former East Germany.

When a young student, Marita had gone on a camping holiday to Czechoslovakia where she had met and fallen in love with a West German student. But this was to turn into something very different from a typical holiday romance. Her new boyfriend asked her if she would like to live in the West, and Marita, curious of life under capitalism and the possibility of being with her new lover, said 'yes'.

On returning to her home city of Dresden after the holiday, Marita soon recognised the signs of Stasi interference. The neighbours suddenly ignored her, a university place was withdrawn without explanation. Her new boyfriend was a Stasi agent – her neighbours were informing the Stasi of her every word and move.

In desperation Marita attempted to flee from East Germany, but she was caught on the border and taken to the prison at Hohenschönhausen where she was interrogated and held for five years. She was released only when the government of the DDR handed her over to West Germany in return for hard currency.

After the reunification of Germany, Marita returned to Berlin where she now lives with her family. She calmly told us her story without any bitterness towards those neighbours and friends who betrayed her to the secret police. Yet the prison at Hohenschönhausen is surrounded by apartment blocks where the people who worked as guards and interrogators in the prison still live in considerable comfort. Marita's situation highlights the fact that although the Cold War is now over, its remnants are still around us and the impact it had on people's lives continues.

The USSR and the communist regimes of Eastern Europe are no more but there still exist states that claim to be communist and groups who claim Marxism as their inspiration. China may have embraced economic capitalism but its political system is dominated by the Communist Party. Cuba is seen as an example of how communism can be utilised to achieve social and economic progress in the developing world, its health care and education attracting particular praise. North Korea remains as a last bastion of hard-line Stalinism, led by the erratic and unpredictable Kim Jong Il. Thus communism still has the potential to provide tensions in world affairs. In 2002 US President George W. Bush declared that North Korea was one of the countries making up the 'Axis of Evil', those rogue states who threaten world peace. International relations at the start of the twenty-first century have been dominated by the USA's 'War on Terror'. Conflict continues, this time with a new 'bogeyman' replacing the communist one.

Thematic review: making a substantiated judgement on an issue or interpretation

The topic you have studied in this book covers a long period of time. It is, therefore, important to stand back and review the period as a whole. This unit has been looking at the nature of conflict and the factors that have caused tension as well as those that have reduced it. The concepts of change and continuity and cause and consequence have underpinned the focus of this study. You need to be asking yourself not only what happened but why it happened and why it happened when it did and not earlier or later. Change is brought about by a range of factors, but you should be asking yourself which factor is the most important. What is the role of each factor and how do they work in combination to produce the events that occurred? Were any events critical turning points in the period as a whole? Thematic review questions, spanning the whole time period, will help to focus your thinking. These are the thematic review questions that relate to *A World Divided: Superpower Relations 1944–90*. You can probably think of more, but these are key ones to start you off working in this way.

- How far were relations between the superpowers in the period 1944–90 influenced by the personalities of the leaders of the USA and USSR?
- To what extent was conflict between the superpowers the result of ideological differences?
- How significant was nuclear weapons technology in influencing the nature of conflict between the superpowers during the Cold War?
- To what extent did economic realities affect superpower relations in the period 1944–90?
- How far was superpower rivalry the result of geo-political factors?

Choose one of these thematic review questions that you plan to answer. Working through this section will make much more sense if you have an actual question in mind.

Answering a thematic review question

There are two key approaches to answering a thematic review question: *select* and *deploy*.

Select   You need to select appropriate material from sources and your own knowledge.

Deploy   You need to deploy what you have selected so that you answer the question in as direct a way as possible.

Unpacking 'select'

All of the thematic review questions are asking you to provide evaluation in order to reach a substantiated judgement. They ask 'How far . . .', 'To what extent . . .', 'How significant', which means that you will have to weigh up the evidence given by the interpretations you have selected. You will, therefore, have to select interpretations that give you a range of differing perspectives. For example, referring to three perspectives that agree with each other will severely limit your opportunity to discuss, debate and evaluate. You will need to select interpretations that pull in different directions so that you can weigh up the evidence that they use and its value. This will help you reach a reasoned, supported conclusion.

So now go ahead.

1 Look back through this book and select the sources that you think will give you the appropriate range of balance in terms of interpretations.

2 Make notes of the knowledge you will need to use to contextualise the sources and create an argument.

You can't, of course, simply use the sources in an answer to illustrate points and provide proof that an interpretation or argument is valid without assessing the value of the interpretation and the evidence it highlights. You therefore need to evaluate the sources you have selected and use that evaluation to create the argument you will be making when you answer the question. You have already had practice at doing this, but here is a reminder of some of the questions you will need to ask of a source before you can turn it into evidence.

- What is the *thrust* of the interpretation? What does it say that relates to the question I am answering?

- What evidence is used in the *content* of the source to support its interpretation? What is the nature of the evidence that is it using?

- What is the *perspective* of the interpretation? Does it focus on individuals and their importance or the context within which they operated? Is it likely to be from the perspective of an orthodox, a revisionist, a post-revisionist or a Soviet historian? Has the background of the author influenced the interpretation? Is the date of publication significant? Was the author able to access the full range of sources for this topic?

- What material from your own knowledge supports the interpretation given?

- What material from your own knowledge leads you to modify, challenge or reject the interpretation given?

Now you have your selection of source material and own knowledge, you need to think about it as a package. Does it do the job you want it to do? Does it supply you with enough evidence of different points of view so that you can show you have considered what weight the evidence will bear in reaching a reasoned, supported conclusion? In order to do this effectively, you need to *cross-reference* the sources, showing where they support each other and where they differ. You should then provide an explanation of the differences and attempt to resolve them as part of your own argument. Can differences be explained by perspective, date of publication, nature of evidence used? What evidence gives your view more weight?

This will be the key feature that makes your argument convincing.

Unpacking 'deploy'

The key to deploying material effectively is relevance. You must address the specific question asked and sustain your relevance throughout the answer. Always ask yourself, 'How does this paragraph take my answer to the question further?' What are you trying to do that relates directly to the question? Make the relevance of your answer explicit at all stages. Do not rely on the reader to work out how your material might be relevant. If you find that a section of your answer does not relate to the specific focus of the question, be ruthless and remove it. You may need the time and space for more relevant material.

You have already had a lot of practice at essay planning and writing, so this is just a reminder of the main things you need to bear in mind.

Plan

Plan carefully how you are going to construct your answer and make out your case. Remember the saying 'Failure to plan is planning to fail'.

Structure

Give your answer a clear, logical structure. It is always a good idea to examine the premise given in the statement in the question first. For example, in answering the question 'To what extent was conflict between the superpowers the result of ideological differences?' it is advisable to assess the evidence that supports the importance of 'ideological differences' first before widening out your answer to consider other factors.

Introduction

Give a brief outline of your argument and how you will develop it. Don't be tempted to 'set the scene' by giving a narrative description. Start as you mean to go on by focusing on the specific demands of the question and presenting your own argument in response to it.

The main body

This section of your answer should be a series of paragraphs that develop your argument by assessing the evidence available. When considering an interpretation, remember to provide evaluation by critical consideration of the evidence that relates to it.

Conclusion

This should pull your case together to provide a reasoned summary of your overall argument. It is essential that you reach a reasoned judgement that addresses the specific question you have been asked to consider. Make sure that your conclusion links to your introduction. Is your argument sustained from beginning to end?

You do not, of course, have to respond to these thematic review questions by writing an essay on your own. You could work collaboratively with others, or use them to prepare for a class debate. Some websites provide opportunities to discuss and debate historical issues with students across the country and abroad. Whatever way you are going to use these thematic review questions, the approach will be the same: select, deploy and make it relevant.

Exam zone

Relax and prepare

Hot tips: what other students have said.

From AS to A2 level

- A2 level History seems like a big step up at first with more demands made on independent reading and more complex source passages to cope with. However, by the end of the first term I felt as if my written work had improved considerably.

- Start reading around the topics studied in class as early as possible. Reading helped me understand how historians present their arguments and use evidence.

- Studying the unit on Superpower Relations helped my understanding of current affairs. I found listening to the news and reading newspapers reinforced my understanding of the topics we studied.

- There are now lots of history programmes on television, even whole channels devoted to history. Although they vary in quality, it is always worth looking out for interesting programmes that relate to what you have studied.

- It is sometimes hard to tell which websites might be useful to look at, but I have become better at ensuring I know who has produced the site so that I can evaluate its material. Many universities have useful websites.

- The more practice source based questions I attempted, the more confident I became and quite quickly I picked up the necessary style and technique required for success.

- Don't get flustered or panic. Ask your teacher if you are not sure. History teachers aren't that scary!

What I wish I had known at the start of the year

- I used the textbook a lot during the revision period to learn the key facts. I really wished that I had used it from the beginning of the course in order to consolidate my class notes.

- I wish that I had taken more time reading and noting other material such as the photocopied handouts issued by my teacher. Reading around the subject and undertaking independent research would have made my understanding more complete and made the whole topic more interesting.

- It helps if you annotate your notes and reading material as you do it. This makes your reading more active and therefore more useful.

- A Level History is not just about learning the relevant material but also developing the skills to use it effectively. I wished that I had spent more time throughout the year practising source questions to improve my style and technique.

- I wish I had paid more attention to the advice and comments made by my teacher on the written work I had done. This would have helped me to improve my scores throughout the year.

How to revise

- I started my revision by buying a new folder and some dividers. I put all my revision work into this folder and used the dividers to separate the different topics. I really took pride in my revision notes and made them as thorough and effective as I could manage.

- Before I started the revision process, I found it helpful to plan out my history revision. I used the Edexcel specification given to me by my teacher as a guideline of which topics to revise and I ticked off each one as I covered it.

- I found it useful to revise in short, sharp bursts. I would set myself a target of revising one particular topic in an hour and a half. I would spend one hour taking revision notes and then half an hour testing myself with a short practice question or a facts test.

- Planning answers to key questions is helpful because it saves time later.

- I found it useful to always include some practice work in my revision. If I could get that work to my teacher to mark all the better, but just attempting questions to time helped me improve my technique.

- Sometimes I found it helpful to revise with a friend. We might spend 45 minutes revising by ourselves and then half an hour testing each other. Often we were able to sort out any problems between us and it was reassuring to see that someone else had the same worries and pressures at that time.

Refresh your memory

Revision checklist

The following provides a useful list for checking the information you need to revise for your exam.

Unit 1: The seeds of conflict 1917–44 (general context)

- The differences between capitalism and communism.

- The tensions that existed between the USSR and the US in the 1920s and 1930s.

- The strains that existed in the Grand Alliance during the Second World War.

Unit 2: How did the Cold War develop between 1944 and 1953? (Section B/context for key controversy)

- The key features of the situation in Europe at the end of the Second World War in 1945.

- The attitudes of the USSR, the USA and Britain to Europe in 1945.

- The ways in which relations between the superpowers deteriorated in the period 1945–47 with reference to

  a)   the Yalta Conference

  b)   the Potsdam Conference

  c)   Soviet actions in Eastern Europe in 1945

  d)   Churchill's 'Iron Curtain' speech

  e)   the Truman Doctrine and the Marshall Plan

  f)   the Berlin Blockade, 1948–49.

- The impact of the communist takeover of China on US foreign policy.

- The reasons why the Cold War extended to the Far East after 1949.

- The key features of NSC-68.

- The causes of the Korean War: the reasons why North Korea invaded South Korea.

- The course of the Korean War.

Unit 3: Why did the Cold War between the superpowers emerge in the years to 1953? (Section B/key controversy)

- The role played by Truman in the development of the Cold War.

- The role of Stalin in Soviet foreign policy: the debate over Stalin's motives for expansion.

- The main interpretations on the issue of what caused the Cold War; the value of these interpretations.

- Different interpretations of the extension of the Cold War to the Far East 1950–53.

Unit 4: What impact did the post-Stalin thaw have on superpower relations 1953–62? (Section A topic)

- The impact of the death of Stalin on international relations.

- Peaceful Coexistence: its meaning and the reasons behind it; the role of Malenkov and Khrushchev.

- The response of Eisenhower and Dulles to Peaceful Coexistence.

- The key features of the 'New Look'.

- The impact of Kennedy on US foreign policy.

- The achievements of the 'Thaw': their limitations.
- The Soviet invasion of Hungary, 1956: reasons, US response.
- The Berlin Wall: reasons for tension over Berlin, reasons why the Wall was built, US response.

Unit 5: What role did nuclear weapons have on the conduct of the Cold War 1949–63? (Section A topic)

- The reasons for the arms race: international, national, personal, domestic.
- The key features of the arms race: the developments in bombs and delivery systems.
- The reasons for the Cuban Missile Crisis of 1962.
- Kennedy's actions during the crisis; the resolution of the crisis.
- The impact of the crisis on superpower relations and the arms race.
- The ways in which nuclear weapons influenced the nature of Cold War conflict 1949–63.

Unit 6: How did Sino–Soviet relations change in the period 1949–76? (Section A topic)

- Reasons for the Sino–Soviet Treaty of Friendship, Alliance and Mutual Assistance, 1950.
- Sino–Soviet cooperation during the Korean War and the Taiwan Straits Crisis of 1954–55.
- The reasons why the Sino–Soviet Split occurred after 1958: ideological differences and national interests.
- The role of the personalities of Mao and Khrushchev in the Sino–Soviet Split.
- Evidence of the Sino–Soviet Split: the Ussuri River Dispute, 1969.
- The reasons for the rapprochement between the USA and China after 1969.
- The impact of the Sino-American rapprochement: its achievements.

Unit 7: What were the causes and achievements of Détente? (Section A topic)

- The causes of Détente: the fear of nuclear war, the needs of the USSR, the needs of the USA, the European dimension.

- The role of Henry Kissinger and his approach of realpolitik.
- SALT I: its key features.
- The Helsinki Accords, 1975: its key features.
- The impact of Détente on superpower relations.
- The differing interpretations of Détente and their value.
- The reasons why Détente came to an end: the rise of neo-conservatives, the invasion of Afghanistan.

Unit 8: How did the Cold War come to an end in the 1980s? (Section B/context for key controversy)

- The impact of Ronald Reagan on US foreign policy.
- The Reagan Doctrine.
- The factors that weakened Soviet control over Eastern Europe.
- The New Political Thinking of Gorbachev and its impact on Eastern Europe.
- The reasons for the ending of the Brezhnev Doctrine and its impact.
- The reasons for the fall of the Berlin Wall.
- Factors leading to the collapse of communism in Eastern Europe.
- Factors leading to the collapse of the USSR.

Unit 9: Why did the Cold War come to an end in the 1980s? (Section B/key controversy)

- The role of individuals in the ending of the Cold War: Reagan, Thatcher, Gorbachev and Pope John Paul II.
- Differing interpretations of the ending of the Cold War and their value.

This revision checklist is very knowledge based. Don't forget that in Section B of the examination your skills in handling sources will also be tested.

Result

You have spent a lot of time working on plans and constructing answers to the (a) and (b) questions. So you now have a pretty good idea about how to plan an answer and write a response to the question of the examination paper. But what are the examiners looking for? And what marks will you get?

About the exam

As part of your A2 Level History course you are required to carry out a study in depth, in this instance *A World Divided: Superpower Relations 1944-90*. You will be required to gain a firm understanding of the chronology of the topic and of the key issues, problems and debates associated with it. You will also be required to explore the nature of challenges and conflict both within the period and relating to the societies and political systems studied, and will do this by working with secondary sources that provide differing views about historical controversies.

At the end of your A2 course you will take a written exam and you will need to answer two questions. The sources will be supplied with the paper.

- In Section A you will need to reach a substantiated judgement on a historical issue or problem. You will have a choice of two questions, and this question will be worth 30 marks.

- In Section B you will need to compare source material to explore an issue of historical debate, reaching a substantiated judgement using your own knowledge. There will be a choice of two questions and this question will be worth 40 marks.

The exam will last 2 hours. Make sure you plan your time carefully and allow enough time to answer both questions thoroughly.

Section A

These essay questions, from which you choose one of them to answer, will have an analytical focus that will require you to reach a substantiated judgement on a historical issue or problem. For example, questions are likely to be worded with the instruction 'how far/to what extent . . .' and to be followed by either a statement or an interpretation that you are asked to weigh up.

Section B

In this section you will be provided with five or six secondary sources that total about 350–400 words. You will then have to answer one question from a choice of two. Each question will ask you to discuss two or three of the sources while exploring an issue of historical debate, and to reach a substantiated judgement based on the sources and your own knowledge.

Questions are likely to be worded with the instruction 'How far do you agree with the view that . . .'. You will also be instructed to 'Explain your answer using the sources and your own knowledge of the issues related to this controversy.'

Section A

What will you have to do, and what marks will you get for doing it?

This question tests your ability to recall, select and deploy information and your ability to understand key concepts and features. There are 30 marks available for this section. You will be working at one of five levels. Try to get as high up in the levels as you can.

Level 1
1–6 marks

- You are able to produce a series of simple statements.

Knowledge will be generalised with few examples. The answer will not be made relevant to the question.

Level 2
7–12 marks

- You are able to produce answers with some development using examples.

The range of examples is likely to be limited. There may be some attempt to link the material to the question but it will not be made explicit.

Level 3
13–18 marks

- You are able to produce an answer that shows an understanding of the question and what it is getting at.

The answer will, however, drift into irrelevance at times or be based on material that, although developed in places, is limited in its range.

Level 4
19–24 marks

- You are able to produce an analytical answer that shows a clear understanding of the focus of the question.

The answer is drawing out key points with detailed knowledge used to develop an argument. There may still be some drifting from the specific question or a lack of balance with some aspects dealt with briefly, but the answer shows some attempt to evaluate the evidence used in the argument.

Level 5
25–30 marks

- You are able to produce a sustained analytical answer.

The answer is a well-structured argument that discusses the evidence used to support/reject/modify the statement in the question. The answer evaluates the evidence for the argument.

Now try this question:

- How far would you agree that the Sino–Soviet Split that developed between 1958 and 1969 was the result of ideological differences?

Guidance notes

Remember that in order to weigh up a statement or interpretation you need to look at the following:

- Explain the statement/interpretation.
- Outline the evidence that could be used to support the statement/interpretation and discuss its validity.
- Outline the evidence that could be used to reject/modify the statement/interpretation and comment on its validity.
- Come to a developed, reasoned judgement that presents your own argument.

N.B. The best answers will show that the student has thought seriously about the issue/problem and has a well-supported, reasoned argument of their own in relation to the question they have been asked.

This argument will be *sustained*, i.e. be present from the introduction to the conclusion. Thus, especial care is needed when you write your introduction.

The argument will be based on sustained *critical evaluation* of the evidence. This will require the value of the evidence to be discussed rather than just a list of the evidence itself.

Now use the marking criteria to assess your response.

How did you do?

What could you have done to have achieved higher marks?

The examiners will not be nit-picking their way through your answer, ticking things off as they go. Rather, they will be looking to see which levels best fit your response, and you should do the same when assessing your own responses.

Section B

What will you have to do, and what marks will you get for doing it?

This section tests your ability to recall, select and deploy information and to understand key concepts and features. This objective carries 16 marks. You are also being tested for your ability to analyse and evaluate differing interpretations in relation to their historical context. This objective carries 24 marks. Thus, Section B has a total of 40 marks. You will be working at one of five levels. Try to get as high up in the levels as you can. The examiners will be marking your answer twice: once for knowledge and a second time for source evaluation.

This is what the examiners will be looking for as they mark the ways in which you have selected and used your knowledge to answer the question:

Level 1
1–3 marks

- You are able to produce a series of simple statements.

Knowledge will be generalised with few examples. The answer will not be made relevant to the question. Links to the sources will be few or indirect.

Level 2
4–6 marks

- You are able to produce answers with some development using examples.

The range of examples is likely to be limited and this may be linked to the sources. There may be some attempt to link the material to the question but it will not be made explicit.

Level 3
7–10 marks

- You are able to produce an answer that shows an understanding of the question and what it is getting at.

There will be some links between own knowledge and the sources. The answer will, however, drift into irrelevance at times or be based on material that, although developed in places, is limited in its range.

Level 4
11–13 marks

- You are able to produce an analytical answer that shows a clear understanding of the focus of the question.

The answer is drawing out key points with detailed knowledge used to support analysis of the sources. There may still be some drifting from the specific question or a lack of balance, with some aspects dealt with briefly, but the answer shows some attempt to evaluate the evidence used in the argument

Level 5
14–16 marks

- You are able to produce a sustained analytical answer.

The answer is a well-structured argument that discusses the evidence used to support/reject/modify the statement in the question. The answer evaluates the evidence for the argument.

This is what examiners are looking for as they mark your source evaluation skills.

Level 1
1–4 marks

- You are able to understand the sources at face value and use them to identify points.

There will be no integration of the sources with each other or with own knowledge – they will be treated singly and separately – when coming to a conclusion.

Level 2
5–9 marks

- You are able to understand the sources and can use them to develop points relevant to the question.

There will be some linking together of the material from the sources. The answer will reach a judgement based on limited support from the sources.

Level 3
10–14 marks

- You are able to interpret the evidence from the sources, drawing out key points from the evidence in the sources.

The answer develops points that both support and challenge the interpretation under discussion and shows an awareness of the nature of the debate that the interpretation relates to. The answer may well be unbalanced with not all aspects covered, but there is a clear attempt to reach a reasoned answer supported by information and argument from the sources.

Level 4
15–19 marks

- You are able to interpret the sources with confidence, showing an understanding of the basis of the arguments offered in the sources.

Answers will relate the interpretations offered by the sources to their wider context by using own knowledge to discuss the arguments presented. Judgements will be reached that integrate the sources and own knowledge to support a well-developed and sustained argument.

Level 5
20–24 marks

- You are able to produce a sustained evaluation of the sources to present a fully reasoned argument.

The interpretations offered by the sources are discussed and evaluated with the validity of the interpretation assessed by reference to own knowledge. Thus sources and own knowledge are effectively integrated to address the full demands of the question.

Don't forget to take care with your English. The quality of your communication can be used by the examiner to decide which mark to give you within a level. Quality of communication is about more than spelling. It is about whether your answer is well-structured with paragraphs and clear sentences.

Now try this question.

- How far do you agree with the view that the aggressive actions of the Soviet Union were the main cause of the Cold War extending to the Far East between 1950 and 1953? Explain your answer, using the evidence of Sources 1, 2 and 3 and your own knowledge of the issues related to this controversy.

Source 1

The Soviet push for influence had run up against its limits, what with the success of the Marshall Plan, the failure of the Berlin Blockade, the formation of an independent West Germany, and the organisation of NATO. Asia looked more promising: the Chinese had shown that nationalism more easily aligned with communism there than in Europe; and as Stalin had none too subtly suggested to Liu Shaoqi (the Chinese Deputy Leader) there might be opportunities beyond Chinese borders. We now know that Stalin saw the situation in Indochina, where Ho Chi Minh was seeking Soviet and Chinese support in his war against the French, as one of them.

From John Lewis Gaddis, *We Now Know* (published in 1997)

Source 2

The Korean War was the first major military confrontation of the post-war Cold War. Indeed, the Korean War saw armed conflict between US and Chinese military forces and also, for the first and only time in the Cold War, armed combat (in the air) between Soviet and US military forces over the Korean peninsula . . . The decision by North Korea, with the support of both Moscow and Beijing, to unite the peninsula under communist rule through the invasion of the south in June 1950 was a major factor in ensuring that the proposals for militarising US foreign policy, embodied in NSC'68, were implemented by the Truman administration.

The Korean War was seen by the Truman administration as an act of aggression directed and planned by Moscow, as part of its global strategy. However, local domestic factors were the primary causes of the war and in this sense the Korean War originated in the rival projects of national unification and social-economic transformation . . .

From Richard Saull, *The Cold War and After* (published in 2007)

Source 3

It was Asia, with its simmering revolutionary nationalism, that taught Stalin a lesson: you can make the revolutionary process serve your foreign policy, but only at your own risk and with serious, unintended consequences. Soon dramatic developments in the Far East forced Stalin in a way he perhaps had never expected or planned.

On Sunday, June 25, 1950, the North Korean army invaded South Korea in an attempt to reunify the country by force. 'The North Koreans wanted to prod South Korea with the point of a bayonet,' Khrushchev recalled. Molotov remembered that the Korean War 'was pressed on us by the Koreans themselves. Stalin said it was impossible to avoid the national question of a united Korea.' The most dangerous conflict of the Cold War, which the West interpreted as blatant, Soviet-made aggression, a possible prelude to invasion in Europe, was not Stalin's brainchild. Yet the Kremlin leader supported North Korea's aggression, since he decided it would advance the geopolitical position of the Soviet Union in the Far East and strengthen the prestige of the USSR as a revolutionary vanguard.

From Vladislav Zubok and Constantine Pleshakov, *Inside the Kremlin's Cold War* (published in 1996)

Guidance notes

These questions can be quite challenging to answer because they require you to integrate the sources with your own knowledge while discussing and making a reasoned judgement on an interpretation. The key features of a good answer will be:

- a discussion of the issues raised by the sources that shows a clear understanding of the arguments they present

- an integration of sources with own knowledge: own knowledge will be used to test the validity of the views expressed in the sources

- relevant discussion of all aspects of the controversy raised in the question.

- a developed, reasoned judgement that presents your own argument in relation to the question.

As with answers in Section A the best answer will contain arguments that are *sustained* and include *critical evaluation* of the interpretation offered in the question.

Now use the marking criteria to assess your response.

How did you do?

What could you have done to have achieved higher marks?

The examiners will not be nit-picking their way through your answer, ticking things off as they go.

Rather, they will be looking to see which levels best fit your response, and you should do the same when assessing your own responses.

How will I time my responses?

You have 2 hours to answer two questions. Both Section A and Section B give you a choice of questions.

Take some time, about five minutes, to read the paper carefully and think about your choice of questions.

The Section A question carries 30 marks and the Section B carries 40 marks. You should therefore aim to spend more time on the Section B question, about 1 hour and 10 minutes, compared with about 50 minutes for Section A. Remember that this includes reading and planning time.

Always conclude each answer with your overall judgement so that your answer reads as a coherent response as a whole. This is important even if you find you have not got enough time to cover all aspects in the detail you wanted to.

You have now had a lot of practice in planning, writing and assessing your responses to the sort of questions you can expect to find on the examination paper. You are well prepared and you should be able to tackle the examination with confidence.

Good luck!

References

Acheson, Dean, speaking in the US Congress, April 1947

Akhromeyev, Sergei and Kornienko, Georgi, *With the Eyes of a Marshall and a Diplomat: A Critical View of Foreign Policy of the USSR Before and After 1985*, 1992

Alliluyeva, Svetlana, *Twenty Letters to a Friend*, 1967

Bahr, Christian, *Divided City*, 2008

Bowker, M. and Williams, P., *Superpower Détente: A Reappraisal*, 1988

Bowker, M., *Russian Foreign Policy and the End of the Cold War*, 1997

Bragg, Christine, *Vietnam, Korea and US Foreign Policy*, 2005

Brandt, Willy, *My Road to Berlin*, 1960

Brezhnev, Leonid, *Pages From His Life*, 1978

Brown, Archie, *The Gorbachev Factor*, 1996

Brzezinski, Z., *Power and Principle*, 1983

CCP, official report presented to Stalin, 4 July 1949

Chuev, F., *Molotov Remembers*, 1991

Churchill, Iron Curtain speech, 1946

Clifford, J. Garry, 'History and the End of the Cold War: A Whole New Ball Game?', *Organization of American Historians*, vol. 7, Fall 1992

Cumings, Bruce, *The Origins of the Korean War*, 1981

DDR Government, *Deutsche Geschichte Band 9: Die antifaschistisch-demokratische Umwälzung, der Kampf gegen die Spaltung Deutschlands und die Entstehung der DDR von 1945 bis 1949*, 1961

Dennis, M., *The Rise and Fall of the German Democratic Republic*, 2000

Dennis, M., *The Rise and Fall of the German Democratic Republic*, 2000

Dobrynin, Anatoly, *In Confidence*, 1995

DOIA, Extract from the Truman Doctrine, 1947–48

Dulles, John Foster, statement, 1954

Dunmore, T., *Soviet Politics 1945–53*, 1984

Eisenhower, D., *Mandate for Change*, 1963

Eisenhower's memoirs

Feis, H., *Churchill-Roosevelt-Stalin: The War They Waged and the Peace They Sought*, 1957

Fitzgerald, Frances, *Way Out There in the Blue: Reagan, Star Wars and the End of the Cold War*, 2000

Gaddis, J. L., *Russia, the Soviet Union and the United States*, 1990

Gaddis, John Lewis, *We Now Know*, 1997

Gaddis, John Lewis, *The Cold War*, 2005

Garraty, John, *The American Nation*, 1991

Garthoff, Raymond, *The Great Transition: American–Soviet Relations and the End of the Cold War*, 1994

Gelman, Harry, 'The Sino–Soviet Dispute in the 1970s', in Ellison, Herbert (editor), *The Sino–Soviet Conflict: A Global Perspective*, 1982

Hahn, W.. in *Post-war Soviet Politics 1945–53: The Fall of Zhdanov and the Defeat of Moderation*, 1982

Hanhimaki, J. M. and Westad, O. A., *The Cold War*, 2003

Hickey, M., *Korean War: The West Confronts Communism, 1950–53*, 1999

Higgins, Hugh, *The Cold War*, 1974

Home Office, *Protect and Survive*, 1980

Jian, Chen, *Mao's China and the Cold War*, 2001

Judges, S., *Superpower Rivalry*, 1994

Kennan, George, 'Long Telegram', 22 February 1946

Khrushchev, letter sent to Eisenhower, 7 September 1958

Khrushchev, N., *Khrushchev Remembers*, 1971

Kissinger, Henry, *The White House Years*, 1979

Kissinger, Henry, *Diplomacy*, 1994

Kwitny, Jonathan, *Man of the Century: The Life and Times of Pope John Paul II*, 1997

Mao, 'On People's Democratic Dictatorship', a statement issued on 30 June 1949

Marks, Colonel Donald M., 'The Ussuri River Incident as a Factor in Chinese Foreign Policy', *Air University Review*, July–August 1971

Marshall, George, at Harvard University, June 1947

Mastny, V., *The Cold War and Soviet Insecurity: The Stalin Years*, 1998

McCagg, W., *Stalin Embattled 1943–48*, 1978

McElvoy, Anne, *The Saddled Cow*, 1993

McNeill, W. H., *America, Britain and Russia: Their Co-operation and Conflict 1941–46*, 1953

Mikes, George, *The Hungarian Revolution*, 1957

Molotov, *Problems of Foreign Policy*, 1949

Nagy, Imre, telegram sent to the Secretary General of the United Nations, 1 November 1956

Nixon, Inaugural Address, 20 January 1969, *Presidential Documents*, vol. 5, 1969

Nixon, Richard, *Memoirs*, 1978

NSC-68 United States Objectives and Programs for National Security NSC 68, issued in April 1950 by the National Security Council

Painter, David, *The Cold War, An International History*, 1999

Partial Test Ban Treaty, 1963

Ponomaryov, B., *Official History of the USSR*, 1959

Reagan, Ronald, speech delivered to the US National Association of Evangelicals, 8 March 1983

Reagan, Ronald, speech on communism delivered to US business people, September 1987

Reagan, Ronald, *Ronald Reagan: An American Life*, 1990

Rees, David, *A Short History of Modern Korea*, 1988

Reynolds, David, *Origins of the Cold War in Europe*, 1994

Roberts, Geoffrey, *Stalin's Wars*, 2006

Sakharov, Andrei, *Memoirs*, 1990

Saull, Richard, *The Cold War and After*, 2007

Schlesinger, *Origins of the Cold War*, 1967

Schlesinger, Arthur M. Jr, *A Thousand Days: John F. Kennedy in the White House*, 2002

Schweitzer, Peter, *Victory*, 1994

Service, R., *A History of Twentieth Century Russia*, 1997

Shaw, George Bernard, letter written to the *Manchester Guardian*, 2 March 1933

Stalin's reply to Churchill's Iron Curtain speech, published in the Soviet newspaper *Pravda* 10 days after the speech was delivered

Stone, David, *Wars of the Cold War: Campaigns and Conflicts 1945–1990*, 2004

Stueck, William, *Rethinking the Korean War*, 2002

Varsori, A., 'Reflections on the Origins of the Cold War' in Westad, O. A., (editor), *Reviewing the Cold War*, 2000

Volkogonov, D., *The Rise and Fall of the Soviet Empire*, 1998

Vyshinsky, Andrei, speech to the UN General Assembly, September 1947

Walker, Martin, *The Cold War*, 1994

Weathersby in *Korea 1949–50, To Attack or Not to Attack? Stalin, Kim Il Sung and the Prelude to War*, 1995

Williams, William A., *The Tragedy of American Diplomacy*, 1959

Yergin, D., *Shattered Peace: The Origins of the Cold War and the National Security State*, 1980

Zedong, Mao, *The Selected Works of Mao Zedong on Foreign Affairs*, 1994

Zhisui, Dr Li, *The Private Life of Chairman Mao*, 1994

Zubok, V. and Pleshakov, C., *Inside the Kremlin's Cold War*

Zubok, Vladislav, 'Why did the Cold War End in 1989? Explanations of "the Turn"', in O. A. Westad (ed.), *Reviewing the Cold War*, 2000

Glossary

Appeasement   The policy adopted by Britain towards Germany in the 1930s. It involved negotiating with Hitler and trying to reach accommodation with his demands for territory where they seemed reasonable.

Axiomatic   Based on a principle that is considered to be a self-evident truth.

Berlin Wall   Built in 1961 to halt the flood of refugees escaping from communist East Germany into capitalist West Berlin. This huge concrete structure became the ultimate symbol of the East-West divide. The order to build the Wall was given by Ulbricht, the East German leader, and was implemented by Erich Honecker.

Bipolar   The idea of the world being divided into two power blocs: those of communism, centred on the USSR, and the West, centred on the USA.

Bolshevik   The name of the political party that seized power in Russia in October 1917. It had been led by Lenin since 1903. The Bolsheviks were believers in communism. In 1925 they changed their official name to the All-Union Communist Party.

Brinkmanship   The policy of threatening to use nuclear weapons and going to the brink of nuclear war in order to put pressure on your opponent in the hope that they back down.

CIA   Central Intelligence Agency: the US agency for collecting information on foreign actions that affect US interests.

Coalition government   A government made up of the representatives of more than one political party. They were often set up in the countries of Eastern Europe immediately after the Second World War in the interests of national unity but provided a useful foothold for the communists to gain control.

Cold War   The term given to the conflict that existed between the USA and the USSR after the Second World War. It was a conflict that involved economic measures, non-cooperation and propaganda but no direct armed fighting between the two sides. Thus, despite a breakdown in relations between the superpowers, 'hot' war was avoided. With the advent of nuclear weapons, both sides used a range of less destructive methods of conflict.

Comecon   An organisation controlled by the USSR, set up in 1949 to coordinate the economies of communist countries. It was largely a reaction to the Marshall Plan. Economic aid was limited, but the organisation was able to ensure that a Stalinist state-owned economy was imposed on the countries of Eastern Europe.

Cominform   An organisation controlled by the USSR, set up in 1947 to coordinate communist parties throughout Europe. Its propaganda was virulently anti-American.

Comintern   An organisation set up in 1919 to facilitate contacts between communist groups throughout the world. The Soviet government was able to control its activities, and the West feared it was being used to undermine capitalism and spread communist revolution. It was also known as the Third International, as it replaced the Second International that had existed before 1919.

Containment   The US policy of actively seeking to prevent the spread of communism. It was heavily promoted by George Kennan's 'Long Telegram' and became the basis of US foreign policy under Truman.

Coup d'état   A violent or illegal takeover of government.

De-Stalinisation   The attempt by Khrushchev, the Soviet leader, to move away from the policies of Stalin. Khrushchev criticised Stalin's use of terror and his economic policies of concentrating on heavy industry and forced collectivisation in agriculture. Khrushchev's actions encouraged those in Eastern Europe who wanted reform to push for change.

Détente   A more permanent relaxation in tension. The term was used to describe the improvement in superpower relations that existed after the Cuban Missile Crisis until the Soviet invasion of Afghanistan in 1979 led to a deterioration in relations.

Dispositional   Refers to an explanation based on natural inclination and temperament.

Dollar imperialism   A term used by Molotov to describe Marshall aid. He saw the financial aid as a mechanism by which the USA would gain control over Europe and exploit it for America's economic interests.

German Democratic Republic (GDR)   The official name of the communist state established in 1949 in the former Soviet zone of Germany. It is commonly referred to as East Germany, sometimes known by its initials GDR or in German DDR.

Gerontocracy   Rule by the elderly (geriatrics). The term is used to describe the Soviet leadership in the years 1980–85, i.e. the last years of Brezhnev, Andropov and Chernenko.

Great Leap Forward   The campaign, launched by Mao in 1958, to increase production in industry and agriculture. The campaign involved building dams, reservoirs and roads, setting up small-scale steel and iron furnaces in country areas and establishing communes as the best way of organising agriculture. The campaign was an economic disaster and at least 17 million died directly as a result of these policies.

'Hot line' telephone link   A system of direct communication between the leaders of the USA and the USSR. It was set up in 1963 in response to the Cuban Missile Crisis. Its aim was to prevent misunderstanding during a crisis.

Ideology   A set of ideas and beliefs that forms the basis of an economic or political system. The Cold War involved conflict between two competing ideologies: communism and capitalism.

Imperialism   Building an empire of dependent states.

Iron Curtain   The name given to the figurative line that divided the communist East from the capitalist West in Europe. The term was made popular by Winston Churchill in 1946 when it was used in a speech at Fulton, Missouri.

Iron Fist   A term used by Truman to describe a tougher approach to the USSR. It was a reaction to the approach adopted by Roosevelt, his predecessor, which was seen by Truman as too soft on communism.

Isolationism   A policy of keeping out of conflicts in foreign affairs and not getting involved in military alliances. After the First World War the USA adopted a policy of isolationism towards Europe.

Marshall Plan   A plan to provide American financial support to war-torn Europe. It was drawn up by George C. Marshall, the US Secretary of State, in 1947. All countries in Europe were eligible for Marshall aid, but the conditions attached made it impossible for the communist states of Eastern Europe to apply.

Massive retaliation   A phrase popularised by Dulles, Eisenhower's Secretary of State. It implied the use, or at least the threat, of nuclear action against any aggressive move by the Communist Bloc.

McCarthyism   The wave of anti-communist feeling that spread through the USA in the early 1950s. It is sometimes referred to as the Red Scare and was encouraged by sections of the Republican Party, most notably by Joseph McCarthy.

Militarised counter-revolution   Those policies implemented by Ronald Reagan as US President to undermine the forces of communism. It was a much more aggressive strategy than Carter's policy towards the USSR and included extensive re-arming and providing covert help to those fighting against communist forces or governments.

Military-industrial complex   The term given to the powerful bloc created by links between the armed forces and those sectors of the economy reliant on defence orders.

NATO   The North Atlantic Treaty Organization, a military alliance of the USA, Canada and most of Western Europe. Set up in 1949, it was an organisation to defend the West during the Cold War.

New Look   The name of Eisenhower's foreign policy that took a hard line against communism based on an increased role for nuclear weapons to further containment.

Nuclear Test Ban Treaty, 1963   A treaty that banned the testing of nuclear weapons above ground and below water. It was signed by the USA, Britain and the Soviet Union and was a measure of the desire to limit nuclear destruction after the Cuban Missile Crisis. It was, however, only a partial ban: testing underground was permitted. France and China refused to sign the treaty.

Permanent Revolution   The name of the policy vigorously promoted by Trotsky, who saw the need to spread world revolution as the priority after the Bolshevik Revolution of 1917. Trotsky argued that without world revolution the revolution in Russia would not survive.

Ping-pong diplomacy   The term given to the tentative contacts between the Chinese and US governments in 1971 whereby sporting links between the two countries were used as opportunities to start diplomacy.

Politburo   An organisation made up of the leading members of the Communist Party. It was the key decision-making body in the Party and provided the leadership of the Soviet Union. In practice it was often dominated by the General Secretary.

Post-revisionist historians Those historians who were critical of both the traditional and revisionist approaches to the Cold War. They sought to move away from the issue of who was to blame to one of looking at the process by which conflict developed.

Purges (the) The wave of terror that Stalin and his supporters used to remove enemies. The targets were so-called enemies of the state and included leading Communist Party politicians such as Bukharin, Kamenev and Zinoviev. Many members of the Soviet armed forces were also purged, as was the secret police themselves. The purges reached a peak of activity in the years 1936–39.

Revisionist historians Those historians who challenged the traditional view of the Cold War that Stalin was responsible for its development. They have tended to be more critical of US policies, seeing the actions of the US government as playing an important role in escalating conflict.

Roll back The policy of pushing back the frontiers of communism and liberating states where communism had been imposed by force. It was a term that gained currency in the 1950s and marked a more assertive US stance than that of containment, which had dominated American government thinking since 1945.

SEATO The South East Asian Treaty Organisation formed in 1954: a defensive treaty designed to restrict the expansion of communism in the region. It was made up of Western states such as the USA, Britain, France, Australia and New Zealand and their close allies. The organisation never gained much respect from the independent nations of South East Asia.

Second Front The name given to the idea of a campaign against Nazi Europe in the west in addition to the Russian Front during the Second World War. Stalin put pressure on Britain and the USA to open up a front against Germany in France that would distract Germany from the Russian Front and thus help to relieve the pressure on the USSR. This proposed new front in France was known as the Second Front.

Secretary of State The head of the department of the US government that conducts foreign policy.

Securitate The Romanian secret police under Ceausescu.

Stasi The East German secret police.

Structuralist view Approach to explaining historical change that stresses the importance of structures and organisations in influencing the behaviour of individuals and leading to events occurring.

The Thaw The term given to the easing of superpower relations that occurred after the death of Stalin in 1953 and came to an end with the Cuban Missile Crisis of 1962.

The Velvet Revolution A term used to describe the collapse of communism in Czechoslovakia in 1989. The communist regime was brought down by widespread demonstrations and protests that involved little violence.

Totalitarianism A concept used to explain the nature of the dictatorships that had emerged in the 1930s. It focused on a political system by which total control was gained over the economic, social and political life of a nation. It highlighted the use of propaganda and terror as methods of social control. The concept was developed by political scientists in the USA and was used to describe Nazi Germany, Fascist Italy and Stalinist Russia.

Treaty of Brest-Litovsk, March 1918 The Treaty that the Bolsheviks signed with Germany in order to pull Russia out of the First World War.

Truman Doctrine A policy statement issued by the American president in 1947. It stated that the USA would aid any country or government under attack by armed minorities. It was aimed at preventing the spread of communism.

USSR The Union of Soviet Socialist Republics, also known as the Soviet Union. The USSR was introduced in 1923 as the official title of the areas of the old Russian Empire that were now under communist control. It was made up of 15 different republics but was dominated by Russia, the largest in size and population. The USSR collapsed in 1991.

Warmonger Someone who wishes to provoke war. Stalin accused Churchill of this after his Iron Curtain speech

Warsaw Pact The organisation set up in 1955 to coordinate the military forces of the Soviet Bloc in Eastern Europe. The organisation was established by the Treaty of Friendship, Cooperation and Mutual Aid, signed in Warsaw, the Polish capital.

West (the) The term given to the capitalist countries of western Europe and North America during the Cold War. The United States was the principal power of the West.

Index

Page references in *italics* indicate illustrations.